D0221221

Frontierswomen
THE IOWA EXPERIENCE

Frontierswomen

THE IOWA EXPERIENCE

GLENDA RILEY

THE IOWA STATE UNIVERSITY PRESS, AMES

1 9 8 1

For Sean

GLENDA RILEY is a professor of history at the University of Northern Iowa in Cedar Falls. She has published widely in professional journals on the subject of the early feminist movement in America, on various aspects of frontierswomen in the trans-Mississippi West, and on the teaching of women's history. In recent years, Professor Riley has received grants from the University of Northern Iowa, the Newberry Library in Chicago, and the National Endowment for the Humanities.

© The Iowa State University Press. All rights reserved

Composed and printed by The Iowa State University Press, Ames, Iowa 50010

No part of this publication may be reproduced, stored in a retrieval system, or transmitted, in any form or by any means, electronic, mechanical, photocopying, recording, or otherwise, without prior written permission of the publisher.

First edition, 1981

Library of Congress Cataloging in Publication Data

Riley, Glenda, 1938–
    Frontierswomen, the Iowa experience.

    Bibliography: p.
    Includes index.
    1. Women—Iowa—history.   2. Frontier and pioneer life—Iowa.   I. Title.
HQ1438.I7R54   305.4′2′09777   80-28298
ISBN 0-8138-1470-7

Photographs courtesy of Iowa State Historical Department, Division of Museum and Archives, unless otherwise noted.

305.42
R57

C O N T E N T S   82-657

PREFACE

IN working with women's history students over the past decade it has become increasingly apparent to me that one of the most neglected aspects of the story of American women is their participation in the settlement and development of the western frontier. While encouraging students to pursue information on women in the West and accelerating my own efforts to learn more about frontierswomen, I discovered that they are either invisible in the scholarly literature or are presented in terms of stereotype and myth. The "saint in the sunbonnet," the "madonna of the prairie," and the "pioneer in petticoats" are archetypal frontierswomen. Such images have done more to cloud than to illuminate women's true involvement in the western experience.

The stereotype frontierswomen suffered, withered, and frequently died when subjected to the harsh circumstances of the frontier environment. Or, also according to myth, they demonstrated spunk and mettle, became courageous survivors triumphing over even the harshest conditions of frontier living. The seeming naivete of such images gave me pause. Could either of these generalized, one-dimensional interpretations explain the roles and emotions of all frontierswomen? When I examined the source materials, I was assured of the inaccuracy and, in many cases, the falsity of the traditional image of the frontierswoman. Frontierswomen's sources have been virtually ignored by the image-makers. Instead, stereotypes have been based upon what largely male writers and historians *thought* the West must have been like for women.

I am convinced that the stereotypes and myths about frontierswomen must be tested against their own diaries, letters, and memoirs to gain an understanding of the myriad of questions surrounding their lives. Due to the mass of such material, I decided it would be most fruitful to concentrate on a detailed study of one specific frontier region. In 1976 *The Palimpsest* (published by the Iowa State Historical Department—Division of Historical Society) devoted an entire issue to my initial attempt to discern realities of

Iowa frontierswomen's lives in combination with a previously unpublished reminiscence by an Iowa woman. The editor, L. Edward Purcell, was enthusiastic about my efforts and urged me to undertake a book-length study of Iowa frontierswomen.

As I pursued frontierswomen's source materials further I began to understand why many scholars have chosen to overlook them. They are widely scattered in state and local archives, they are not separately catalogued, and in some cases they have been retained by the families—even when the rest of the family papers were donated to archival repositories. (Sadly, women's papers often have not been considered important enough to donate.) My project expanded to include improving the availability of frontierswomen's documents. The manuscript librarian at the Iowa State Historical Society in Iowa City, Joyce Giaquinta, was particularly helpful in this regard by creating a distinct catalogue category for women's manuscripts. In addition, the editor of *The Annals of Iowa,* Judith Gildner, eagerly published a series of frontierswomen's documents in that journal. And the families of the women who left diaries, letters, and memoirs aided me with biographical information and their permission to publish the documents.

During this phase of the project I discovered that documents produced by certain types of frontierswomen remain difficult or even impossible to locate. Diaries, letters, and memoirs written by ethnic and black women are few in number while materials left by Indian women, such as oral interviews, seem to be nonexistent. I am hopeful that ethnic, black, and Indian women's sources will gradually appear in archives and libraries, just as other frontierswomen's source materials have come to light in recent years. In the meantime, however, assessing the history of these groups on the Iowa frontier is a tenuous venture. As a result, I have chosen not to attempt to include Indian women in the scope of this study. I have included ethnic and black women, but only in the generalized terms dictated by the dearth of source materials regarding them.

Despite these difficulties, my commitment to the study of Iowa frontierswomen increased. In 1976 it received support from the University of Northern Iowa through a Summer Research Fellowship and in 1977 through a Professional Development Leave. Continuing assistance was extended by the Dean of the Graduate College, H. Ray Hoops. The Newberry Library in Chicago provided additional research support during the summers of 1978 and 1979.

Throughout the study I depended upon the friendly competency of the staffs of the University of Northern Iowa Library, the Iowa State Historical Society in Iowa City, the Iowa Historical Library of the Division of Museum and Archives in Des Moines, the Iowa State University Special Collections, the University of Iowa Special Collections, the Luther College Library Manuscript Collection, and the Newberry Library in Chicago, as well as that of numerous local archives.

My colleagues in the Department of History at the University of Northern Iowa and particularly Donald R. Whitnah, department head, offered continuing encouragement. As the book manuscript began to take shape, two of my colleagues, Leland L. Sage and David A. Walker, generously contributed their time and expertise to it. Others who read portions of the work are Robert E. Belding, John R. Christianson, Grace Ann Hovet, Louise Moede Lex, Sandra L. Myres, and Thomas G. Ryan.

My mother, Lillian Gates, and my son, Sean Riley, aided the project by undertaking technical tasks, as well as by their unflagging patience and support. Diligence and a sense of perfection were demonstrated by the typist of the manuscript, Lois Pittman. And whatever polish the final product can claim was added by the careful editing of Judith Gildner, managing editor, Iowa State University Press.

I am appreciative of the combined efforts of all those who aided in strengthening the study, broadening its scope, and eliminating many of its errors. In the final analysis, I alone am responsible for those errors of fact and interpretation which remain.

INTRODUCTION

THE settlement of the American frontier has provided one of the richest and most colorful themes in the history of the United States. This saga of people fulfilling what was widely believed to be America's manifest destiny has been told and retold in many varied forms. It is clearly a significant part of the heritage of the people who were born, or chose to become, citizens of the United States. Upon closely examining the history of the American West, however, it is dismaying to discover that the focus is preponderantly on the activities and achievements of men.

Unfortunately, most historians of the West have been oblivious to the presence of women in frontier society. In 1893, in an address to the American Historical Association, Frederick Jackson Turner stated,

> The wilderness masters the colonist. . . . It takes him from the railroad car and puts him in the birch canoe. It strips off the garments of civilization and arrays him in the hunting shirt and the moccasin . . . he shouts the war cry and takes the scalp in orthodox Indian fashion.[1]

In a 1922 presentation to the Mississippi Valley Historical Association, George F. Parker, another western historian, similarly declared,

> I define the American Pioneer as the man who . . . crossed the mountains from the thin line of Atlantic settlement. . . . I mean the man who . . . swept on through the passes. . . . This man steadily solidified his settlement. . . . To me, this man reflects the character of the most effective single human movement in history.[2]

As recently as 1974, historian T. A. Larson, in a review of western history textbooks, discovered that male-oriented interpretations of the frontier still prevail. He found little or no mention of pioneer women, although the authors of the texts were reputedly experts on the history of the frontier. "In short," Larson concludes, "standard textbooks used in college and university courses in Western History come close to ignoring women entirely.''[3]

This long-standing tendency to see the West in terms of the male experience is complicated by the fact that most frontierswomen did not fill highly visible roles, but labored quietly behind the scenes in traditional, and usually unremarked, tasks. Larson points out that most western women "did not lead expeditions, command troops, build railroads, drive cattle, ride Pony Express, find gold, amass great wealth, get elected to high public office, rob stages, or lead lynch mobs."[4] Instead, they often worked a fourteen- to sixteen-hour day at domestic chores. This not only made them essentially invisible, but it left them little time to record their thoughts and activities in the diaries and journals that are the source materials of history for later generations. When women did record their activities and feelings, the resulting documents were too often judged insignificant or even embarrassing. It is impossible to detect how many families removed a woman's "ramblings" from their papers before donating them to an historical society or archives.

Before the renaissance of the American feminist movement in the 1960s, women's lives were generally regarded as unworthy of study. Since then, feminist protests have helped focus attention on women in American history in general. Yet as late as 1972, a researcher of American history textbooks bitterly complained, "The message of these texts is obvious: to 'make history,' one ought to be born a male."[5] In 1976, another study charged that "sexism is still endemic in most of the American history textbooks offered to the college market in the past few years."[6]

Attitudes must undergo specific changes in order to fully rectify this unfortunate situation: historians must reject the prevailing idea that dominant (meaning male) realms of activity are the only ones deserving examination. The difficulty of collecting women's source materials can no longer be rationalized as a deterrent to scholarly investigation into women's lives. The myths and stereotypes regarding women which have resulted from the attempt to keep them subordinate to male-directed history must be identified and revised.

All these areas are being attacked with force and a modicum of effectiveness by both feminists and historians of women. Scholarly journals devoted to women's studies, manuscript collections, microfilm series, and conferences on women's history are all promising signs of change. How these forces for reform will affect the interpretation of the American West is as yet unclear. A few scholars are beginning the huge task of reconstructing women's experience on the frontier. A solid effort is being made to collect pioneer women's source materials. Artifacts in the form of personal and household items offer a kind of mute evidence; diaries, letters, and memoirs, which are gradually being rescued from libraries, attics, and other storage places, speak of women's lives from the past.

Until recent years, these personal records have not been deeply explored because, as Ray and Victoria Ginger have noted, "it is easier to work with published polemics than to begin the enormous task of ferreting out the everyday lives of the anonymous."[7] Another commentator added that if the "common man" has been virtually ignored by historians, then "what must be the case of the 'common woman?' "[8] This slighting of women's "grass roots" sources has created a lamentable breach in historians' credibility. They have failed to present the full story of the American experience. One writer recently contended, for example, that because pioneer women's "struggles and successes . . . have been too long dismissed as trivial by our historians," we "owe it to ourselves and to our children to retrieve our own history."[9]

In an attempt to repair that breach, this study endeavors to shelve inaccurate models and paradigms in favor of exploring the daily lives of Iowa's pioneer women. What they confided to their diaries, what they wrote to their families and friends back home, what they recalled in later years at the insistence of their children and grandchildren, is blended with more formalized data such as contemporary newspapers, census reports, and secondary accounts. The goal is to portray the lives of real frontierswomen and challenge the legitimacy of the colorful but unauthentic typologies of them.[10]

The story of Iowa's pioneer women starts around 1830. The first white woman to settle in Iowa was in all likelihood Maria Stillwell, wife of Moses Stillwell, who came to what was known as the Half-Breed Tract near Keokuk in 1828. The Stillwells were illegal squatters on government-owned land. The following year, Hannah Galland, wife of Dr. Isaac Galland, moved into the same area and shortly gave birth to a daughter who is traditionally recognized as the first white child to be born in Iowa. Not until after 1832, when the Black Hawk Purchase Treaty provided for the removal of the Sauk and Mesquakies from a section of eastern Iowa, was the territory inundated by settlers.

Migration into Iowa quickly reached substantial levels by the mid-1830s. Since the "new purchase" in Iowa consisted primarily of farmland, it was attractive to family units, and women were therefore a major part of Iowa's population from the beginning of settlement. Due to its burgeoning population, Iowa's pioneer period formally ended in 1870 when the United States Bureau of the Census declared the Iowa frontier closed.

Comparing Iowa's population figures by decades dramatically indicates the rapidity of its growth. Iowa's population of 43,112 in 1840 shot up to 192,214 in 1850; to 674,913 in 1860; and to 1,194,029 in 1870. Iowa's expansion was also clearly illustrated in terms of people per square mile. Using 55,475 square miles as a base figure for Iowa, the number of people per square mile jumped from 0.8 in 1840 to 12.2 by 1860.[11]

The swift increments in Iowa's population underscore the supposition that its frontier met with a relatively quick demise, perhaps even before 1870. When the statistics are broken down by counties, however, a slightly different conclusion emerges. Settlement was not uniform; some counties were heavily populated while others were sparsely settled. In 1870, Scott County (with Davenport) had 84.8 people per square mile, Lee County (with Keokuk) had 72.6, Des Moines County (with Burlington had 65.6 and Dubuque County (with Dubuque) had 64.8. These four eastern Mississippi River port counties contrasted sharply with four western rural counties for the same year: Lyon County had 0.3 people per square mile, Sioux County had 0.7, Ida County had 0.5, and Osceola County showed no figure at all.[12]

The wide variations in settlement patterns make the 1870 state average of 21.5 people per square mile invalid in determining the existence of frontier conditions for Iowa as a whole. Some areas did not come near the average while others far exceeded it. Moreover, the same four western counties underwent a growth spurt either during the last five years before the terminal date of 1870 or sometime after that date. Therefore, they had frontier conditions up to or after the Iowa frontier was officially closed.

This is not to suggest that only western counties lagged behind in settlement while the eastern counties were completely populated. Some western counties such as Pottawattamie (with Council Bluffs) and neighboring Mills County had more people per square mile by 1870 (17.6 and 19.6 respectively) than did some of the eastern counties such as Howard with 13.1 and Grundy with 12.7.[13] Although the total aggregate shift was westward, frontier migration was not the sweeping westward tide that the legend of the West would lead one to believe. Rather, some people became disillusioned with the West and moved back East; some moved from county to county or out of Iowa entirely in a search for the best land; some left farming altogether for urban pursuits. Geographer Michael P. Conzen estimates that between 1840 and 1895, "when the westward movement was in full swing, probably one out of every four local migrants filtered toward the modest urban centers of the state."[14] This rural-urban migration eventually resulted in higher concentrations of people per square mile in Johnson County (with Iowa City) and Polk County (with Des Moines) than in the rural counties immediately surrounding them.

The strong pull exerted by pioneer Iowa's towns and cities in all probability has been overlooked due to their limited size as well as the overwhelmingly agrarian nature of the state. Pinpointing urban concentrations helps to establish the fact that frontier conditions existed in certain parts of Iowa concurrent with urban conditions in other parts. This meant that Iowa still had some frontier influences through 1870 although its total population figures appeared to prove otherwise. This explains how Iowa could spawn the city of Dubuque, which Mary Ann Newbury described in 1854 as a "pleasant spot" and a "place of much intelligence,"[15] yet in 1857 could also provide the setting for the brutal clash between white settlers and the Wahpeton Sioux at Spirit Lake.

The definition of a frontier is not dependent solely on statistical data, but on other more elusive qualities. Most historians who attempt to confront the issue of what constitutes a frontier have rejected the idea of statistical measurement and focus attention instead on the concepts of place, process, and people as definitions of frontier status. Most of these commentators have concluded there was no one frontier; rather, there were many frontiers, such as a cattle frontier, a farmer's frontier, and an urban frontier, among others. Moreover, the frontier has been defined differently by distinct groups of people. The Native Americans' frontier, for instance, came into being when their culture clashed with that of white society, while foreign-born pioneers experienced two frontiers simultaneously when they came to America and the West.

In this sense, then, the study of the Iowa family farm frontier presented here concentrates on what might be termed a female frontier. It necessarily omits American Indian women due to the paucity of source materials, but does make some attempt to consider certain aspects of black and foreign-born women's lives within the limitations of extant resources. Its major focus, however, is white frontierswomen in Iowa between 1830 and 1870. The reconstruction of this slice of the larger female frontier, which covered all parts of the American West to a greater or lesser degree, is intended to be one step towards an understanding of the full implications of women's participation in Americans' westward movement.

Frontierswomen
THE IOWA EXPERIENCE

CHAPTER ONE

Bending the Grass

THE name *Iowa* evoked connotations of hope, optimism, and promise for literally thousands of people in the early 1800s. They envisioned a promised land, a land of milk and honey, a magic land of opportunity where their dreams could and would be fulfilled, if not in their lifetime then at least in their children's lifetime. They gossiped about Iowa's rich soil, daydreamed about the better life it surely proffered, and imagined themselves actually setting out on the long and arduous trek toward its golden prairies.

On the other hand, they carefully weighed the cost of reaching out for what seemed like a panacea. They would have to sell their farms or businesses, leave friends and family, commit themselves to the initial hardship and labor that was necessary to make the dream of the prairies a reality. Only after an anguishing process of alternating between doubt and hope did aspiring pioneers sever their ties at home in order to begin the often painful process of transplantation to Iowa.

That many people made the decision to move to Iowa is borne out by statistics, reports of contemporary observers, and by newspaper accounts. In 1855 the *Eddyville Free Press* noted that the annual spring migration to Iowa had just begun. "Thousands and tens of thousands will flock to our borders this coming year," it boasted. "We bid them welcome."[1] A few years later, in the summer of 1862, Mary Alice Shutes concluded a travel diary chronicling her family's migration from Ohio to Iowa with the remark,

> Our wheels have bent the grass towards the west for quite a spell. Not that our wheels were the first and neither will they be the last to cause the grass to lean towards the west.[2]

Although she was only thirteen years old at the time of her family's move, Shutes was an astute observer. She had already experienced enough of the westward trail, to realize that her own family was but one miniscule element in the rapidly growing western population. Shutes's world view, however, was not sufficiently broad for her to know that her family's geographical origins made them typical Iowa bound migrants. She was not as interested in her place of origin as she was in her destination, but for contemporary historians the question of migrants' origination points has become a potentially valuable tool in understanding the historical development of Iowa.

Several scholars have attempted to penetrate the mass of census data in order to determine Iowans' origins and thus better understand the cultural baggage they transported to the prairie with them. When historian Allan G. Bogue studied midwestern settlers through selected census figures, he learned that they came from the Ohio valley states, the southern states, the middle states, the New England states, and from other countries. Bogue's findings substantiate an earlier contention of Iowa historian Frank Herriott that migration did not follow latitude lines from east to west as so many observers had thought. More recently, several other investigators have confirmed Bogue's and Herriott's theses by identifying large numbers of southerners and foreign-born in early Iowa.[3]

Related to Iowa migrants' place of origin is their mobility history; that is, the places and the number of times they settled before and after their settlement in Iowa. Bogue notes that intermediate stops were not recorded by census takers who were only concerned with origin and present residence in Iowa, yet several historians have demonstrated that most migrants made several moves in the course of their lives.[4]

Women's manuscript sources validate migrants' varied points of origin and multiple moves. The Archers represent a typical case. They made their first move from Ohio to Waterloo, Iowa; next lived in Jones County, Iowa, for a short time; briefly tried Missouri and Illinois; then permanently settled in Lee County, Iowa. The Welchs, on the other hand, were originally southern-based. They left South Carolina for Richmond, Indiana, where after a short time they decided to move again to Van Buren County, Iowa. Eventually their final destination was Jefferson County, Iowa. The Laceys came from the middle states. Their trail led from New York to Illinois to Chester, Iowa, and finally ended in Storm Lake, Iowa. Similarly, the Motts made one long initial move from New Hampshire to Winneshiek County near Decorah, Iowa, which was soon followed by a succession of local moves. The Korens were immigrants from Norway who settled in Decorah. And the Egberts, who moved on from Iowa to California, as well as the Belknaps, who left Iowa for Oregon, both reflect the fact that many families settled in Iowa only as an intermediary point in their overall pattern of migration and settlement.[5] Unfortunately, neither census studies nor case studies indicate the relative proportions of women migrants from the various origination points, nor the weight the factor of gender may have carried as a possible variable in pre-Iowa and post-Iowa migration patterns.

The tendency to overlook frontierswomen has also created a problem in determining women's motivations in deciding to migrate. Women are too often simply lumped together as lesser (although admittedly necessary) appendages to the male undertaking of "going West." The resulting stereotype of the female migrant as an appendage of the male migrant especially clouds our ability to understand the motivation of the unmarried woman moving west. What made her decide to move on her own rather than in conjunction with other family members? It has generally been assumed that the unmarried female relocated only to *become* an appendage; in other words, she moved west to marry one of the surplus male settlers already in Iowa. Although it is perhaps a bit exaggerated, the following story reported in a national magazine in 1844 reflected the prevailing attitudes of the time towards single female settlers.

> A western newspaper says . . . that the arrival of 41 ladies, all at one time, in Iowa, has caused "a sensation." We think it should. But the manner of "paying addresses" and getting "hitched," is what we want to come at. It is said to be done in a business-like way. . . . When a steamboat-load of ladies is coming in "at the wharf," the gentlemen on shore make proposals to the ladies through trumpets, something like the following:— "Miss with blue ribbon on your bonnet, will you take me?" "Hallo thar, gal with a cinnamon-colored shawl! if agreeable we will jine." The ladies in the meantime get ashore and are married at the "hotel," the parties arranging themselves as the squire sings out, "Sort yourselves! Sort yourselves!"[6]

Although this witty piece was probably exaggerated for the sake of humor, many women did in fact go west with the intention to marry. As early as 1837, the (Dubuque) *Iowa News* reprinted an item from the *Philadelphia Ledger* which promised young, single women that "every respectable young woman who goes to the west, is almost sure of an advantageous marriage, while, from the superabundance of her own sex in the east, her chances for it are not greater than those for a disappointment." And almost twenty years later, an Iowa writer remarked that, "According to this last census, the number of males exceeds that of females some 16,000. Let the Yankee girls take the hint when they see these figures."[7]

Such thinking obviously reflected a society in which women were expected to marry and in which the preponderance of women actually did marry. Despite the emergent feminist movement of the 1840s, marriage was still seen by most Americans as the only appropriate be-all and end-all of a young woman's life. After all, how else could she find love, protection, and the opportunity to fulfill herself through motherhood. It is not surprising, then, that many young women capitalized on the population imbalances in Iowa to further their own marital plans.

In spite of the stereotyped image of women as dependent and weak, many ambitious single women did head for the Iowa frontier as laborers, missionaries, and teachers. Catharine Beecher, an early advocate of improved education for women, in particular encouraged groups of women teachers to move west because she saw employment opportunites for them and because she regarded women as civilizing influences necessary to a new society. In addition, some unmarried women moved, as did men, to take up land—although the data on them are incomplete at best and impressionistic at worst. Curiosity butts its head against John B. Newhall's 1846 guide to Iowa which listed for women the single occupation of dairymaid, against gazetteers and almanacs which listed women in occupations primarily as seamstresses and dressmakers, or worse yet, against Iowa census reports which sometimes categorized Iowa women as "not gainfully employed."[8]

If assessing the motives of the single woman is difficult, the task of unearthing the motives of married women (or women otherwise part of a family unit) is almost impossible. Because such women were dependent members of family units, their part in the decision-making process was usually obscured by the family decision. One rather tenuous supposition argues that many women simply submitted to the will of determined husbands, their only motivation being to obey or please their husbands. Because income production was the husband/father's ascribed duty in nineteenth-century society, he made the decision as to how and where that income would be produced and the rest of the family had to acquiesce.[9]

Certainly, nineteenth-century society cast men in the role of breadwinners, initiators, and decision makers, but women's manuscript sources do not uphold the idea that they had no part in the decision-making process. Evidence shows that women in family units ran the gamut from acceptance of, identification with, or support of, to initiation of the idea of settling on the Iowa frontier. As these women explained their reasons for migrating to Iowa, the emotion which most often surfaced was one of optimism rather than bitterness. And like their husbands, they too were sensitive to the pushes and pulls which caused their friends, neighbors, relatives, and ultimately themselves to decide to uproot their ties, their lives, and their families. The pushes—those conditions existing at home which caused people to think about the possibility of moving to a new area—exerted themselves forcefully. The pushes came and went over a long period of years or descended with the suddenness of a storm; they persuaded with rationality or with grinding emotion; they attacked the health or perhaps the purse strings; but in the final analysis, they resulted in a firm and final decision to head towards Iowa.

For some people, the push was the poor health of a family member which hopefully could be restored in a more favorable climate. According to Lydia Arnold Titus, when illness struck her mother in 1847, her father, "thinking that a change of climate might help her, decided to go West."[10] Improved health was apparently a key element of the favorable stereotype of the West, for many people came to a similar conclusion.

AMONG the western areas, Iowa was particularly noted for its supposedly salubrious climate. Considering the harsh Iowa winters, it is not clear just how such a picture was projected. Perhaps Iowa's long periods of sunshine influenced the favorable image or maybe there was some inferential logic applied which assumed that if Iowa was good for corn it was good for people. At any rate, many health-seekers flocked to her borders. Oran and Maria Faville abandoned their careers in women's education in the East in 1855 to move to Mitchell County, Iowa, with the hope that prairie living would improve Oran's health. Whether or not Iowa fulfilled such hopes is unknown but there are at least a few cases on record such as the Hauns who moved *out* of Iowa due to poor health, aggravated in Catherine Haun's estimation by "the intense cold of Iowa."[11]

Another push came from a gnawing dissatisfaction with the system of black slavery as practiced in the South and some sections of the East. Many people who disagreed with the principle of enslaving another human being were casting about for an area where they could be free of slavery's taint. During the 1840s and 1850s antislavery sentiment grew in Iowa; this was eventually manifested by the establishment and successful operation of Underground Railroad stations in Iowa. Thus, Iowa became attractive to many abolitionists and antislavery proponents of varied backgrounds and persuasions. Whether these dissenters found Iowa as liberating as they had hoped is doubtful, for slavery seemed to spread its poison even to the far side of the Mississippi River. The intense nature of the controversy knew no boundaries and seemed to shadow the settlers wherever they went. Joanna Harris Haines vividly remembered the "rumpus" she created as a young girl by singing an antislavery song on the boat en route to Iowa. She also recalled her hurt and dismay at the alienation and "sense of loneliness" her family suffered in Lee County due to their firmly rooted abolitionist sentiments.[12] Hatred, like poor health, apparently continued to plague settlers despite the promise of freedom held out by the vast expanse of the prairies.

In addition to poor health and opposition to slavery, economic liabilities forced people to move west. Heavy taxes were the bane of many. When combined with soil exhausted by long-term abusive practices, the burden of taxes convinced many people that their efforts needed redirection. Some decided that their accumulated debts were too great to bear any longer, others suffered severe losses during the country's several economic panics of the mid-nineteenth century, while others began thinking about westward migration as a result of the financially depressed aftermath of the war with Mexico.[13] Sometimes, several of these factors combined in a way that made a westward move seem imperative. Haines's description of her father's decision to move to Iowa falls in this category.

> He extended too much and then mortgaged his farm to secure a note for a relative. The fall of prices following the Mexican War and the general depression ensuing was too much for him. He lost his holdings and decided to seek his fortunes in Iowa, tales of which were most alluring.[14]

In the face of such disconcerting circumstances, the choice to try their luck in Iowa was not an agonizing one for this family.

Other people were urged to leave their homes because of their dislike of prevailing political leaders and governments. One young Canadian couple immigrated to Iowa because, as their son later explained,

> My father was too much of a liberal and my mother too much of a Yankee ever to be contented under monarchical rule. And so for a number of years the question of emigrating to "the states" was agitated.[15]

When they heard about the "New Purchase" (Black Hawk Purchase) in Iowa they decided to leave Canada in 1839 in favor of a new, and presumably less politically controlled home in eastern Iowa's Linn County.

But the story of Iowa-bound migration cannot be told solely in terms of pushes, for certain pulls were being exerted as well. In conjunction with the pushes, the pulls created a climate of opinion in which almost anyone could find some justification for his or her decision to take to the trail. Literally thousands of letters from those already in Iowa flowed to friends and relatives back East every year. The overwhelming majority of these brimmed over with assurances of prosperity and happiness for settlers to the new land. Haines's parents felt very comfortable with their decision to go to Iowa because their son, who had moved there in 1851, sent letters home radiating enthusiasm. As a result, they "had no doubts as to whither they should journey when the financial disaster compelled them to give up the old farm." Other letters begged for the company of family and friends on the frontier, often wheedling, imploring, and pleading loneliness. Parents became distracted by worrying about the well-being of their children, grandparents longed to see newborn grandchildren, brothers and sisters were anxious to learn how their siblings had fared, while friends and neighbors wanted to recreate the warm bonds of friendship that had once sustained them. That many people responded to beckonings from loved ones is manifested by the Iowa pioneer woman who remarked that her family had come to Iowa due to her sister's "letters of entreaty."[16]

In a sense, these personal epistles were a kind of private propagandizing carried on by individual letter writers reflecting their own personal needs and desires. They were reinforced on a much grander scale by more organized propagandists who had ambitious, specific, and usually profit-oriented objectives in mind. Land companies, newly spawned transportation lines, and various media joined in a concerted effort to sell, and at the same time to idealize the frontier of the farmer. In 1837, the *Iowa News* unreservedly proclaimed that in its territory "one remarkable characteristic of matters and things is perpetual excitement." Describing the burgeoning towns, the throngs of emigrants, and the energetic people, the *News* concluded, "it is seldom that a person who has resided for some years here, can ever content himself to return and live in the east."[17]

What resulted from this propaganda was a huge, if unintended, hoax. Discontented and unhappy people everywhere were led to believe that the trans-Mississippi West was what Henry Nash Smith later termed the "Garden of the World." They were urged, in the name of "progress, civilization, and Christianity" to migrate, multiply, and work hard; the rewards were guaranteed to outdistance their wildest dreams. They had only to come with "strong minds and willing hands to work" as the *Eddyville Free Press* phrased it in 1855, and they would "be abundantly blessed and rewarded."[18]

How could they doubt? How could they hesitate? The spirit of hope symbolized by the American frontier swept over them, washing away their reservations. Reason, a sense of reality, even sanity deserted the minds of otherwise rational people when the image of the frontier was invoked. They were urged to believe that, in the words of a typical mid-nineteenth-century magazine article, the West was "the paradise of the poor"—a "blooming field" for the "really poor man." The eulogies were seemingly endless.

In a strange way, the potential Elysium offered by the West became fixed in many people's minds as another New World. As Europeans had once seen America as a fresh start for their troubled society, now disillusioned people in many countries saw the American West as yet another new beginning. Annette Kolodny analyzes this phenomenon with insight:

> . . . what the American West had provided . . . was the repeated invitation
> to experience pastoral realities, a continuation of the invitations issued to
> Europeans with the discovery of the New World . . . the West was a
> woman, and to it belonged the hope of rebirth and regeneration.[19]

Of course, at the time of settlement most would-be pioneers were not aware of the effect of propaganda, myths, and stereotypes upon their own thinking. Few were blessed with the gift of introspection towards their own actions and their era; so it was with most migrants. One Iowa woman vaguely diagnosed her father as being "spurred by the spirit of the time," but for the most part the pioneers tended to interpret the lure of the West in concrete terms that they could easily understand and assimilate.[20]

Most settlers responded to the promise of Iowa's relatively cheap, easily accessible, and incredibly fertile land. Iowa boasted acre after acre of rich black soil, since classified as one-fourth of all Grade One land in the United States. Understandably, then, many pioneers equated the pull of the West with its ability to provide productive farmsteads.

The theme of fertile and inexpensive (or even free after the Homestead Act in 1862) land was thus reiterated over and over again. The newspapers hammered it into people's minds day after day and year after year. The *Waterloo Courier* on March 19, 1868 reprinted a story from the *Des Moines Register*: "Wanted—thirty seven thousand five hundred farmers! Let the news be scattered. Let the home hunting immigrant . . . be informed that a free home awaits him in Iowa." Presumably, by 1868 most immigrants would have heard stories about Iowa's land, but Iowa was then engaged in peopling her northwest counties and was intent on repeating the message about land to all who would listen.

Throughout Iowa's pioneer period, the repeated theme of rich land had a significant impact. The manuscript sources again and again sing what soon becomes a monotonous song—the acquisition of productive Iowa land. The Willis family heard so much "of the great, unoccupied prairie region of the Iowa country" that they finally invested their paternal grandfather's land warrants from the War of 1812 in Iowa farm land. In another case, Hosea Newton responded to the enticement of Iowa land after being exposed to frequent reports from his friends about its opportunities. He finally made an exploratory trip in 1856, bought 160 acres of prairie at one dollar twenty-five cents per acre, thus committing himself and his family to a future on an Iowa homestead. Alvin and Sarah Lacey, finding that Illinois land was out of their financial reach, "decided to go farther west where land was to be had almost for the taking." Predictably, they chose Iowa, which, "with its broad prairies and fertile lands, was beckoning. Milton and Lydia Moore moved four times: "lured by the tales of better and newer land, he was ready to set out in quest of the ever-receding paradise of the frontiersman."[21]

Most pioneers moved only after an interval of forethought and planning. This period usually involved the procurement of farm land; therefore, it was necessary for someone in the family to make an exploratory trip into Iowa to locate and purchase the family's new homesite. Since women were charged with the care of the children, it was not usually feasible for them to serve as the family emissaries. The harsh travel conditions of the time, as well as the difficulties of dealing with land agents and lawyers, further mitigated against many women of that era attempting such a task.

So it was usually left to the men of the family to venture into the unknown territory in order to entrust the family fortune and future to a strange, but auspicious, piece of land. Because this advance journey was often long, enhausting, and fraught with physical danger, it had to be planned carefully. One young woman retained graphic memories of her father's initial trip to Iowa: "I remember well his preparations for that trip—how mother looked after every button on his coat, and how she sewed a peculiar band inside his shirt. In this was stitched the money with which the relative who had no land warrants wished him to pay for their land."[22]

It was common for a single agent to deal for more than just his own immediate family. Emery S. Bartlett scouted land for his parents, his brothers and sisters, and his intended bride, while G. Hiram Shutes procured land for his wife and children as well as for his unmarried brother. The actual migration to the farming frontier of Iowa often involved extended family units which included many laborers. The 1838 Iowa Territorial Census data demonstrates that migrants settled in households which averaged five to six members with a ratio of four men to three women overall. The census data also stress that most people were attached to a family; few people lived alone.[23]

Of course, not all people who settled in Iowa were farmers and certainly not all family members undertook farm work. However, the 1840 Territorial Census did bear out the preponderance of pioneers engaged in agricultural pursuits. Occupations listed were as follows:[24]

Mining	216
Agriculture	10,728
Commerce	349
Manufacturing and Trade	1,594
Navigation of Ocean	9
Navigation of Canals and Rivers	80
Learned Professions	348

Summary statistics given in the state census of 1880 confirm that the agrarian-oriented migration persisted throughout Iowa's frontier period. The gross number of farms in Iowa rose from 14,805 to 61,163 in 1860, and to 116,292 in 1870.[25]

With the aid of historical hindsight, one can see that the land could not continue to absorb agrarian families at this rate. In 1800 there were 104.2 acres of land for every man, woman, and child in the United States. By 1870 this figure had only shrunk to about half, or about forty-eight acres per person, because even though the population had grown significantly, the United States added new land areas which offset this growth.[26] The relatively slow decrease of the people-land ratio created a false sense of openness in the West. Saturation of available lands and eventually overpopulation would result from continued emphasis on raising large families. This was especially true for areas like Iowa which did not develop much industry or urbanization to absorb surplus population. But in the pioneer era this problem was too embryonic to be of any concern to the frontier farmers who tended to regard bigger families as literally more hands to work rather than as more mouths to feed. They were understandably unaware of what kinds of problems the idealization of the large farm family might cause for future generations.

The need for familial labor combined with the growing belief that the large family was virtuous in itself, became a rallying cry of land promoters. As a result, the path leading to Iowa was crossed by more families and higher proportions of women and children than were the routes leading to nonagrarian frontier areas. Unfortunately, no one at the time had the foresight to gather formal census figures for the trek itself; extrapolation from later census data and the statements of contemporary observers provide clues to the composition of migratory groups. The family structure of the caravans crossing the trail was apparently quite noticeable. One observer commented:

> So far as I could learn no person in all that multitude traveled alone, or unattached to a family; and the very few unmarried men among them each was usually, if not in every case, a member or a near relative of the family to which he was attached.[27]

This description is corroborated by Bogue's study of census records. It theorizes that "the 'typical' pioneer . . . was apparently a married man between the ages of twenty-five and forty-five who had started his family before he moved to the . . . Iowa frontier."[28] This profile of the "typical" pioneer can be supported to some extent by common sense. Not only would the established family be able to provide essential farm laborers, but they would often be in a better position to finance the move than would a younger family. Despite the popular belief that anyone could escape to the West, the very poor rarely migrated. The investment in transportation, animals, tools, seed, provisions, and land was formidable and demanded that pioneers have some means of raising capital such as selling household goods and land, using land warrants or soldier's pay, or negotiating a loan. It is reasonable to suppose then, that the more mature family would be a common sight on the trail, and would frequently provide a "core" for younger and/or unattached migrants as well.

The end of the trail, of course, did not mark a corresponding end of capital investment. Land, as relatively inexpensive as it was, still required a sizeable outlay, usually in cash. If not already paid for by the family's advance agent, it had to be paid for at the time of possession, but either way it necessitated some kind of financial wherewithal. When the Shutes family arrived in Iowa, Mary Alice was surprised to see her father pull "a canvas sack from somewhere" and count out "one thousand dollars in gold to pay for the land and some more to pay the Judge for legal fees."[29]

Land was a major investment, but it was only the first in a long series of outlays, particularly in Iowa where farming entailed certain specialized expenses, such as breaking plows to rip through the tough web of prairie grass roots and fencing to protect the crops from wandering stock. If the Iowa settlers had intended to live as subsistence farmers, they possibly could have gotten along with less land and equipment. But most of them planned to produce a surplus for the market which in turn would produce more capital to be invested in additional land and equipment. With these goals in mind, they had to have a fair amount of land and equipment in hand to begin with.

For these reasons Iowa-bound migration tended to involve families who were capable of raising sufficient capital to undertake the journey, procure land, and start farming. Two other significant characteristics distinguished this migration. First, most of the settlers were traveling over parts of the country which were comparatively well settled, a factor which created a certain amount of ease for them in that they could occasionally buy supplies along the way and could sometimes stay in inns or campgrounds. References to fresh produce, friendly shopkeepers, and rudimentary campgrounds established specifically for the covered wagon people abound in the diaries and letters of the migrants. This is not to say that their time on the trail was easy, but there is little in their history—either factual or legendary—to compare with the tragedy of the Donner party, who perished in the snow-choked passes of the Sierra Nevada Mountains in 1846.

Also, because of the settled nature of the countryside through which they traveled, Iowa migrants had relatively little to fear in the way of confrontations with Native Americans. Land treaties, President Andrew Jackson's removal policy, and outright genocide had essentially cleared the portion of the United States lying northeast of the Mississippi River of Indians. Second, increasing industrialization and technology of the period supplied these pilgrims with a choice of modes of transportation. The covered wagon, popular legend to the contrary, was not the only means of conveyance.

Riverboats were frequently used by travelers. When the Harrises—James and his wife and seven children—came to Iowa from Pennsylvania they chose to go virtually the entire way by river: "First down the Allegheny to Pittsburgh; thence down the Ohio River on the steamboat, 'the Diadem' to Cairo; thence on the 'New England' up the Mississippi to Keokuk." Although they traveled in deck passage for reasons of economy, they remembered it as a speedy and enjoyable trip, often made pleasurable by the company and song of the other passengers.[30]

Rail routes offered another possibility. When they left New Hampshire in 1855, Joseph and Alma Mott chose a rail route all the way to the Iowa border. They began their journey by railroad first to Boston then on to Niagara Falls where they crossed the suspension bridge into Canada. From there they continued on the railway until the end of the rail line on the Mississippi River across from Dubuque. For the last lap of the trip they took a steamboat to Lansing in northeastern Iowa and finally traveled overland by stage to their final destination of Decorah. In 1858 Hosea and Mary Ann Newton traveled west by rail from Connecticut. From Fair Haven they took a stagecoach to the dock where they boarded a steamboat to New York. There they boarded "the cars" for Chicago. After visiting a few days there, they again boarded the railway for Davenport. They then rode to the end of the railway line in Louisa County, Iowa, where they hired a man with a team to take them to their new home in Keokuk County.[31]

Through advertising, improved facilities, and multiplied routes, railroads and steamboats attracted more and more migrants. But despite their attractions, the steamboats and rail lines had some serious drawbacks. Space limitations curtailed the settler's needs and desires to transport necessary household goods, farm implements, seed, stock, and even clothing. Because such goods were more in demand and thus more expensive in Iowa than back East, the unequipped settler could expect difficulty in obtaining goods as well as increased expense in paying for them. Boat and railway fares were expensive and often became prohibitive if more than two or three members of the family were making the trip.

The majority of Iowa's pioneers traveled in covered wagons. Although slow and awkward, the commodious wagons accommodated family members, goods, equipment, and animals. The journey might take considerably longer than it would by boat or rail, but the travelers would enjoy the initial advantage of having belongings, seed, and stock with them in a territory which had little surplus to spare. And in many cases the prairie schooner, as it was called, even became a temporary home for the settlers when the trail ended.

Obviously, something as crucial as a wagon had to be selected and provisioned with great care, patience, and cooperation. The mental and physical efforts of almost every member of the family were focused on the wagon for weeks, or even months preceding their departure. They realized that an oversight or lack of attention to a minute detail could make the difference between survival or disaster. So they worked on the wagon as a team, but like any effective team they divided the labor according to the skills of their members.

Because of their long experience with machinery, the men of the family usually made the actual selection of the wagon. They chose from two basic types: the large Conestoga Wagon, which was approximately fifteen feet long, five feet wide, and five feet deep, or the smaller, lighter emigrant wagon, which measured about ten feet in length, four feet in width, and two feet in depth.[32] Their choice was predicated upon how much they wanted to carry and how fast they wanted to travel, but in either style they looked for a sturdy, well-constructed box which would not shake apart on some particularly rough stretch of trail. Once the wagon was secured, the men were expected to equip it with running gear as well as to select and train suitable animals to haul it and its contents hundreds of miles through sun, dust, rain, mud, and even snow.

Production of the cloth top for the wagon was assigned to the women of the family due to their familiarity with fabrics and their skill at needle. This was a long-term job since the top frequently was stitched by hand. In planning a wagon cover, Kitturah Belknap explained, "Will make a muslin cover for the wagon as we will have a double cover so we can keep warm and dry; put the muslin on first and then the heavy linen one for strength. They both have to be sewed real good and strong and I have to spin the thread and sew all those long seams with my fingers."[33] According to her, women's time and expertise were the two ingredients needed to produce a roof that would successfully shelter the family from inclement weather during the long months of their western journey.

After the basic wagon was selected, careful planning and long hours of labor were devoted to equipping the wagon box. The degree of thoughtfulness and efficiency expended in this task could also spell disaster or success for the migrants. All of the family's needs had to be assembled and packed in that limited space. This meant that the usefulness of every item they owned or purchased had to be critically scrutinized.

Equipment included all the clothing, food, cooking utensils, bedding, medicines, and tools that might be necessary to sustain family and animals along the trail as well as seed, farm implements, and furniture to carry them through the beginning phases of establishing a farmstead. Equipping the box was a chore shared by both men and women. The men usually readied such items as firearms, tools, and furniture. They also used every possible space on the outside of the wagon box to hang buckets of grease for the axles, barrels of water for the stock, and spare parts for the wagon. Then they busied themselves training the team that was to pull the wagon, as well as preparing the family's other stock for their long journey ahead. Women took the primary responsibility for preparing items of food, clothing, and medicine. Kitturah Belknap left a detailed account of her preparations for an overland journey, preparations which consumed all the spare moments she could wring from her many routine duties during an entire winter.

> I have to make a feather tick for my bed . . . the linen is ready to go to work on, and six two bushel bags all ready to sew up . . . have cut out two pair of pants for George . . . I have worked almost day and night this winter, have the sewing about all done but a coat and vest for George. Will wash and begin to pack and start with some old clothes on and when we can't wear them any longer will leave them on the road.[34]

With the experience of a previous migration behind her, Belknap knew what would be needed. She dipped enough candles to last a year; prepared a complete medicine chest; packed homesewn sacks with flour, corn meal, dried fruits and other foodstuffs; assembled dishes and cooking pots; and cooked enough food to last the first week. Her final preparation was to put together a workbasket of sewing so that she wouldn't have to spend any idle moments during the trip! Her husband George, in the meantime, built an ingenious camp table, practiced with the oxen he had purchased to pull their wagon, and prepared the stock for travel.

Belknap was particularly pleased with the camp table since it perfectly complemented the homey ambience she was determined to maintain on the trail. She had already decided to start off with "good earthern dishes" although she was realistic enough to bring tin dishes as back-ups in case the earthen ones got broken. She also had made "four nice little table cloths." With these accoutrements, she declared that she was "going to live just like I was at home."[35]

When fully loaded, a prairie schooner must have been an impressive sight indeed. It has been estimated that they ranged from 1,500 to 2,000 pounds, not counting the additional weight of their human passengers.[36] Many wagons had an assortment of farm animals tied to the back end or confined in crates that were lashed to the sides. And many wagons had individualized refinements, depending on the needs and inventiveness of their owners.

The Belknaps prepared a secure spot for Kitturah's rocking chair so that she could ride comfortably while sewing. They then arranged for a miniscule play corner for their young son to play in and devised a clever folding bed which would allow them to sleep in the relative comfort of their wagon rather than out-of-doors. The Shuteses also arranged their wagon in such a way as to accommodate Ann Shutes and her infant at night. A common practice, which soon became an accepted part of trail lore, was the sewing of canvas pouches to the inside of the wagon cover. The Hauns found their "pockets" invaluable for small items which needed to be kept in easy reach, such as cooking knives, firearms, and toilet articles.[37]

Emigrant wagons were usually selected by families with shorter distances to cover, but they too were experts at using every possible inch of space. Mary Moore McLaughlin described the wagon she traveled in as a child. It was "a low, long-coupled, straight-box, two-horse wagon, made roomy and comfortable by an extension of the wagon bed over the wheels." Although it was relatively limited in size, it was crammed with many items, including some things that were apparently family treasures. McLaughlin especially remembered "mother's little cane seated rocker, our family pictures and books, one bureau, and a jar of honey." Like most other families, the Moores made every effort to create additional space. They hooked a small table upside down on top of the feed box at the back of the wagon to hold "the cooking utensils, the dinner box, the stove rack used for campfire cooking, and two splint-bottom chairs." When it was unhooked it quickly converted into a convenient and comfortable dining area.[38] Although the Moores' wagon sounds as if it was already performing exceptional service, it managed to accommodate a rather sizeable human cargo as well. The wagon transported a family of six perched about on various seats, boxes, and items of furniture. Usually the parents rode on a spring seat in front while the four children spent the day in the back of the wagon. Mary's memories were not of discomfort, but rather of the sights that greeted her eyes on the days when the weather permitted the canvas to be "rolled up to allow us to see the country through which we passed."[39]

All of the necessary packing, preparing, and arranging would have been a much simpler process if the migrants could have just loaded their existing belongings and supplies into their wagons and departed for the frontier. But word-of-mouth, emigrant guidebooks, and their own good sense indicated that only certain supplies would see them through their venture. It is understandable then that the sifting and sorting process usually took anywhere from three months to a year before departure and often involved getting rid of as many things as were newly acquired. Bartering and bargaining were carried on among potential migrants and their neighbors with everyone hoping that a deal would be concluded to his or her own satisfaction.

One popular way of disposing of household "truck," as it was called, was to hold a public auction. Advertised beforehand in local newspapers and by handbills, auctions usually attracted the curious as well as the serious buyers. One young woman, Mary St. John, mentioned in a diary that her father went to considerable trouble to organize an auction to sell the family furniture. "The things," she decided, "sold as well as could be expected."[40]

An alternative was simply to give away items which were no longer of use. Family, friends, and neighbors became the recipients of useful items as well as some of dubious worth. Despite their nature, many of these items were family or personal treasures whose value was not great enough to justify occupying space in an already crowded wagon. When the Shuteses began to give away many of their possessions, young Mary Alice noted in her diary that, "we are finding it a little rough to have to give away a lot of things we have owned since we can remember." Poignantly, she added that these things were "valuable to ourselves only, mostly sentimental value."[41]

Another possibility was to trade an item for something which would prove more useful on the westward trek. A cherished iron kettle and crane in exchange for a light, folding camp stove; some split fence rails for wagon wheels; a party dress for a handpieced quilt were all common exchanges. Catherine Haun was bemused by the furious trading among her friends. "The intended adventurers," she wrote, "diligently collected their belongings and after exchanging such articles as were not needed for others more suitable for the trip, begging, buying or borrowing what they could, with bouyant spirits started off."[42]

In spite of all the advice which circulated, the migrants' good intentions, and warnings to the contrary, most people still tended to take far more than their wagons could possibly carry. With its sides bulging and its wheels creaking, a swollen wagon soon overburdened the animals forced to drag it overland. When people understood that their expectations of wagons and teams were unrealistic, they traded everything possible and discarded the rest. Consequently, the wayside was littered with cooking ware, furniture, and many luxury items. Catherine Haun explained that when they left Iowa they purposely took many extra goods along to sell for cash upon arrival in the Far West. "The theory of this was good," she said, "but the practice—well, we never got the goods across the first mountain."[43] These discarded articles were appropriated by other settlers or by Native Americans who must have eventually recovered a veritable treasure trove of washstands, mirrors, what-not shelves, and other similar trappings of European civilization.

If it was so difficult for the pioneers to leave their cherished possessions behind, it must have been emotionally wrenching for them to part with their families, friends, and neighbors. Unlike modern society where the average person moves many times in his or her life, most nineteenth-century Americans were accustomed to being part of a region, a town, a neighborhood, and a kinship network. Many of these people shared value systems, social life, customs, and traditions. They shared the joy and the tragedy of births, weddings, and deaths in each other's families. They called upon each other for help in times of crisis. And they gathered together to pray or to celebrate a holiday.

A family's decision to leave this comfortable web was not only traumatic for them, but also for those who would be left behind. The announcement that a family was leaving initiated a transition period during which both the soon-to-be pioneers and those remaining at home attempted to adjust to the idea of separation. The rituals recognizing the impending departure included dinners, dances, family visits, and special church services, all designed to wrap the migrant family in a warm cloak of good wishes and friendship of the people they had known for so many years.

Defying their brave attempts to invest the coming break with a festive air, the actual departure usually presented a heart-rending scene. In the murky early morning light, people gathered around the migrants to help them load their wagons, to serve them breakfast, to grasp their hands one last time, and to wish them luck in the new country. Sleepy-eyed Mary Alice Shutes peered through the dim light of a predawn bonfire to discover that a great number of her family's relatives and friends had come to see them off and to cook breakfast as a "final display and effort of friendship." She sensed the strain in the air: "The younger kids know something unusual is going on but don't understand it like the older folks do. . . . Some of the older ones seem to welcome the solitude away from the fire . . . they have said their goodbyes and are just waiting." Although she sympathized, she did not really understand.

From her perspective as a thirteen year old, she was thinking more of the excitement of the "good lark ahead of us" than of those people who would be left behind.[44]

It was a common practice for some friends to ride along with the migrants and their wagon for the first few miles in kind of an extended goodbye ceremony, but as the outskirts of town were reached, these riders gradually dropped back and returned home, leaving the travelers to begin the expedition on their own. Waving one last farewell to their friends and to the life they had known, the would-be pioneers finally confronted the rigors of the trail which would lead them to a promising, if unknown, future.

Fortunately, they did not lack company on their journey for there were many settlers heading towards the Iowa frontier during the mid-nineteenth century. In fact, Newhall portrayed the Iowa-bound migration as a mass movement. He claimed that in 1836 and 1837,

> The roads were literally lined with the long blue wagons of the emigrants slowly wending their way over the broad prairies—the cattle and hogs, men and dogs, and frequently women and children, forming the rear of the van—often ten, twenty, and thirty wagons in company. Ask them, when and where you would, their destination was the "Black Hawk Purchase."[45]

In 1840, Isaac Galland added the rather extravagant claim that "the rush of immigration to Iowa has greatly exceeded anything of its kind heretofore experienced in any other part of the United States."[46]

The huge, distended wagons forced their iron-covered wheels into the earthen trail leaving tracks that were reinforced by thousands of wearying footsteps of both people and animals. By the time the migrants converged on Iowa the marks of their passage were clearly etched on the prairie. Recalling her family's move in the 1860s, Mary Moore McLaughlin later wrote, "I can see now the two tracks of the road, cut deep by the wagon wheels and washed out by the rains."[47] These tracks became a kind of map for those who followed as well as a testimonial to those who had already completed the demanding journey.

Whenever the opportunity presented itself, migrants would join with another family to swap information, to exchange bits of trail lore, or to travel together for as long as their routes coincided. McLaughlin remembered that at times they traveled alone, but when possible, they joined with other "movers." She remarked that they "were always glad to have company, especially when fording swollen streams, for then we could double up teams and take turns in making the crossing."[48]

Although the Iowa trail was not characterized by wagon trains as was the cross-country migration to the Far West, some people did travel in groups.

When the Willis family announced their intention to relocate in Iowa, they were surprised and pleased to find that "most of the immediate relatives soon sold their homes, loaded their goods into wagons, and started for Iowa" with them. They traveled as a group, helping each other whenever they could by "fording streams, wading through mud, and enduring untold hardships" together. Many years later, Mary Willis Lyon recounted her version of that westward journey to her granddaughter. Even though she had been a young girl at the time and many years had intervened, she insisted that she could still remember "the great bows of the old ox-drawn wagon, and can feel yet the lurch and chug of the big wheels, as they struck the ruts and hummocks along the way."[49]

The Harris family put together a very similar kind of caravan. Numbering ten people, they moved along in two huge covered wagons pulled by yokes of oxen as well as in a two-seated buggy pulled by a team of horses. Because they attempted to get a jump on the summer migration season by leaving in late winter, the Harris party endured much cold weather. Even years later, Joanna Harris Haines's memories of the trip centered on the cold weather as well as the need to travel with care for her "mother was suffering from a severe attack of lumbago." In spite of the hardships, she concluded that, "save mother's distress, we enjoyed the journey."[50]

A SIGNIFICANT portion of the migrants were children. Any attempt to determine the proportion of migrant children is thwarted once again by the lack of specific census data. Although their actual numbers remain a matter of conjecture, mention of their existence is liberally scattered throughout women's sources.[51] There is little indication that anyone thought it unusual for a child to make the demanding trip, even at a very tender age. In 1869, when Lydia Arnold Titus and her husband resolved to make Iowa their new home, her young sister and her husband announced that they were going along. Both couples sold their farms and stock, "keeping only a wagon apiece and four horses," to transport themselves and their four children. Lydia had an eight-year-old daughter, a three-year-old son, and a ten-month-old girl, while her sister had a six-week-old baby girl, yet neither woman felt that moving the young children was an extraordinary undertaking. They were not alone. There were many others, such as the Archers, who with four wagons were moving nineteen people, thirteen of whom were children between the ages of two and the early twenties. Some women commented on how they thought their children felt about the trip. Lydia Arnold Titus, as a case in point, was convinced that "it was a great adventure to the older children just as my trip from New York had been to me, but the babies were too young to care much about it."[52]

Other women later recalled how they felt as trail children, although admittedly their memories may have become fonder with the passing of time. One woman, reminiscing about her days on the road, remembered the trail as a great adventure. "Maybe it was hard for the grown folks," she stated, "but for the children and young people it was just one long, perfect picnic." Another echoed this sentiment: "It was a wonderful trip for us children."[53]

As a matter of course, children were expected to carry out a good share of the trail work. This would not necessarily have jaded their perception of the trip, however, since they were long-accustomed to doing a portion of the family's tasks. In fact, the novelty of the trail and the warm sense of shared endeavor probably relieved what might have otherwise been onerous chores.

On the trail both boys and girls acted as "outriders." Mounted on horseback, or on foot with a switch in hand, their major responsibility was to look after the cattle and other stock. Because roadside grass appealed to cows who really were not all that enthusiastic about what was turning out to be a very long walk, the children were constantly prodding and pleading with recalcitrant stock to keep them on the move. One woman recalled that "there were three of us children old enough to run along behind or ride Jim and we took turns in herding our livestock, which frequently paused to graze by the wayside."[54]

Mary Alice Shutes and her brother Charles were initially very excited about their role as "cowboys" but they quickly learned to detest their two un-cooperative and sluggish cows. Since their father was determined to get the cows to Iowa, he ignored Mary Alice's and Charles's complaints and tied one cow to each child's horse. After unsuccessfully trying to drag the cows along by ropes, Mary Alice and Charles persuaded their father to tie the cows to the tailgate of the wagon instead. Shutes explained,

> The idea of having a cow on one end of a rope and Charles or me on the other end did not work. When Bossy did not want to move, a jerk on the rope was not enough to prove to Bossy who was boss. It took the team on the wagon to prove to Bossy who was the boss.[55]

When the cows' hooves cracked and their udders went dry, Hiram Shutes finally relented and sold them. For days afterwards, Mary Alice kept looking back at the end of the wagon in disbelief. "Oh," she jotted in her diary, "no cows is good." While Mary Alice helped cook, wash, and care for the younger children, Charles helped tend the horses, maintain the wagon, and stand his share of the nightly watch. They generally fared better in these tasks than they had with their balky cows, although Shutes found that caring for the younger children could also be troublesome. One day she reported that "they took orders fine so not so bad a day after all," but at another time she wrote, "what a relief to get Archie and Howard into their quilts. They just were everywhere they were not supposed to be"[56]

For the most part, trail children managed their chores with equanimity and found time for play as well. Along the way they explored, fished, joked, and swapped stories with children of other parties. They gathered wildflowers, picked berries, and darted through the prairie grass playing games of tag or hide-and-go-seek. The trail replicated a slice of society in motion, and the children managed to intersperse work with play just as they had done at home.

The real hardships for trail children most often came in the form of threats to their physical well-being. The possibility of accident, illness, and disease constantly hovered over the travelers. Although they carried some medicines, they knew that the services of a doctor would be virtually unobtainable in case of serious trouble. Elisha Brooks always remembered the starkness of the situation when illness hit him and the other children of his party. "A picture lingers in my memory," he said, "of us children all lying in a row on the ground in our tent, somewhere in Iowa, stricken with the measles, while six inches of snow covered all the ground and the trees were brilliant with icicles."[57] Similarly, Mary Alice Shutes recorded in her diary the terror her family faced when sleepy young Archie bounced off the wagon and barely escaped having his head crushed by the wagon wheel. "Am sure luck is with us," she wrote with a sense of relief upon finding out that Archie was dazed but otherwise uninjured.

For trail women, the problem of protecting their children from physical harm was in all probablility the most distressing aspect of child care. Although they were constantly vigilant, illness and accident took its toll. Within a few years the westward trail was marked not only by wagon wheel tracks but by small hastily dug graves as well. How many children perished because of trail conditions and how many would have succumbed in normal situations is a question that can never be fully answered.

Evidently, the migrants themselves did not see trail hazards as being much greater than those experienced in their former homes for they persisted in undertaking the trip with babies and children. In some cases, optimism displaced the threat of adversity. One couple traveling with two infants was described as "young and full of hope and made light of the hardship." In other cases, a spirit of necessity prevailed. As one pioneer woman summed it up, "then I never thought about its being hard. I was used to things being hard."[58]

This stoic observation offers a softer perspective of the epic tales of hardship faced by pioneers both on the trail and later in their new frontier homes. For most nineteenth-century Americans life was difficult no matter where they lived. One woman said that her parents survived the crude conditions of the road because "their early lives had been spent amid such surroundings."[59] The trail *was* demanding, but at least it offered the hope of rewards for the deprivation and toil.

The labor of women migrants was crucial to success on the trail. They were charged with the awesome task of preserving their homes and families during the unsettling time in transit. Being en route did not change or lessen the jobs designated as women's work. Rather, women had to continue, in the primitive conditions of the trail, taking care of their families as they had always done. It is to the credit of most trail women that during the time in which the wagon was their only home and the trail their only backyard, they cared for the needs of their families in as homelike a setting as they could possibly manage to recreate.

The easiest problems for them to resolve were their families' sleeping arrangements. The wagon presented itself as an obvious "bedroom" and many of the wayfarers took advantage of its minimal protection. The Titus party was delighted to find that its two wagons "were roomy enough for all." Most groups reserved space in the wagons for the most needy members: the aged, the ill, the small children, or the women with infants. The Harris party developed another alternative; whenever an inn could be located, the women of the party boarded there while the men slept nearby in the wagons. Others used tents, deserted houses, or simply slept outside, using a variety of quilts, feather ticks, or corn husk mattresses to shield them from the chill air and the unrelenting hard ground. Most campers combined a night watch with an all-night fire to protect their camp. Mary Alice Shutes mentioned that "the men folks arranged about turns for night watch to watch the stock and keep the fire going as a warning for intruders to keep away." Later in her diary she reported that they had "a nice campfire going to keep wild animals away—mostly the small kind." The eerie shadows created by the flickering fire combined with the noises of a wilderness night must have provided a strange and even scary backdrop for the travelers. Recalling the nights she spent in the wagon as a small child, McLaughlin vividly remembered that, "as the twilight settled into darkness, the wolves came slinking around the camp; and while they howled we children snuggled closer together in our beds in the wagon box, begging father to build the fire higher."[60]

Occasionally, travelers were fortunate enough to be afforded shelter for a night by a friendly family who remembered its own trip west. For Kitturah Belknap one such instance of hospitality was particularly welcome. The Belknap party crossed an eighteen-mile-long stretch of prairie in the swirling snow during which Kitturah drove the team so her husband could herd the stock. "I thought my hands and nose would freeze," she related. "When I got to the fire it made me so sick I almost fainted." Luckily, they were taken in by a family of eight people living in a tiny, isolated cabin. Belknap thawed out her frozen provisions for dinner and then, sick with a toothache, she bedded down on the floor with the other five members of her family. She and the others in her party arose at four A.M. to eat breakfast without disrupting their hosts and set off for more miles of snow-covered prairie somewhat refreshed by the brief interval spent indoors.[61]

The Shuteses accepted hospitality from a family who had come to Iowa in the 1840s and had been helping migrants ever since. The Shuteses had just been chased out of a deserted log cabin by what the children called ''striped kitties,'' but which were more correctly identified by their father as skunks. After their narrow escape, they were more than happy to spend a night in the host family's barn and to be treated to a breakfast of buckwheat cakes, fresh side pork, and coffee. Mary Alice was especially pleased with the meal because ''you could eat your fill with no smokey taste.''[62]

Mary Alice's observation on the breakfast illustrates the fact that women had a much harder time feeding their families than they did figuring out where they could sleep. Women tackled the arduous job of meal preparation by developing a trail-craft, the ingenuity of which rivalled the woods-craft or plains-craft of their male counterparts. Using reflector ovens, prairie stoves, or just campfires, they concocted meals which ranged from adequate to elegant.

Lydia Arnold Titus was particularly adept at campfire cooking. She ''fried home-cured ham or bacon with eggs'' while she ''boiled potatoes or roasted them in the hot ashes.''[63] The Lacey family had a cold lunch from a big barrel that mother Sarah had packed with suitable provisions, but at night she also insisted upon cooking them all a hot meal over a campfire. She prided herself on always offering them ''meat or eggs and a warm vegetable for all, as well as pie or cake.''[64] Mary Moore McLaughlin recalled a homey mealtime:

> . . . father would bring water, build a fire, and take down the little green table and the splint-bottomed chairs from the back of the wagon, while mother prepared the meal. We were at home on the prairie with prairie chicken for supper![65]

Another woman's diary referred to cooking over an open fire, cooking in the rain, and cooking food on Sunday to be eaten during the first part of the following week. On one particular Sunday, her project of fixing beans was interrupted by a sudden rain shower. ''Wasn't it a shame'' she lamented. ''Mine were almost done when a shower came up and drove me into the wagon. The beans taking advantage of my absence burned up. Nothing was left for me but to cook more.'' Like many trail women, she augmented her cooking facilities with whatever resources came to hand. At one camp spot she made biscuits after obtaining permission to bake them in a nearby house and at another she prepared eggs on a borrowed campstove.[66]

For pure creativity, however, Kitturah Belknap deserved congratulations. Using a Dutch oven, a skillet, a teakettle, and a coffeepot, she devised meals which were just like ''at home.'' These regularly featured her salt-rising bread, which she worked at in between her other chores.

> When we camped I made rising and set it on the warm ground and it would be up about midnight. I'd get up and put it to sponge and in the morning the first thing I did was to mix the dough and put it in the oven

and by the time we had breakfast it would be ready to bake. Then we had
nice coals and by the time I got things washed up and packed up and the
horses were ready the bread would be done and we would go on our way re-
joicing.[67]

Butter for the bread was not a problem for her either. When the cows were
milked at night, she strained the milk into little buckets which were covered
and set on the ground under the wagon. In the morning she skimmed off the
cream, put it in the churn in the wagon, and after riding all day she had "a nice
roll of butter."[68]

Belknap further supplemented her family's meals with foodstuffs bought
along the way. She would keep her eye out for a farmhouse where she might
purchase a head of cabbage, potatoes, eggs, or other fresh foods. She soon
learned that "where there were farms old enough to raise anything to spare,
they were glad to exchange their produce for a few dimes." Another woman
recorded buying bread from farmers along the route, gathering wild nuts, and
being given milk by traveling companions with cows. Others bought items such
as eggs and fresh ham from local storekeepers who were so anxious to attract the
settlers' business that some of them even built sheltered campgrounds for the
travelers.[69]

As travelers neared Iowa, the task of food preparation was complicated by
decreasing fuel supplies. The prairies did not readily yield wood for their fires
so the pioneers often had to purchase wood. When wood was totally
unavailable, they twisted hay, prairie grass, or slough grass into "cats." This
made an extra job for the women and children who had to spend hours producing fuel by collecting and twisting the hay or grass, but it was perhaps more
agreeable than collecting animal excrement, euphemistically called cow-chips
or buffalo-chips, for use as fuel.[70]

Limited water supplies on the prairie necessarily made it hard for women
to wash clothing and bedding. When the rain barrels were full, when a farmhouse with a well was located, or when a stream was reached, the women and
girls seized the opportunity to refresh garments dirtied and worn by traveling in
heat and dust. Jane Augusta Gould's note about clothes washing was typical.
"At four P.M. I commenced and did a real large washing—spreading the clothes
on the grass at sunset." At a later point in her diary she expressed shock
because, while they were "laying over because it was the Sabbath," she
discovered that "the women were doing up their week's washing."[71]

Gould's observation offers an insight into women's work on the trail in the
sense that their tasks were often out of step with the rhythm of other trail work.
Rest periods for the men and younger children, such as meal stops or evenings,
were the very times when women began their chores. Occasionally, men would
help with the cooking or other domestic tasks, but more often they relaxed or
mended harnesses, while the women cared for the children, washed clothes, or

prepared food. The younger children used the time for play. One woman remembered that her mother prepared the evening meal while "we children raced and romped enjoying our relief from the long hours in the wagons."[72]

This pattern created a tremendously wearying situation because the women were not relieved of duties once the caravan was again on the move. Child care of course continued, but women also performed many of the so-called male tasks such as driving the team and herding the stock. Catherine Haun called it lending "a helping hand." She explained, "the latter service was expected of us all—men and women alike." Belknap frequently took over the lines and drove the team to free her husband to tend the unruly stock. And Mary Lyon's mother routinely drove the wagon part of each day so that her husband could stretch his legs by walking behind it. When their wagon became mired in the mud, she even mounted their horse and with "the baby in her arms" and her small son astride behind her, guided the horse in rescuing the wagon.[73]

Despite the prevalence of this kind of grit, some women never completed the journey. There were a few who, regretting their decision or finding themselves unable to cope with the demands of migration, voluntarily turned back. The trail had a certain number of misfits; not only women but men as well sometimes decided to terminate the venture. As one woman pointed out, "some like the new country, but others . . . returned to their native States."[74] The truly unfortunate were those women who were stricken by illness, died in childbirth, or suffered accidents and never saw the end of the route which had promised them so much.

SOME scholars argue that the work which women performed and the suffering they endured on the trail did not guarantee their inclusion in the larger aspects of the undertaking such as decision-making. They claim that in consequence women soon became alienated and disheartened by the migration experience.[75] If Iowa women had regrets or reservations, they generally avoided discussing them. Perhaps they realized that any domestic routines they could recreate, any assistance they could offer, any supportive feelings they could express were all hedges against the disintegration of family unity under the duress of migration. Most seemed to understand that their efforts, whether in the material or psychological realms, were absolutely essential to subduing the trail and getting their families to the promised land.

More often than complaint, a sense of equanimity was expressed by Iowa women. This was apparent in Gould's remark that it was "decidedly cool camping out and cooking by a campfire, but we must do as we can." It was also reflected in Shutes's statement that "we have a lot of weary miles behind us. Glad to have done it but would not care to do it over again, or very soon anyway.'' The harshness of the trail environment was often leavened by a spirit of fun. Singing, dancing, and courting were all part of the picture as the settlers moved closer to their new homes. The following diary notations were not uncommon. Jane Augusta Gould: ''I hear the merry notes of a violin. A general cheerfulness prevails.'' And Esther Pillsbury: ''We spent the evening singing and talking. Will played on the fiddle.''[76]

Had these women become totally embittered, they probably would not have been as awed and delighted as they were by the prairie country which gradually enveloped them. One exulted that ''the prairies were just one great flower garden.'' Another remembered how her family learned to love the open prairie as they traveled across its broad expanse. Another emphasized that she could not adequately describe ''the magnificence of the wild flowers that made the prairies for miles in all directions one gorgeous mass of variant beauty.'' And yet another called it ''a perfect garden of Eden.''[77]

Naturally, the geography and climate of the new land were not always pleasing. Women pioneers recorded their battles with sun scorched prairies, biting snowstorms, mud sloughs, and particularly, wide streams and rivers. Rivers could usually be forded or ferried across with comparative ease, but in some cases, especially after storms, their depths or flooded conditions presented a great barrier to settlers, wagons, and animals. In 1832, Caroline Phelps and her husband William were stymied by flooded Sugar Creek, which they finally crossed by swimming on horseback and floating on driftwood. In the process, Caroline, who already had an eye swollen shut by an infection, was knocked down and kicked in the forehead by a frightened horse. She roused herself sufficiently to pick up her baby and get them both across the creek, after which the men of the party brought their wagon across in pieces. Her good spirits were not adversely affected for she remarked, ''We had a good supper and a good bed . . . the next morning I was quite refreshed.''[78]

Even if they escaped perils of crossing smaller rivers, most Iowa-bound migrants had to confront the Mississippi River. Bridges across the Mississippi were not constructed until the late 1860s due to the bitter opposition of steamboat companies and ferry operators. Throughout most of the pioneer period railroads and highways alike ended abruptly on the east bank leaving the settlers to traverse the river by boat or ferry.

For most people, crossing was a time-consuming, but interesting event. When the Shuteses reached the Mississippi, they learned that they had just missed a bad flood which had prevented crossing of any kind for several weeks. ''Not just too much water,'' they were informed, ''but too much trash and big trees that would smash anything in their way.'' Fortuitously, Hiram had been advised to arrive ahead of his party and get his name ''in the pot'' for a place on the ferry so the wait would be less than a day. When the Shuteses left their camp spot and approached the ferry, they were quickly caught up in the excitement of throngs of people, escalating noise levels, animated talk of high water, and piercing blasts from the whistle of the steam-powered ferry. As they gradually edged up the loading plank, the men took responsibility for the wagons, the children led the blindfolded horses, and the mother shepherded the small children. Once out upon the swirling waters, Mary Alice Shutes felt that her mother had "the real job sitting on a chair holding the baby and Howard." After several uneventful hours, they left the ferry and moved onto "Iowa dirt."[79]

For some travelers, the crossing was not easy. In the mid-1860s a woman, coming to Iowa with four children under age eleven to join her husband, was appalled to learn that cracking ice in the Mississippi River prevented teams from transporting any more settlers over it that winter. She was told she would have to wait until the ice cleared and the ferries began to run again. Faced with four exhausted children and a diminished cash reserve, she decided to join a few others who were walking to Iowa over the groaning ice floes. She picked up the baby, distributed the luggage among the older children, and set out. Her daughter later recounted their perilous crossing:

> I can see yet, as in a dream, that great expanse of gray ice. Even then it was cracking, and as we went on there was a low grinding sound . . . we were constantly warned not to crowd together or we would break through. Mother who, with all her burdens, was clipping along with the rest would call out cheering and encouraging me to come along. I don't think she had realized how wide the river was, how far the distant shore.[80]

When her children asked her what had given her the courage to keep going across the splitting ice, she replied, "I was thinking of your father and all he had been writing about you children growing up in Iowa."[81]

The Mississippi River was a dramatic, but not an unfitting, introduction to a frontier which would continue to tax the bodies and the wills of pioneer women. In a sense, the journey on the trail served as a dress rehearsal for their subsequent attempts to create a home on the Iowa sod. Women who survived the trail had already survived one kind of a frontier—a community in flux.[82] In the process, many women learned to adjust their work, their emotions, and their life-styles to meet constantly fluctuating circumstances.

In challenging the trail, multitudes of hardy women unconsciously challenged a widespread nineteenth-century stereotype concerning the nature of the "weaker" sex. The social myth, predicated upon a belief that women were weak, emotionally insecure, and capable of existing only within the confines of a home tucked away from the realities of a harsh world, was trampled in the dust of the trail.[83] Although the westward journey broke and embittered some women, too many emerged from it intact, or even strengthened, for the myth to be successfully transplanted to the western scene. As they emerged from the restraints of the stereotype, women often came to be esteemed as valuable partners in the frontier experiment.

CHAPTER TWO

Women's Workplaces

WHEN the journey finally ended and the weary pioneers came to rest on the piece of Iowa sod that was to be their new home, they quickly observed that the promised land was going to require a lot of taxing, backbreaking work in order to fulfill its promise. Because the economy of Iowa was primarily based on family farms, the initial tasks at hand included breaking land, planting crops, building dwellings, and producing domestic goods. With all these chores demanding immediate attention, there was little time either to rest from the trip they had just completed or to prepare themselves for the new life they were about to begin.

The various jobs were hurriedly assigned to family members according to traditional notions of men's and women's work. Men turned to the fields as their workplaces. Because they had less strength and were charged with the care of babies and younger children, women turned to the home as their workplaces. In this realm, the frontier had more shocks for women than men. Certainly men had to deal with a harsh work environment in terms of stubborn prairie sod and climatic extremes, but at least their working environment existed. Many women, however, discovered that their working environment, the family home, either did not exist or was woefully inadequate. This situation was further complicated by the fact that the fields by necessity had to have first claim on investments of time and money while the home had to wait. Thus, women were cast into the frustrating role of workers without workplaces.

Many scholars of the West conclude that this situation created tremendous anomie, helplessness, and stress, both psychologically and physically, for the pioneer woman. After all, they reason, her work was crucial to the family's survival and an adequately equipped workplace was a necessity. Yet, by herself, she was powerless to create or improve her workplace because she lacked strength and technical skill. Heaped upon these factors were nineteenth-century dictums regarding domesticity as a woman's highest calling—a profession she could not practice without a workplace.[1]

The mythic image of the pioneer woman which results from this kind of logic is two-sided: she was a "saint in a sunbonnet" for surviving such conditions or she was victimized and eventually "broken" by them. Either way, the lot of the pioneer woman appears one-dimensional and grim. From the sentimentalized works of Iowa-born novelist Hamlin Garland to the more scholarly work of western historians, a picture of a beleaguered frontierswoman has emerged to haunt later and more fortunate generations of Americans.[2] The myth includes reverential homage paid to the poor women who watched their husbands and sons labor to create arable land while they themselves were essentially bereft of place and direction.

The evidence for pioneer Iowa, however, does not support this view of women. It suggests instead that scholars have dealt more in myth and stereotype than they have in fact; that researchers underestimated, to the point of distortion, the ability and stamina of frontierswomen to provide for themselves and their families. To be sure, some women retreated from the frontier in despair and fled back East, but so did some men. And some frontierswomen became depressed and hopeless in the face of their living conditions, but so did some men. Such cases, although highly visible and deserving of sympathy, were not fairly representative of the general population of frontier Iowa.

The "typical" Iowa pioneer woman had been a farm wife or daughter before migrating. She had already learned how to cope with arduous tasks, rudimentary equipment, and adversity. When she left her farm home for Iowa she carried with her experience, skills, and some of the equipment she would need in her frontier home. If she traveled by covered wagon, she had the additional advantage of learning trail skills during the transition period. This allowed her time to fully comprehend the meaning of the phrase "westward migration."

Once in Iowa she might be disappointed, as indeed many were, but it is fallacious to suppose that she could only function happily and effectively if her workplace replicated the one she had left behind. Surely this was not true of the frontiersman who turned to his workplace, the fields, only to be confronted by tangled webs of prairie grass roots, breaking plows, prairie fires, locusts, grasshoppers, and other unexpected factors. Like him, she learned to adapt and to improvise. She could not afford to do otherwise if she cared about her own survival and that of her family. As one woman stoically commented, "When we got to the new purchase, the land of milk and honey, we were disappointed and homesick, but we were there and had to make the best of it."[3] Like her, most Iowa frontierswomen "made the best of it," exhibiting ingenuity and an intuitive grasp of how to use the resources at hand in the process.

For some of these newly arrived Iowans, the covered wagon which carried them to their new home literally became their new home. Just as earlier settlers in the Ohio valley had torn apart log rafts to build their first cabins, the prairie settlers looked to their wagons as potential housing. The wagons were more easily converted than the rafts had been for they were already arranged, to some degree, for sleeping and cooking. Once the seed, tools, farm implements, and firearms were unloaded, wagons even became commodious. One Grinnell settler of the 1850s remarked on the prevalence of these early shelters. "There was not a shed, or fence, or even a hitching post on the prairie," he later told his family, "all horses being tied to wagons, in many of which people were still living."[4]

Even if the wagon was not used as a house, it was seldom discarded, but was put to all kinds of supplementary purposes. It sometimes became an extra bedroom for a large family crammed into a small cabin. The Shuteses, for example, had to compact the seven members of their family into a twenty-four-by sixteen-foot cabin, so "Uncle Charley" was more than happy to have the family wagon turned over to him as his bachelor quarters. In other cases, the wagon was used as an outbuilding or a storage shed for tools, clothing, or food. During their first winter in Clay County, Albert and Abbie Benedict found their wagon to be indispensable. After partially dismantling it, the men used the running gear to haul lumber in for the frame of their sod shanty while the women used the covered box as a "root cellar" in which to store the winter's supply of meat and other foodstuffs.[5]

Besides the prairie schooners, another quick housing resource involving less than ideal conditions was sharing another family's home. When the Newtons first arrived in Iowa in the 1850s they owned land devoid of buildings so they "boarded out" with their nearest neighbors for the three months it took to haul in lumber and construct the first building on their treeless land. In 1854 the Grinnells spent their first Iowa winter in a tiny room built onto the side of one of the few existing houses in the area. And in the 1860s the Laceys moved into the Loomis's "little shack" so that the men could "pool their resources and break prairie together."[6]

Another alternative was to rent or buy houses left vacant by settlers who had moved on to a better home or to another region of the frontier. Although abandoned houses were often in a state of disrepair, many homeless migrants were glad to move into them, at least for the time being. Lydia Arnold Titus and her husband, their three children, her sister and husband, and their baby all lived in a rented two-room house in a town composed of "a few frame store buildings and a handful of small houses" until they could buy land and build on it. But like many other women of the era, Titus seemed to be much more interested in the possibilities of the future than the inconveniences of the present. In later life her primary memories of that first year in Iowa centered around the "fine prairie land" that they purchased at $6.25 per acre—land that fulfilled their hopes for it by jumping in value to over $300 per acre in the years following the Civil War.[7]

Young Kitturah Belknap, her husband George, and her in-laws took up a claim with a two-room hewed-log house already standing on it. Kitturah set up housekeeping in one room while her relatives crowded into the other room. Kitturah's notation on this awkward situation was brief and practical. "We unloaded and commenced business," she wrote. "Made us some homemade furniture and went to keeping house."[8]

Not all women adopted a stoic attitude towards such situations. When the Shuteses reached their dilapidated cabin in Carroll County, Mary Alice's diary entry registered both shock and resignation. "We walked over to the cabin door," Mary Alice recorded. "It does not look much like home right now but no one said a word." The Peitzke's first farm near Riceville, with its old log house and shed for straw, left much to be desired too. According to their daughter, Matilda, "The house was about 12 by 18 all in one room, with one door and one window. There was a low upstairs all in one room without a window. The roof leaked in many places." Margaret Archer Murray was also distressed about the poor condition of her family's old four-room house where her first baby was born about the same time that her mother and brother moved in. She remembered that they wintered together with difficulty: "We all lived practly in one room as kitchen was to cold the north Sill had roted and lift a hole that one could throw a cat out through."[9]

Even in a state of disrepair, many dwellings were probably more comfortable than the abandoned outbuildings that some pioneers converted to home. The Laceys bravely moved into a corncrib; their only defense against Iowa's climate was provided by the spare blankets and bedding that were nailed up over the slats. Sarah Carr Lacey's daughter later remarked that because her mother was "accustomed to making the best of things" she was able to make it "fairly livable." The Willis family did not fare quite as well living in a crude structure which was "utterly desolate" and "gave ample evidence of having been used as a stable, rather than a human dwelling place." Some years later, Mary Willis Lyon recalled that it had been very easy for her to understand why her mother, "remembering the pretty little white house back in Ohio, sat down and wept."[10]

Since options in temporary housing did not always present themselves to arriving migrants, many had to erect a hasty shelter from whatever materials might be available. In those regions of Iowa where timber was accessible, this generally meant a rough-hewn log cabin which in its initial form was usually little more than a shack. Because the demands for labor in the fields competed with the demands for shelter, the "cabins" were often built with great dispatch but little planning. One family built its shelter in a day's time. It had "a frame of two by fours at top and bottom, with boards running perpendicularly nailed to them, a roof sloping one way, a door, and two windows." After observing this rudely constructed hut, a neighbor characterized it as a "lean-to without anything to lean to."[11]

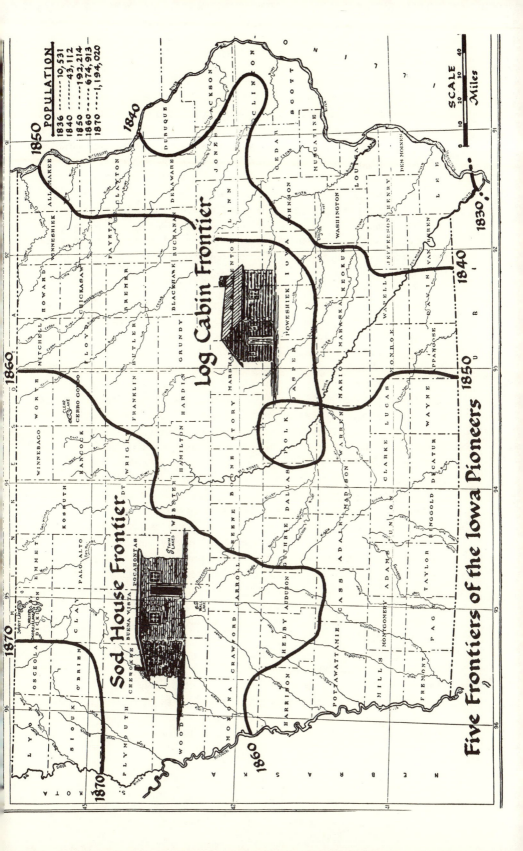

Five Frontiers of the Iowa Pioneers

Some of the other early experiments were not much sturdier. One family built a structure of poles covered with elm bark. To their dismay they soon discovered that the bark roof curled in the sun so rapidly that it had to be replaced every few days. Even when the bark was fresh, they concluded that it was not much better than no roof at all in keeping the elements out. Another family did slightly better. Mary Ann Ferrin Davidson remembered that her family built a cabin as high as one of them could reach, then roofed it with clapboards held on only by the weight of poles. "We were," she wrote, "glad to take shelter within its rough walls, without having a chimney or floor made in it; for there came a heavy rain storm that lasted nearly a week."[12]

Clearly, these primitive shelters were only seen as temporary by Iowa settlers. Women could not work in them effectively and families could not live in them comfortably for very long, but they could be tolerated for a short time. Therefore, most pioneer families endured their first homes while anxiously working towards the day when a house-raising would follow the land-breaking.

Frontierspeople usually planned a modest one-room cabin, sixteen by eighteen feet, with floors of packed dirt or handhewn puncheons (pieces of split logs with roughly smoothed surfaces), possibly with a small root cellar underneath. Wood was used exclusively in construction in many areas of Iowa.

Some people, such as Joseph and Mary Ann Davidson and George and Kitturah Belknap, were able to prepare all the lumber and lathing they needed from the trees growing on their own land, only having to travel and pay for such items as nails, which they could not produce themselves. As more settlers moved into Iowa, however, the sparse woodlands could not supply all the building needs. When Joseph Mott went to a nearby sawmill and hauled back green lumber for his family's home in 1855, he counted himself among the fortunate. Tales of bringing lumber ten, twenty, or even fifty miles across the Iowa prairie in order to build a house were becoming quite common.[13]

When the time actually came to build the house, as many hands as possible were enlisted. Men siphoned off time and energy from the fields, which they diverted to the house-raising. Children proved useful in carrying tools, holding logs, and chinking in the spaces between logs. Women learned skills and assumed tasks that in their former homes might have been considered unwomanly. And if there were neighbors in the area, they were asked to participate in a house-raising "bee" complete with food, drink, and fellowship to speed the work along.

Susan Dubell's recollections of her first home provide an excellent picture of the type of cabin that typically resulted from these efforts. It was "a one-room house, built of logs with the bark on, roofed with clapboards." The logs had been cut to a prescribed length, notched at the ends, and then fitted together. The cracks between the logs were chinked with pieces of wood as well as a clay and water mortar. The roof consisted of log rafters fastened with wooden pins and covered by clapboards. These clapboards, approximately three feet long and six inches wide, were split logs put on in layers held by long poles laid over them and fastened together at the ends.[14]

Dubell recalled that the cabin boasted two windows, but that the glass was so defective it distorted the reality of the outside world. The only door was made of boards held together by crosspieces called cleats. Unlike most cabin doors, it was held by iron hinges rather than leather or wooden ones. It fastened with a wood latch held in place by the proverbial latchstring, which was pulled in through a small hole to lock the door or left hanging outside to welcome guests. The floor was of sawed lumber probably held in place by pegs, as was the rest of the house, for no nails were used except in the windows and door.[15]

Although Dubell's house was representative, there were many variations. One Iowa woman depicted her childhood home as "a small farm house of one and a half stories, sealed with lumber in the living room and bedroom, but unfinished upstairs except for the floors." In early Algona, the Moores lived in a sixteen- by twenty-foot cabin with a split log floor and clapboard roof which also served for a "post-office, town hall, boardinghouse, and meeting house." And Sarah Kenyon wrote to her mother-in-law about a rather unusual stone house, which she described as "the dampest frostiest hole I ever saw."[16]

According to May Lacey Crowder, her family's first real home was "on a very pretentious scale" because "it measured sixteen feet wide by eighteen feet long and was a story and a half high." The first floor had two rooms; one of these was a combination living room, kitchen, and pantry while the other was a small bedroom. The upper floor was one large room divided by curtains which created "sleeping quarters for us children and for anyone else who chanced to pass by when night was approaching."[17]

Crowders' judgment that such a house was "pretentious" for her area of Iowa during the late 1860s reflects the relative values of a time and place. Women not only had personal perspectives on what they considered adequate housing, but they frequently adjusted their standards to fit the expectations of the area of the frontier in which they lived.

At first they expected packed dirt floors. That was all that was available in the early stages of settlement. Later, puncheon floors of split logs laid flat side up became preferable because they were cheaper than lumber and easier to maintain than dirt. As Sarah Welch Nossaman told her daughter, "We did not think of such a thing as plank for floors. Your father split puncheons and hewed them and made a floor of them."[18]

Settlers who could afford it, and had access to a mill, often chose the smoother, more finely finished plank floors. Mary Alice Shutes, who immediately noticed that her family's new home had a dirt floor, was very relieved when her father announced that he would "get a slab floor in that building just as soon as we can find the slabs." The slab floor was apparently a high priority for the Shuteses, because within a few days of their arrival Hiram measured the twenty-four- by sixteen-foot cabin for planking and set off for a nearby mill. Mary Alice was resigned to "use it as it is for a few days." While Mary Alice anticipated a plank floor as a step up, Elisabeth Koren regarded the one in her first Iowa home as a step down. Having just moved from her family's well-established home in Norway, she was not very impressed by the floors in her Decorah cabin. "The floor consists of unfinished planks," she jotted in her diary, "which bob up and down when walked on."[19]

A Webster City family felt favored to have even a partially planked floor. They reserved the area covered with wood for the beds, spinning wheel, loom, and cupboards while they used the earthen section for the daily chores. With a great sense of the practical they saw that the eighteen-inch space disrepancy between the wood planking and the dirt formed a ledge which could be used as a bench. They concluded that they were twice blessed because not only did they have some wood flooring, but they also had a built-in bench, which would allow them to manage with fewer stools in their crowded quarters.[20]

Cellars were another matter of perspective and preference. Most families included, or eventually added, some kind of cellar under the floor. They were used as general storehouses for goods such as soap, candles, and foodstuffs. Susan Dubell explained that her cellar, like most others, was just a hole dug in the ground with earthen walls, reached by a trap door and a stout wooden ladder. In a similar manner, the Peitzkes used a shallow hole under their house as a cellar and when they needed some of the potatoes or other food items stored there, they simply lifted up one of the wide boards in their floor to gain access to it. The Lacey's cellar, used to store milk, butter, and vegetables, was reached by a door from the pantry and dirt steps into the cellar wall and was banked on the outside with earth several feet up the walls of the house to prevent food from freezing in the cellar.[21]

In Palo Alto County, a group of Irish settlers developed what they believed to be a definite improvement on the usual type of cellar. They built "root houses," as they called them, outside of the house. They roofed them with logs covered with another layer of clay and sod. Root houses had no outside opening, but were reached by steps or ladders from inside the cabin. This arrangement allowed heat from the fire in the cabin to enter the root house, thus preventing frost from entering and destroying the valuable produce stored there.[22]

Families who acquired such improvements as smooth wood floors or commodious storage cellars no doubt considered their environment superior to earlier living conditions which may have included dirt floors and a dismembered wagon box as the only storage facility. Yet the next generation would look back on wooden floors and earthen cellars as primitive aspects of earlier homes. Because living conditions and attitudes toward them changed so rapidly, judgments about the crudity of pioneer homes should be kept in historical perspective. A careful reading of frontierswomen's source materials indicates that what was anathema to one might well be a refinement to another.

The long-standing assumption that frontiersmen had to continue investing time, energy, and capital in their workplaces (the land) long after the initial groundbreaking, while all frontierswomen sat by helplessly waiting for the promised day when there would be something left over with which to renovate and improve their workplaces (the home), must be approached more critically. The data from Iowa suggest that the assertion that land and tools received a major share of available capital, while the home got little or none, is a partial truth whose impact was offset by intervening variables not usually considered.

Of course, farming *was* literally a sunup to sundown occupation, with only horses, hand tools, and occasional hired labor to ease the way. Women often mentioned the tremendous amount of time that men had to invest in farm labor. One talked about the wheat crop, which had to be hand-cut with a cradle: "That was real hard work swinging a cradle all day." She also noted that sheaves were bound by hand and haymaking was done by cutting the grass by hand with a scythe. Another woman referred to her father cutting "all the wheat with a cradle and the hay with a scythe" while her brother "bound all the grain, and raked up all the hay with a homemade hand rake." Yet another described how grain was handsown by the farmer who carried a sack across his shoulder and walked his fields scattering the seed before him.[23] And in addition to time, farming required continuous outlays of capital for land, machinery, seed, animals, and other capital goods. Even when better machinery was developed to reduce the farmer's time spent in the fields, the apparent advantages were often outweighed by the machinery's cost. An 1864 advertisement for the latest McCormick Reaper and Mower in the *Fairfield Ledger,* for example, quoted a price of "$155 and upwards, according to terms."[24]

On the other hand, not all farmers operated at a subsistence level. Many profited or even prospered; indeed, that was why they came to Iowa in the first place. Many pioneer men were anxious to use spare time to provide a nicer home for themselves, their spouses, and their children. When the Laceys moved into their home, it lacked doors and windows, but Alvin Lacey set up his workbench in the second story where, in moments stolen from farm work, he planed the lumber for window frames and doors. Another Iowa man devoted his spare hours for years to get shingles "split and shaved to cover the roof" and to replace the ladder to the room upstairs with a stairway.[25]

Pioneer women were not incapable or unwilling to undertake the heavy tasks involved in improving their homes. One young girl mentioned that her mother did the lathing as well as sharing the work "of getting out stone and digging the cellar." Another woman helped dig a well and "stoned it up" herself. Another said that she and her two young sons dug the earthen cellar for their home while the men did the haying. And two daughters mixed clay mortar for the fireplace and assisted their mother while she "laid up the stones with her own hands."[26]

Both men and women often exhibited qualities of patience, persistence, endurance, and optimism which carried them through the long and sometimes uncertain years required to complete a frontier home. Kitturah and George Belknap are a perfect illustration. In 1841 Kitturah recorded in her diary that after two years of hard work she and George had most of the necessary materials gathered for the frame house they were planning. Since there was no saw mill closer than fifty miles, the lumber had been prepared by George from their own trees. "Everything from sills to rafters," she wrote, "are hued with the broad axe." The winter had been devoted to making shingles. "While I spun flax," Kitturah recorded, "George brought in the shaving horse and shaved shingles and we burnt the shavings and both worked by the same light."

In the summer of 1841 a carpenter was hired to lay out the work and then her husband and his father began to build the house "after the corn was layed by till harvest." During the fall of 1841, the roofing and siding were put on the twenty-four- by sixteen-foot dwelling that was to have one general room and two bedrooms. In October, Kitturah noted that they were "at the house again. Have it all enclosed and rocks on the ground for the chimney. Now it is time to gather corn." In November she remarked, "we will spend another winter in the little log house." The summer of 1842 was spent in lathing, plastering, and constructing the chimney. In September she recorded, "Time moves on and here it is September and the new house is about ready to live in this winter." Finally, in November, 1842, she rejoiced, "Everything is about done up and we have moved in our own house."[27]

Kitturah spoke for many pioneer women when she expressed her joy at overseeing her own home. "It is real nice to have things all my own way," she wrote at one point. At another she declared, "It seems real nice to have the whole control of my house; can say I am monarch of all I survey and none to dispute my right." Despite her positive attitude, the finish work on the house was to continue over a period of years. It was not until the spring of 1847 that she said, "We are fixed nicely in our home now." At the time of writing, she was blissfully unaware that by fall of the same year she would be sewing a wagon cover in preparation for a move to Oregon.[28]

Belknap's case was not atypical in this respect for many families chose to move farther and farther West. This meant that women and men had to survive successive relocations. At this point evidence is inconclusive whether such moves tended to wear women down or whether they were able to handle moves with increasing efficiency due to past experience. The two cases which follow show that two women, Sarah Carr Lacey and Abbie Mott Benedict, readily and happily accepted their many and varied moves.

Sarah Carr Lacey, married in 1858, spent her first two years of married life and bore her first two children in her sister-in-law's home. In 1860, Sarah, her husband, and their children migrated to Iowa where they made a home first on the trail then in an empty corn crib. Within the year, they moved into a log cabin that had one room and a loft, where a third child was born in 1861. During the Civil War her husband served in the Union army and she lived in the cabin, supporting her three children with the produce of the nine cows she purchased. By 1869, the Laceys were on the trail again, this time to northwestern Iowa. Here they shared a makeshift shack with another family while they cleared land and built a home. By late 1869 they moved into their half-built, new frame house. Ten years later the house was torn down to be replaced by a larger dwelling, and here her narrative ends.[29]

Abbie Mott Benedict, who moved twenty-one times during her first twenty years of marriage, is an even more striking example of a woman who survived frequent relocations. After making a home in sod huts, log cabins, and frame houses, she and her family settled down on one farm for nine years, "the longest time we ever lived in any one place, up to that time." When the farm became a financial burden, the Benedicts moved to another farm where they finally found success, happiness, and for the first time in their married life, freedom from debt. "We were now so well situated," Abbie reminisced, "that in honor of the event Albert in his characteristic way, named the farm 'Safeside,' feeling that we were now on the safe side of things in general." The following year they built a new house where they lived out their lives. In her words, they "had followed what Hamlin Garland calls 'The Middle Border' long enough."[30]

These stories illustrate the trauma of dislocations that frontierswomen had to deal with. In the case of Lacey and Benedict, each woman's faith in the future was justified; farm production did increase and working environments were eventually improved. These women embodied the frontier version of a success story to which most pioneers aspired.

On the Iowa prairies, settlers did not always start out in a log cabin or frame hut. Due to the treeless nature of many regions, numerous settlers lived in sod huts. Humble sod dwellings, however, are usually omitted from the mythical image of frontier opportunity, since many observers viewed them as symbols of unrelieved poverty whose inhabitants were quaint, yet often painful to see. In reality, however, many pioneers willingly started out in a "soddie." Since the northwestern portion of Iowa was primarily prairie with very little timber, it necessarily began as a sod-house frontier. This did not, however, automatically impose any limits on future production and income. Perhaps the aura of poverty surrounding the sod-house frontier attended early assumptions that land covered by prairie grass was not very productive. Although productiveness of such land was soon proved, the negative view of the sod house remained. Historian Everett Dick, for example, portrayed the sod hut as an "unpromising, ugly hole in the ground" which portended "utter loneliness and drab prospects." Here again, Iowa does not fully conform to such an interpretation. Abbie Mott Benedict found life in a sod hut "desolate" and "windswept," but at the same time she pointed out that it was very warm during the harsh Iowa winter. And, it effectively sheltered her family from a raging prairie fire and from a blizzard which killed several people.[31]

Benedict's report gives an excellent picture of a sod house in pioneer Iowa. She explained that wood was brought from twelve miles away to build the frame of the fourteen- by twenty-foot hut. A heavy post with a fork at the top was set at each end to provide support for the ridgepole. Additional posts were set along the sides and at the corners as wall supports, leaving space for only one door and two windows. Then a prairie sod breaking plow was used to turn and cut the previously untouched sod around the hut. The resulting strips of sod were cut into lengths of two and one-half feet which were then laid up around the wall supports like large brick. The roof was thatched with slough grass covered with a layer of sod. The Benedict soddie had some welcome accoutrements: a board floor, a trap door, and a small cellar. A partition created a bedroom while a platform over the partition provided more storage area for foodstuffs, particularly flour. The Benedicts spent one winter in their soddie, "proved" up their claim, and in the spring began construction on a proper frame homestead.[32]

Unlike the Benedicts, most people constructed their sod houses over a hole dug into the flat prairie or into the side of a hill. One such structure started with a three-foot-deep hole which measured sixteen by thirty feet. Rafters were raised from its banks to a twelve-foot-high ridgepole, then were covered by squares of sod. A floor of rough boards and a chimney made from turf completed this primitive but effectual shelter. Another soddie, protruding from a hillside, was described as a "large, roomy cave in the hillside" which was "warmly banked up, and inclosed in front, and was as comfortable as the most costly a place when the wild winter winds whistled across the prairie."[33]

Considering Iowa's climatic extremes, it is significant that the warmth of sod huts was so often touted as one of their major advantages. Some settlers even maintained that water did not freeze in a soddie during the coldest Iowa winter. Another point in their favor was the minimum capital investment involved in constructing sod houses. One person claimed to have built a sod house for two dollars and seventy-eight and one-half cents around 1870, a reasonable investment for the poorest of homesteaders.[34]

Certainly these soddies had little else to recommend them. They lacked aesthetic value, afforded little space or privacy, and were difficult to keep clean. Most sod-house dwellers, however, considered their soddies to be only temporary homes. Like the many other Iowa settlers living in shacks, lean-tos, and cabins, the sod-house people saw their rough homes as a necessary beginning to life on the frontier. Just because a sod hut looked miserable did not mean its inhabitants *were* miserable. One Iowa frontierswoman, thinking back on her life in a soddie, summed up the issue of relative happiness this way:

> When we think of those dugouts or shacks now, it is hard to realize how one lived. There was a hole dug down three feet or more in the ground and then a frame of whatever you could get made over that and sometimes only the sod (which was very tough) cut in squares and built up. There were no floors, or partitions, unless made of bed quilts. . . . But I can not help but say there was more general happiness to be found in some of these shacks than was found in their more pretentious homes afterward.[35]

Whether cabin or sod hut, few of the pioneer homes could be accused of pretension. In fact, by modern standards they didn't even include the necessities. Solutions to bathing and hygiene are not fully known since women of the nineteenth century did not usually discuss such matters, even in their personal diaries. One Iowa woman did break with convention when she frankly explained that "outhouse accommodations were the thick brush or a couple of fallen tree-trunks; one for men, one for women."[36] Babies' diapers, menstrual periods, and sexual relations were taboo topics and are mentioned only in the vaguest of phraseology, if at all.

Some pioneer women did feel unconstrained enough to talk about the problem of getting dressed in a small home which accommodated a large family as well as frequent visitors. One account said that the men dressed before the women awoke; the men then went outside "to check the weather" thus leaving the women a few minutes alone in which to get dressed. For some people, this lack of privacy caused discomfort. In her two-story home, Elisabeth Koren hastily performed her toilet before the men descended from upstairs. "I hurried to dress myself before the men came down," she told her diary. "One must watch his chance." For others, like the Benedicts, the lack of privacy was a cause for humor. There was only one room in Abbie's sister's home so on one occasion her sister's husband Ed went outside to change his clothes, rather than embarrassing his houseguests. "Forever after," she remarked, "the boys referred to 'out of doors' as 'Uncle Ed's bedroom.' "[37]

Although by modern standards, pioneer homes seem unattractive and inefficient, the creativity and resourcefulness of many pioneer women transformed these humble dwellings into reasonably efficient workplaces and comfortable homes. When walls were nonexistent, women created them by hanging dividers made of curtains, blankets, or sheeting. Occasionally calico was used, although Benedict believes that many settlers avoided these kinds of "walls" because "calico curtains were sometimes expensive and very toney for pioneers."[38] Evidently, some pioneer women could create space in their tiny homes for a variety of purposes. Matilda Peitzke Paul remembered a neighbor's cabin, the back room of which had been turned over to the children of the area as a school, leaving the family a living room of fourteen by sixteen feet and a small bedroom separated only by a curtain. It must have been very small indeed for she wrote that "this bed-room had walls on 3 sides of the bed with just room for the bed to fit in, and curtains across the front with about one foot of standing room between curtains and front of bed." A trundle bed under the bigger bed and the family's clothes hanging from pegs in the walls filled the last few inches of space in the room.[39] Another woman remembered a similar arrangement in her aunt's log cabin in Mahaska County. She recalled,

> The style of bedstead used then was so high from the floor to the bed rail that there was ample room under a bed to store many trunks and chests and boxes and bundles. It was customary to hang a valance around which hid all these unsightly things. . . . Women in that day and stage of the country's history, learned how to manage and utilize room.[40]

The interior surfacing of the side walls was also a matter of concern to many pioneer women. The chinking between the logs or boards was relatively fragile and needed continued maintenance if drafts were to be avoided. When the Shutes family reached their cabin they discovered that kindly neighbors had attempted to lighten their tasks by rechinking the inside of the cabin. In another instance, the diary entry of a young pioneer girl indicated that rechinking was a chore which frequently fell to the children of the family. In 1862, she noted, "heard Emma recite her lessons and corcked up around the logs of the room."[41]

Nicely surfaced walls were a priority with many. One woman's home was entirely lined by tarred paper, which she felt had a neat appearance and was good insulation as well. Other pioneer women resorted to cheap and available newspapers for wall covering. A young bride in Algona was delighted when she received "a quantity of old newspapers" with which she promptly papered the walls of her small cabin. Another woman who had wept at the sight of her new home soon made it bright and cheerful by papering it with clean newspapers.[42]

When lime was available, it was preferable to newspapers for surfacing interior walls. Although it was more expensive, it was bright, clean-smelling, and uniform. Even when applied to the interior of a sod hut it gave the appearance of smooth plaster. Liming did, however, require a certain amount of knowledge and skill. According to Susan Dubell, the lime was "slacked" for several hours or perhaps for a day before the whitewashing was to begin. Slacking was done by combining kiln-burned limestone with water in an iron pot and letting it "boil" from its own internal heat. Gradually, it became a "smooth, snowy white mass" to which more water could be added until the proper consistency was attained.

In the meantime, the women removed the furniture from the house. When the lime reached a satisfactory consistency, they began the actual liming with an old broom or a special whitewash brush. Dubell observed that "an expert did not splash the floor and woodwork very badly, but when the whitewashing was done the windows had to be washed, the floor scrubbed, and the furniture carried in again." To keep the limed walls fresh and uncracked, this process had to be repeated every spring and, when possible, every fall as well.[43]

A few women were fortunate enough to have a home with a lathed and plastered interior. Kitturah Belknap explained that she and her husband were able to finish their home in this manner because both laths and lime were extracted from their own land. Although lathing and plastering produced a more refined wall covering than some of the other methods, it often had its drawbacks too. When Emery Bartlett built a home for his bride, Hannah, he soon learned to his chagrin that the walnut siding he had nailed to the studding warped so badly that "one could almost run their fingers between the boards." Combined with a single coat of thin plaster, these walls gave little protection from Iowa's cold winds.[44]

Like the Bartletts, many pioneers soon became disenchanted with the inability of their homes to withstand the onslaught of Iowa winters. The first homes naturally had the greatest problems, and to their credit, women tried everything they could think of to protect their families. When the Archers built their first cabin they were unable to procure a door, so Elizabeth Archer "fastened a quilt in the opening to keep out the snow and as much cold wind as possable." Another woman lamented that her cabin had only "rag carpets hung over the opening at night to protect you from the cold air, the house being only sheeted up."[45]

Even in relatively well-built homes, cold was a constant problem for the homemaker. One woman remembered frost on the wall behind the bed all winter long. Another recalled snow drifting onto the loft beds as she and her brothers and sisters slept. And Sarah Kenyon wrote home, "I guess I shall friz here. Mary swept off a heeping dust pan of frost off of one window this afternoon." Sarah recalled that during the past winter her floors would turn to ice when mopped and her table would freeze during dishwashing. With equanimity she added, "Mr. Barnard froze his great toe one night when it happened to get out of bed when he was asleep."[46]

Kitturah Belknap constantly combatted the snow which drifted into the loft of her first home and then slowly dripped on the people below as it melted. She was particularly dismayed when a snowstorm hit the house just hours before the Sunday meeting was to be held there. She noted in her diary,

> It snowed and blowed so the upstairs was so full of snow Sunday morning that we had to shovel it out and build big fires to get it dryed out so it would not drip before meeting time. We took up some of the boards and shoveled snow down and carried it out in the washtubs (barrels of it).[47]

The infamous Iowa blizzards placed an especially severe strain on these early homes, some of which could withstand such pressure while others could not. During an 1863 blizzard, for instance, the small stove in the West Wilson home could not accommodate the entire family so the children were kept in bed for days to stay warm, a wise precaution in a storm so severe that it froze several of the neighbor's oxen to death while they were still standing on their feet with their tails to the storm.[48]

Other early homes were able to comfortably withstand even the worst Iowa winters. One woman credited her small house with adequately protecting her family through two consecutive winters of frequent blizzards. She later remembered:

> There were days when we could see only a few feet away because of the blinding snow; and often the cold was so intense that people were frozen to death out on the prairie. During such storms men were sometimes lost while going from the house to the barn. When father went to do the chores he would often tie a rope to the house to guide him back in safety.[49]

Frequently, hard winters were followed by heavy rains in the spring thus placing another burden on the patience and endurance of frontier women. According to Matilda Peitzke Paul, her mother had to use every pot and pan she owned just to keep the beds dry during the rainy season. Furthermore, these heavy rains created dangerous floods, which threatened pioneer homes. In the spring of 1832, Caroline Phelps watched as high water and ice blocked up below her home causing flood waters of the "Demoin River" to rise in her direction. She was hesitant to desert her home, but was persuaded to do so when "the water burst through the back of the chimney" and "the floor was all swimming." She sent her sister and the baby ahead while she stayed to salvage some household goods, but she was trapped by the rising water so that her husband had to carry her out of the cabin on his shoulders. They all camped on a nearby hill in incessant rain for three days until the ice and water began to subside, allowing them to escape to a neighbor's home.[50]

In 1865, the Benedicts' shack was similarly invaded by the overflowing waters of the Upper Iowa River. After grabbing their children and a loaf of bread, they quickly moved upstairs to the part of the structure where another family lived. As they watched, the flood waters swirled into their home below them and floated a large cake of ice into their front yard. Fortunately, that marked the high point of the flood and they were soon able to return to their water-soaked house. Another woman got so disgusted when flood waters forced her family out of its home that she adamantly refused to return to the beseiged cabin. The neighbors provided a happy solution by disassembling the damp house, moving it to a nearby hill, and reassembling it there.[51]

As a matter of course, spring rains and floods were followed by dry, hot summers with their own brand of discomfort and danger. Cooking fires and small unventilated rooms combined to make things particularly uncomfortable for women. Emery Bartlett told his children that "it has always been a mystery to me how Mother endured that long hot summer, with all the family she had to provide for, in that one room used as kitchen, dining room, sitting room and sleeping room, and destitute of almost everything we now consider necessities."[52]

Although the heat was oppressive and inescapable, the constant threat of prairie fires was more frightening. Many householders tried to offset the threat of fire with various precautions. Some carefully trimmed off the hay that hung down at the eaves of soddies, while others carefully plowed fire guards around their soddies or cabins. These guards usually consisted of two plowed strips in the shape of a square, one close to the house and one a "safe" distance away from the house. The grass between the plowed strips was kept "burned off" during prairie fire season.[53]

May Lacey Crowder remembered that her mother always insisted that the men of the family keep the firebreaks around their home burned off, a precaution that saved their lives on one occasion when the men were away hauling lumber for a new cabin. When young May called her mother's attention to the odd orange hue of the sunshine of the kitchen floor, her mother immediately diagnosed it as an approaching prairie fire. Crowder's description of that fire gives a feeling of the helplessness of the pioneers in the face of such an overwhelming menace.

> Soon the flames became visible. The fire was coming with racehorse speed, for the grass was long and heavy and a prairie fire always creates a strong wind. Great sheets of flame seemed to break off and go sailing through the air directly over the house and stables, but nothing inside the firebreaks was ignited and soon the danger was past. The burned-over prairie, however, was drearier than before.[54]

If the pioneer homestead escaped these dangers, there was always the possibility of one of Iowa's infamous tornadoes descending upon it. The Wilsons regularly retreated to a specially dug cave when a thunderstorm approached to protect themselves in case of a tornado. Less cautious by nature, the Archers learned the hard way to respect a tornado. They closed the doors and windows of their two-story frame house and the men braced their bodies against them as the storm approached. Little actual damage resulted but the family was badly shaken. The seriousness of the situation became even more real to them when they learned that in a four-mile stretch just south of them, every house, barn, or building had been leveled by the tornado. The storm left dead stock and huge beams driven three or four feet into the ground. On another occasion, the Benedicts witnessed a "cyclone" with a black funnel-shaped cloud, which hurtled buildings, trees, and other debris through the sky. Although it passed them without touching down, it tore a path of destruction through houses and trees which remained marked for many years.[55]

Besides the elements, various animals and insects were also enemies of homemakers. Since there were no screens, flies and mosquitoes entered the houses at will to feast on the family's dinner or on the family members themselves. Matilda Peitzke Paul claimed that the flies and mosquitoes were so thick that her family "used a little limb, thick with leaves, to keep them off food while we ate." To her, they were "too terrible to dwell on" but she did mention that her family also made a smudge of fine chips gathered by the wood pile to drive the mosquitoes away. Another woman recalled the persistence of the mosquitoes, especially during the night. "The only way we got any sleep was to cover up heads and ears with a thick, heavy cover," she wrote, even though the weather was "hot enough to almost cook eggs." There were also the ever-present bedbugs which Harriet Bonebright-Closz called "crimson-ramblers." Even if a housewife made a weekly ritual of pursuing the pests with a kettle of hot water, a can of kerosene, and a feather, she was seldom successful in dislodging them from the premises for very long.[56]

Snakes also seemed to prefer the hospitality of pioneer homes to the outdoors. According to Sarah Welch Nossaman, "it was not an uncommon thing to get up in the morning and kill from one to three snakes, but they were of garter snake variety, but we would rather they had stayed out if it had suited them as well." Paul, however, remembered many varieties of snakes: "the little green snake, garter snake, hoop snake, spotted water snake and worst of all the poisonous rattle snake which sometimes killed people."[57]

Skunks and wolves made less frequent visits, but were difficult to handle when they did appear. Nossaman noted that "we treated skunks very kindly until they were out of the shanty." She never learned to sleep soundly through the howling of the wolves and the screeching of the owls because they made her feel eerily alone during the otherwise still prairie nights. Other women also feared wolves. Margaret Murray said that her mother was often startled by the many wolves who "came right up and howled around the cabin at night." And Mary E. Ellis stated that she "would not dare to go far after dark here" due to the "many wolves who raided the pig houses."[58]

MATILDA PEITZKE PAUL

(Courtesy Iowa State Historical Department, Division of Historical Society)

It is small wonder that so many families spent hours huddling around the hearth for physical and psychological warmth. Although in some of the early houses the hearth was simply a hole where the projected fireplace would be built as soon as possible, many included fireplaces of stone, rock, or sod which provided a source of heat as well as a cooking fire. The fireplace was usually placed in the middle of one of the end walls of the dwelling. Its sides were tapered in to form a throat above which the chimney was constructed. Rock or stone daubed with clay were frequently used to build the chimney, but if those materials were not available a chimney of sticks covered inside and out by a thorough daubing of mud proved cheap, easy, and workable.[59]

Gradually fireplaces were replaced with stoves of various designs. Susan Dubell recalled that her family had a Premium stove, manufactured in Cincinnati, Ohio. Its pipe ran out through a crude hole in the roof and was only prevented from setting the roof boards on fire by large nails driven into the edge of the boards. Since Rising Sun Stove Polish had not yet made its appearance on the frontier, the rusty red coloration produced by the rain and snow dripping through the hole remained on the stovepipe year around.[60]

Such stoves were widely advertised in the newspapers of the time such as the *Burlington Daily Hawk-Eye and Telegraph*, *The Daily Gate City* (Keokuk), and the *Waterloo Courier*. Often accompanied by pictures, these ads lauded the diverse features of their product. The variety must have been bewildering to the prospective buyer, but did offer many options in purchasing such a significant piece of household equipment.

The Laceys, duly impressed by the importance of selecting a good stove, chose theirs with extreme care. They were delighted to find that it kept them comfortable all winter despite the fact that they lived in a home with board walls located out on the open prairie. They learned that the major problem with their stove was not its heating ability, but keeping it fueled. Although the boys of the family were sent on frequent excursions to the nearby Des Moines River to cut wood, in emergencies the family twisted hay or slough grass into bundles approximately the size of a stick of wood.[61] So many Iowa pioneers turned to this type of fuel that a stove was eventually developed specifically to burn hay or grass. Its design, which incorporated a large firebox with an adjustable weight to keep the fuel burning at a steady pace, was thought by many Iowa pioneers to be the most efficient way of heating a prairie home.

Supplying furnishings for their homes further taxed the industry and inventiveness of frontierswomen and here again they pressed existing resources into service. Lacking carpets, many women simply covered their floors with dry hay. They soon realized that although hay insulated the floors, it was extremely difficult to keep free of bugs and dirt. Another alternative was rag carpets that they wove themselves from old rags parsimoniously hoarded over the years. These were very serviceable and added spots of color to otherwise drab rooms. Eventually, many women acquired manufactured carpets brought into Iowa by the hundreds of dry goods firms which rapidly established themselves in early frontier towns.

Most pioneer women started frontier housekeeping with homemade furniture, occasionally supplemented by a store-bought piece. With great clarity, many later recalled the meager belongings that accompanied them to their homesteads. Phelps said that she had "only a small feather bed and two blankets and one quilt, one skillet and one trunk." Paul's family had slightly more in the way of possessions: "three chairs, cook stove, home made table and cupboard, 2 benches we used in place of chairs, and 2 large wood chests that were brought from Germany, some beds and bedding."[62]

Margaret Murray felt that she had at least the basics when she started housekeeping. They included a small No. 7 cookstove, a fall leaf table and three chairs, a perforated tin door safe used to store dishes and food, a wooden box with a calico curtain to store pots and pans, a wooden water bucket, a bed, a small stand, and one trunk. Lydia Arnold Titus gave a very similar accounting of her first household goods. She listed some plain chairs, two wooden beds, a dry goods box with a curtain used for a cupboard, a cook stove, a kitchen table, and dishes, tub, and washboard which cost six dollars.[63] Another woman's inventory was even more exact:

> 5 coarse sheets, 4 pair of pillow cases, 4 fine sheets, 3 pair of pillow cases, 2 quilts, 2 tacks (comforters), 2 blankets, 1 bed spread, 1 bed and pillows, 1 bed stead, 6 chairs, 1 rocking chair, 1 bureau, 1 dozen plates, a water pitcher, a tin tea pot, a milk strainer, a molasses cup, and a deep dish.[64]

Women were not usually expected to be totally responsible for furnishing the home and many worked in concert with their husbands. Joseph and Alma Mott pooled their skills in a typical manner. He made several four-legged stools with boards to be laid over them to create three bedsteads. She made a plentiful supply of bedding, blankets, and feather beds. Together they hung sheets around the beds to create "rooms" and valances around the bottoms of the beds to improve their appearance. Their scanty household was completed by the purchase of a small cookstove and several chairs from a neighbor who was leaving for Louisiana. Similarly, the Laceys began with a core of several chairs, one Boston rocker, a few dishes, and several cooking utensils. He built a few benches and three bedsteads strung with cord for springs. She made ticks filled with fresh clean straw to serve as mattresses, to which she added the pillows and feather bed which her mother had given her as a wedding gift.[65]

People augmented these plain furnishings as soon as they could but it was sometimes many years before a home was really considered comfortable. Murray pointed out that she didn't have carpets, curtains, or even a rocking chair during the early years of her marriage. She observed that the one factor that saved her from despondency was that her neighbors were not any better off.[66]

It was not just the availability of money that limited purchases; it was also the availability of goods. During the early years of settlement, manufactured furniture was not always easy to find in frontier regions. When Emery Bartlett made a business trip to Iowa City in 1850s, he was commissioned to purchase his sister's wedding bonnet, as well as some articles of furniture. He snapped up the only two bureaus he could find in Iowa City, tied them precariously atop his heavily loaded wagon, and drove home through a January snowstorm to present one to his sister while reserving the other for his intended wife.[67]

When money and furnishings were scarce, frontierspeople tended to exercise their unlimited ingenuity. If four-legged stools refused to stand on uneven floors, three-legged stools replaced them. If real beds were impractical, one-legged pole beds supported by the cabin walls on the sides took their place. If chairs were limited, the hearth or the hay piled in the corner for fuel served as substitutes. These years of shortage were made easier to bear because they were of relatively brief duration for most pioneers. Gradually, luxuries did appear in their homes and there was increasingly frequent mention of a piano or a melodeon, an upholstered chair, or even a marble-topped table.

Advertisements in Iowa newspapers attest to the fact that all kinds of household items became easily obtainable as the frontier became more settled. Merchants hawked their wares at what they referred to as "Eastern" prices. One such ad in the *Burlington Daily Hawk-Eye* appealed to "House-Keepers" to examine stocks of sheets, blankets, and other types of bedding. In 1857, the *Gate City* carried an announcement by O. C. Isbell's Music Room of the first parlor grand piano shipped to Keokuk. Ordered by a customer, it was to be on public exhibition for several days before its delivery. By the 1860s, pianos and organs were as commonplace in the commercial announcements of most Iowa newspapers as were furniture, kitchen goods, and other household equipment.[68]

Even though the really tough years tended to pass rather quickly for most Iowa frontierspeople, one might still expect to find women's diaries and memoirs brimming with bitter complaints or at least with frustrated impatience. Naturally there was some negativism, but there was also much more positivism than the situation might seem to warrant. Joanna Harris Haines characterized her early frontier years this way:

> We lived in a log cabin, of course. But we were always comfortable. We were poor, as we measure worldly possessions today. One thing I particularly remember is that mother always had a plentiful supply of bedding and no matter how cold the winter nights might be we were always warm.[69]

Others were even more graphic about their lives in those early homesteads. "We lived seventeen years in that home," one woman wrote, "with few improvements, as happy as any years of our lives." Another savored the joy of long winter evenings when the family would gather around the fireplace, each with a chore in hand. Yet another was convinced that the pioneers enjoyed life better, had more good times, and were much more appreciative than people in the twentieth century. The classic comment, however, came from the woman who was initially disillusioned when she arrived in "the land of milk and honey." "Oh, how contented we were," she later declared. "I did not think it hard."[70]

Are women such as these, who express positive feelings toward their pioneering experiences in Iowa, a selective and highly biased sample? Perhaps contented women of some leisure had more time and inclination to express positive feelings, while those who underwent hard times were frequently too bitter or fatigued to record their feelings. Women's memoirs are possibly untrustworthy because their authors' reminiscences have been softened by the passage of time. Or the explanation may be that Iowa was a unique frontier, easy in its life-style, and therefore not fairly extrapolated to the lives of women in other sections of the frontier.

Even if all these factors have a degree of validity, the favorable attitudes of many Iowa women towards their pioneer years cannot be rejected out of hand without first considering some of the blind spots that led scholars and other commentators to create the picture of an overburdened and unhappy frontierswoman in the first place. Tangible methodological problems have too often interfered with a balanced interpretation of women on the frontier.

First, there is the definition of nineteenth-century standards of domesticity for women. Even a cursory glance at nineteenth-century newspapers, periodicals, and ladies' journals would initially convince any reader that a "true woman" of the nineteenth century must have practiced domesticity in the highest sense of the word. To Catharine Beecher, a leading proponent of domesticity, it meant "planned" kitchens, professionalized homemaking skills, and the latest training in the domestic arts. Beecher also prescribed a certain religious and moral atmosphere in which children would be raised in a strictly circumscribed manner.[71]

Because a typical pioneer homemaker did not fit into Beecher's idealized scheme, many observers erroneously assumed that a frontierswoman was not fulfilled as a true woman and was thus discontented with the frontier life which thwarted her domestic impulses. But although pioneer women were not achieving domesticity in its ideational sense, they did not demonstrate or verbalize tension about their "failure." The reason for the absence of the stress, so long assumed to be present in frontierswomen, is simple: most other women in nineteenth-century America were not practicing domesticity in its ideational sense either.

While it *is* true that there were thousands of words spoken and written extolling the virtues of domesticity, these were prescriptive (lecturing women on what they ought to do) rather than normative (what women actually did). In fact, much of the talking and writing in behalf of domesticity was intended as an antidote to the opposing trend that was emerging in nineteenth-century American society. More and more women were behaving less and less like the domestic creatures they were supposed to be. Margaret Fuller, the Grimké sisters, and the leaders of the 1848 Seneca Falls Convention for women's rights were just a few of the more dramatic examples of deviants from woman's prescribed sphere. And there were numerous others, such as Sarah Josepha Hale and Lydia Sigourney, who continued to preach the concept of "women's sphere" publicly while abandoning it personally.

In a sense, frontierswomen were themselves deviants from "women's sphere" because they agreed to disrupt homes and families to move them to a situation where high standards of domesticity would be unattainable. But because these women paid lip service to standards of domesticity, while rejecting them by their actions, does not automatically indicate distress and strain on their parts. As historian Julie Roy Jeffrey points out, "Assenting to ideas was not the same as living up to their prescriptions. Domesticity described the norms and not the actual conduct of American women." Jeffrey adds that perhaps frontierswomen were even repaid for their defection from the ideal by regaining an economic importance to the family that many women in settled regions had lost, as well as becoming the shapers of culture rather than its symbolic arbitrator.[72]

It might be hypothesized that frontierswomen did not suffer psychological damage because they had to defer their aspirations to operate a planned kitchen or raise their children in the "proper" manner dictated by the cult of nineteenth-century domesticity, but that they actually found greater satisfaction in the potentially larger roles offered to them in a frontier society. Consequently, the question of domesticity, and its effect on the attitudes of frontierswomen, at the very least deserves more investigation before it is unequivocally accepted as evidence of the oppression of women in the West.

Frontierswomen played their roles on an ever-changing stage, as students of the West must realize. The prevailing concept of monolithic pioneer life results in the fallacy that log cabins symbolize the American West. The fact is that as the frontier evolved into settled communities, the log cabin became a two-story cabin and eventually a frame or brick house with its share of "store-bought" luxuries. It was entirely possible that the woman who began frontier life in a one-room cabin ended it as the mistress of a solid respectable farmhouse. Abbie Mott Benedict, with her twenty-one moves during her first twenty years of marriage, is a good example. She spent her last years both financially stable and physically comfortable. Women who had not yet escaped their shanties could at least look to someone like Benedict and picture themselves in her place in a few years. Thus, the first primitive dwelling was not an end to a pioneer woman's life; rather, it was a beginning.

Another pitfall in the scholarship of the American West is visualizing western migration as a smooth east to west flow with line after line of cabins and soddies marching out across the frontier. As Michael Conzen demonstrated for frontier Iowa, migrations (averaging several per family) were East to rural West, East to urban West, rural West back to East, urban West back to East, rural West to urban West, urban West to rural West, settled county to unsettled county, and unsettled county to settled county.[73] The varied patterns indicate that not all women had to struggle with the deprivations of primitive homesteads. The circumstances of a rural woman would differ markedly from that of an urban woman, while a twenty-year veteran might be starting fresh in a sparsely settled area at the same time that a much younger counterpart moved into an established home in a settled area. It also suggests that many pioneer women had some choices open to them if they really wanted to remove themselves from an intolerable situation. They could (as many actually did) move into the rapidly spreading towns or even return back East. If they were immobilized by finances or some other aspect of their situation, frontierswomen could at least alleviate their suffering by planning for the day when they too could pick up and move to a more amenable setting.

It is a fallacy to perceive all women as belonging to a homogeneous group—in this case, all frontierswomen sharing the same thoughts and experiences. This misconception has caused frontierswomen to be inaccurately stereotyped as farm wives and leaves out recognition of the single women—unmarried, divorced, and widowed—who chose to challenge the frontier without the aid of a man. There were employed women: teachers, writers, postmistresses, station agents, and homesteaders whose incomes supported them or augmented the earnings of their men. And there were army women: wives and daughters of enlisted men and officers who chose to live in military forts rather than face long separations from their husbands and fathers.

Women who did not fit the stereotype—the frontier myth—were probably ignored in contemporary records partly because they were seen as a threat to the legend. Tantalizing glimpses of these women exist in newspapers, census figures, or brief references in someone else's account, yet there are little hard data. Caroline Phelps, for example, briefly referred to her sister who, with her young daughter, deserted her husband. She told Caroline that he was a "disapated [sic] man" who was not providing a decent living for them; beyond that, little or nothing is known.[74] Another illustration is Matilda Peitzke Paul who had much to say about her father's death, yet skimmed over the process by which her widowed mother got their long-planned new home built by using bricks her deceased husband had prepared, employing bricklayers, and putting the oldest boys to work at the task. Nothing is said about her problems as a widow on the frontier.[75]

Social class existed on the frontier, causing a further differentiation of types of women. Some families had sufficient wealth to provide women with "proper" eastern-style homes, domestic servants, and leisure time. Because these women did not go through the cabin-soddie stage, their example gave hope to those who were stuggling toward a better way of life. On the bottom end of the class scale were the domestics, servants, and various kinds of laborers. These were largely foreign-born women or black women who, although they had migrated westward in hopes of improved economic opportunities, often found themselves employed as washwomen, nursemaids, and field help. Not only did their labor lighten the load of the pioneer women who managed to hire occasional help, but their lives made the lives of the cabin–sod-hut women appear less burdensome by comparison. In fact, many of the domestics and laborers aspired to have cabins or sod huts of their own someday.

Of course, not all foreign-born and black women were domestics or laborers. Although the history of black pioneer women is virtually unwritten as yet, there is some information on foreign-born frontierswomen. Many of them had to "step down" in position by migrating from their home country to the American frontier, and all of them had to cope with the dual burden of learning American ways and frontier ways at the same time. It is significant that, in spite of their altered life-styles, many of them felt that they had made the right decision. Elisabeth Koren, as an illustration, was homesick for her home in Norway yet concluded, "This is best."[76]

It is potentially dangerous to interpret the American frontier as a male activity in which women just happened to take part. The questions which must logically be asked then are: (1) how did women contribute to it? and, (2) how were women oppressed by it? By defining the frontier in terms of a male system, women are seen in the context of "contribution" or "oppression" history rather than being viewed objectively. As historian Gerda Lerner points out, "The limitation of such work is that it deals with women in male-defined society and tries to fit them into the categories and value systems which consider *man* the measure of significance."[77]

The alternative is to approach frontierswomen on their own ground and through their own sources. "The true history of women," Lerner argues, "is the history of their ongoing functioning in that male-defined world, *on their own terms.*"[78] In this context, frontierswomen's diaries, letters, journals, and memoirs demonstrate little or no consciousness of themselves as a special group in frontier society. They saw themselves as parts of families, as partners with men, and as economic producers. Their roles and their work were integral with and connected to men's roles and work. Most importantly, they did not see themselves as subordinate, marginal, or auxiliary to the task of conquering the frontier, nor did they perceive themselves as oppressed or exploited.

Some scholars argue that such interpretations are absent from women's sources precisely because women had been indoctrinated into full acceptance of a system that exploited them. But the explanation may be that frontierswomen saw that life was hard for others besides themselves. They lived with the daily knowledge of family members laboring under difficult conditions with only horsepower and crude tools and the realization that life was burdensome for many people, regardless of location. Mill girls, pieceworkers, immigrants, blacks, Native Americans, slum dwellers, eastern and southern farm wives, and prostitutes all did what they had to, to survive in a harsh and demanding world. A former New England woman urged a relative to join her in Iowa ''so you will not have to work in the mill till you are all worn down to a stub.'' Glad to have escaped such a fate herself, she wrote, ''I have never seen the day that I wishes myself East to live.''[79]

In light of all the problems of interpretation of frontierswomen discussed here, certain questions must be posed. What was reality for frontierswomen? What were their workplaces really like? Were frontierswomen relatively better off or worse off than the rest of nineteenth-century America? Where does myth end and history begin?

When placed in her own historical time and place, it was not inconsistent for an allegedly beleaguered pioneer woman to write of her life on the frontier, ''I picture in my mind's eye the happy days when we were young and strong . . . although we were crowded, we were all well and happy so it didn't make much difference,'' or that another could claim, despite the hardships, she ''had a good deal of pleasure in those early days when all was new, and strange, and full of expectancy.'' Was it exploitation or a true sentiment expressed from the sympathetic heart of a young pioneer bride, when, seeing her husband looking ''completely downcast'' because the addition he had ordered added to their rude cabin had not been completed by the time of their arrival, she masked her own dismay with a smile because she ''would not for the world have showed other than a cheerful face on Elias' account''?[80]

By urban twentieth-century standards for housing, workplaces, and workloads, Iowa frontierswomen faced regrettable lives. But, by rural nineteenth-century standards, their lives were not so dire.

CHAPTER THREE

"*Not Gainfully Employed*"

D A T A collected by the United States Census Bureau can often serve as a window on a particular society. Upon close scrutiny, census figures can yield insights regarding what the people of an era were doing and thinking. The data must be used with extreme care, however, if the results are not to be misleading. This is the case with Iowa's pioneer women who sometimes were summarily grouped under the census heading "Not Gainfully Employed." At first glance, this categorization raises some surprising and, in a sense, shocking questions about frontierswomen. Was their labor worth so little that they were not considered workers? Was their contribution to the westward movement so inconsequential that it could be easily dismissed?

Frontier lore, of course, traditionally pictures pioneer women as hard workers. Clearly, frontierswomen were economic producers who manufactured all manner of domestic goods, gave birth to and trained future laborers, helped with "men's work," and generated small amounts of cash income. Why then did census takers damn them with the epitaph "not gainfully employed"? The answer is simple. The census did not recognize the actual work of frontierswomen; rather, it reflected a moneyed society which tended to equate useful work with paid work. During the very early years of American settlement, factors such as barter, trade, subsistence farming, and emergent economic structures made it necessary to judge human labor by standards other than cash income. But as the colonies became more settled and America moved with headlong speed into its own version of the Industrial Revolution, money and the ability to earn it became the standard measure of human worth.

By the 1830s, when Iowa was opened for settlement, the eastern United States was already immersed in a system which separated the "paid" worker from the unpaid. Mill girls were employed, farm wives were not. Nursemaids

This chapter first appeared in slightly different form in the *Pacific Historical Review*, vol. 9, no. 2, pp. 65–92. ©1980 by the Pacific Coast Branch, American Historical Association. Reprinted by permission.

were employed, mothers were not. Businessmen were employed, wives were not. The ability to earn a money income was the distinguishing mark of a gainfully employed person. This concept rapidly became characteristic of American society. According to one scholar, most women performed chores in their homes which, if done for pay, would have been judged as productive, but because they were done in the home were not even seen as economic contributions.[1]

Since this idea that domestic work is not gainful work has been so pervasive and long-standing in America, it is not surprising or shocking after all that census officials often cavalierly extended it to women on the frontier. In the nineteenth-century American East, factories were rapidly taking over women's customary functions of producing foodstuffs, soap, lighting facilities, clothing, and other domestic goods, but in the nineteenth-century West, women still produced these goods in their own homes. Frontierswomen manufactured many goods and purchased little, especially in the early years of settlement, because neither the goods nor the cash to purchase them were readily available. But the frontierswoman was not just a domestic drudge whose life was therefore automatically unhappy. Bypassing any employment she may have held outside the home, she was a full economic producer in her own right; as such, her life often included the same kinds of satisfactions that her male counterpart derived from meaningful labor. In fact, the skills she would need in her life's work were of such great consequence that she spent a good portion of her girlhood in apprenticeship to her mother or to another woman to learn them thoroughly.

By the time a frontier girl was of marriageable age, her greatest personal assets centered around her abilities as a domestic manufacturer. She was rated as a worker in the same way that men were graded as "providers." According to a recent study on frontier marriage,

> . . . the choosing of a mate on the frontier was a matter of economic necessity far and above individual whim. Good health and perseverance were premium assets while the charm and ability to entertain that one values so highly in a society of mechanization and leisure time was only of tangential significance. . . the woman who could not sew nor cook had no place on the frontier.[2]

Mates, then, were chosen in large part as economic partners. It was considered a bonus if they were also compatible. For the typical frontier couple, their wedding day marked not only the beginning of a shared life but the beginning of a shared business venture as well.

Even if a pioneer woman chose to remain unmarried or was pushed into single status by circumstances such as divorce, or the death or desertion of a mate, her skills were still crucial. Census figures indicate that most single women on the frontier were absorbed by other households: parents, children, relatives, or neighbors. In her adoptive family, a woman had to pull her own economic weight by continuing to render a share of household services. As in other parts of the country, these unmarried women were often assigned to the job of spinning flax, wool, and other fibers into thread.

So, regardless of their marital status, women were absolutely necessary to the frontier economy. Only by looking at them in this light can one really understand the impact and importance of the many tasks they performed. The long-standing onus attached to "mere" housework is quickly dispelled by the example of highly skilled labor provided by frontierswomen.

Domestic labor in the frontier was exceedingly diverse. The picture given by one frontier Iowa man of his mother's labors gives some idea of their vast scope.

> Mother bore and cared for the babies, saw that the floor was white and clean, that the beds were made and cared for, the garden tended, the turkeys dressed, the deer flesh cured and the fat prepared for candles or culinary use, that the wild fruits were garnered and preserved or dried, that the spinning and knitting was done and the clothing made. She did her part in all these tasks, made nearly all the clothing and did the thousand things for us a mother only finds to do.[3]

This description clearly indicates that his mother was the chief laborer in the home. It was her responsibility to process the raw materials generated in the fields outside of the home. The woman and her home were the key link in translating unusable raw materials into consumable finished goods. She was, therefore, the equivalent to her family of the factory to an industrialized society.

Of all the products that she manufactured, food required the most continuous attention. In an age when people worked long, physically taxing hours and consumed thousands of calories per day to sustain themselves, food production was naturally the center of domestic activity. Unlike the women of later eras, a pioneer woman could not turn to packaged foods, prepared mixes, or chain restaurants to lighten the burden of feeding a large family many times every day. She had to rely on her own talents and resources for every step from processing through storing to actual preparation.

The first step, processing, began with the gathering of the raw foodstuffs. Many of these, such as corn and wheat, were produced by the men of the family. The women, however, were frequently responsible for vegetables, fruits, herbs, eggs, and milk. Although the men usually did the heavier jobs such as harrowing and planting the vegetable patch, women did the weeding, picking, and "digging taters." Women also gathered wild and domestic fruits beginning with currants and cherries in June, through strawberries later in the summer. Futhermore, planting herb gardens, gathering wild herbs, collecting eggs, cleaning henhouses, and sometimes even milking the cows fell to the lot of the women.

To supplement their gardens, women were constantly on the watch for wild bushes that they might replant, for wild flowers which they could transplant by their doorsteps, or for roots and seeds that some friends or relatives might send them from "back home." The Kenyon family letters often mention the seeds and roots that were exchanged between relatives in the East and the West; both sides of the family felt that the resulting crops were invaluable in providing variety to their otherwise drab fare. Another frontierswoman sent her children to the nearby woods to dig up wild gooseberry bushes which were then planted in neat rows in her own garden. In the same way, she began a plum grove near her house, and finally an apple orchard from some infant trees which her husband ordered for her from Louisa County.[4]

When Sarah Carr Lacey moved to her new home she came well prepared with seeds and roots carefully transported from her previous homestead. She marked off patches in her garden, distributed the seeds to her children, and watched their enthusiasm grow along with their plants. They all worked together to bring wild gooseberry and currant bushes and wild plum and crab trees home from the river bank. Their biggest project was cutting slips from growing trees, particularly willows and poplars, and rooting them in their own soil. Although the trees grew well and hardy, young May Lacey never became accustomed to the "sedate, straight rows of trees" which resulted from the planting.[5]

These various efforts eventually yielded many kinds of produce, particularly fruits and vegetables of almost every description. Combined with the produce of the fields, of the farm stock, and of hunting wild game, they provided a myriad of raw materials which could be processed into many varieties of usable and appetizing foodstuffs.

Naturally, corn was a staple of the Iowa pioneer's diet. It was eaten fresh, but was also stored for use during the long winter months when fresh foods were unavailable. Sweet corn was dried during the hottest days of late August. The ears were husked, scalded, then the kernels were cut off and spread on pans, covered by a mosquito net, and placed on the roof in the sun. If rain should unpropitiously threaten, the pans were rushed back into the house to be placed in the oven for drying. This dried corn would later appear in many forms: cornbread, mush, corncakes, and corn pone.[6] Corn was also commonly made into hominy, a favorite food served with milk and some sort of sweetener. The following description of hominy-making was passed on by Iowan May Ramsay:

> They had a hopper made out of wood up on a stand where they put the wood ashes and made lye. Grandmother would take corn and boil it in lye water untill the shells would come off. (That was in a big kettle out of doors.) Then take the corn to the well and wash it until she had all the lye off. I remember how I watched her and wondered about it. It sure made good hominy when it was washed enough.[7]

Eggs and milk were two other mainstays of the pioneer menu. Milk, of course, was frequently churned into butter. Matilda Peitzke Paul remembered that it was a tedious and time-consuming process.

> . . . the milk was put in pans to cool and left long enough for the cream to come to the top which was about 24 hours, then the cream was skimmed off with this kind of skimmer and kept in a cool place if there was one, until there was enough cream to make several pounds of butter in a dash churn. . . . I remember how I used to dread to have mother call me and tell me to help with the churning. It seemed as if the butter never would come sometimes it did take for hours to churn.[8]

Another woman lived near a creek with a shelving rock under the bank where she kept her milk and butter cold even on the hottest summer days. She was an expert buttermaker and in 1857 when she sent her "roll of butter, daintily marked and as smooth as marble" to the local fair, she easily captured first place.[9]

In addition to these staples, innumerable other foods were processed. Milk was made into cheese in a specially designed wooden cheese press. Tomatoes were covered with red wax and placed in cans. Cucumbers were salted down in big crocks. Cabbage was converted into sauerkraut in huge wooden barrels. Vegetables were cleaned and carefully deposited in the root cellar. Fruits were stored in crocks, were canned, or were cooked into many delicious flavors of jellies and jams. Apples were wrapped in paper or hay, cut up and dried, or cooked into apple butter. Hogs' heads and feet were cleaned for souse. Pork was salted and chickens were dressed down. And the wild meat that the men brought in after hunting was carefully dried or otherwise preserved.

By the end of the fall, the family's cellar had been transformed into a storehouse which would gradually surrender its precious treasure throughout the long winter. Amelia Murdock Wing retained fond memories of her family's well-stocked cellar.

> A barrel of kraut was made in the fall; chunks of pork were salted down; fruit was canned and kept in long, heavy wooden boxes, many kinds of vegetables would be kept there throughout the winter. . . . In our cellar there was a floor of rock, always cleanly scrubbed. There was a long table for use in handling the milk and butter, and a wooden dash-churn stood beside it. There was a large cupboard whose tin doors had holes for ventilation, and this was where the milk, cream and butter was kept. No one had ice in those days, but our cellar was cool.[10]

Although the processing of foodstuffs was primarily a summertime chore, the conversion of food supplies into edible meals was a continual task to be faced day after day, year after year, often with only the most rudimentary kitchen equipment as an aid. During the early years of settlement, the most common cooking utensil across the Iowa frontier was a black iron kettle suspended on an iron crane which swung in and out of the open fireplace. This was complemented by a Dutch oven, which consisted of a flat-bottomed pot with an iron lid. This "oven" was set directly in the hot coals and often covered over with coals. The best cooks could do almost anything with these Dutch ovens including frying venison, roasting a chicken, broiling a squirrel, and baking corn bread, or "dodger," as it was called.

Another common implement was a long-handled frying pan, used over an open fire to fry both meat and flapjacks. Large pieces of meat, such as a turkey, a quarter of venison, or a large cut of pork might be cooked by suspending it over the flame on a tightly twisted piece of string. As the string unwound, it acted as a kind of spit which turned the meat slowly and allowed it to brown evenly. Bread was also baked by the open hearth by spreading the dough over a "johnny-cake" board, propping the board up to face the fire, and then turning it until the heat produced a nicely browned loaf. Sarah Nossaman's directions for this bread give a good idea of the talent and experience required.

> Take a board eighteen inches long and eight inches wide, round the corners off and make the edges thinner than the middle, spread it with well-made corn dough, set it on edge before a hot fire in a fireplace, and it will bake nice and brown, then turn and bake the other side the same way, then you have corn bread that no one will refuse.[11]

Despite the limitations under which they worked, many pioneer women gained reputations as competent cooks, an achievement which was particularly difficult when the few receipt (recipe) books that did exist gave directions in terms of a pinch and a handful. Kitturah Belknap was especially pleased after a fleece-sorting party because her women friends were impressed with her chicken dinner and old-fashioned pound cake. "Now my name is out as a good cook," she rejoiced, "so am alright for good cooking makes good friends." Another Iowa woman discovered that she could earn money to purchase her first store-bought clothes by hiring out as a cook. Working with one other woman over an open fireplace, she prepared all the meals for forty-five men building a mill. For this feat she was paid the grand sum of seventy-five cents per week, which, according to her, "was the best wages that had ever been paid in the country at that time."[12]

Despite the rude conditions, the diversity of some pioneer menus seemed almost unlimited. On one occasion, Belknap treated her guests to stewed chicken, fried cakes, sausage, and mashed potatoes. Another time she prepared a Christmas dinner for twelve people that would tax the dexterity of a modern cook equipped with all the latest appliances. Her bill of fare, as she called it, was elegant and extensive:

Firstly; for bread, nice light rolls; cake, doughnuts; for pie, pumpkin; preserves, crab apples and wild plums; sauce, dried apples; meat first round: roast spare ribs with sausage and mashed potatoes and plain gravey; second round: chicken stewed with the best of gravy; chicken stuffed and roasted in the Dutch oven by the fire.[13]

Pioneer cooks were frequently required to be creative in the face of inadequate tools and shortages of supplies. Harriet Bonebright-Closz recalled that her family lacked the rolling pin essential to biscuit making. They improvised, using a wooden stick, peeled fresh daily. "When it could not be found," she said, "the biscuit dough was rolled with a fresh ear of corn—or mayhap, the cob." Kitturah Belknap often found herself without the kind of fruit that she needed for preserves so she devised a clever imitation. She squeezed the juice from watermelon, boiled it down to syrup, added some muskmelons and crabapples, cooked them with a little sugar, and produced a substance which at least tasted like preserves. According to her, "You have nice preserves to last all winter (and they are fine when you have nothing better and sugar 12½¢ a lb. and go 40 miles after it)."[14]

Most frontier cooks faced problems in obtaining sugar, salt, and spices. Often, herbs from their own gardens sufficed for seasonings, but salt had to be purchased, as did sugar, and both were usually very expensive by pioneer standards. In 1856 Mary Ellis complained that sugar was one dollar for eight to nine pounds and molasses was eighty-five cents per gallon. Another source listed sugar as wholesaling for .098 cents per pound in 1856, .090 cents per pound in 1861, and jumping to .235 cents per pound by 1864 due to the inflationary effect of the Civil War. It is little wonder that frontierswomen did what they could to find substitutes. Sweeteners, of course, were more easily replaced than salt. Women kept their eye out for a bee tree which they might rob of its highly prized honey. They tapped maple trees for sap which was boiled down into maple molasses or converted into maple sugar at a "sugaring-off" session.[15] And they stripped cane to produce molasses, a commodity considered so important that children were often kept home from school to help with the "stripping."

As settlements thickened and frontier towns increased in size and number, the problems of the pioneer cook were somewhat alleviated. Her sparse utensils were augmented by tinware, pewter, and various types of pots and pans. Unfortunately, these had to be scoured weekly with sand and water to keep them in respectable condition. Her open fireplace with its pot and crane was replaced by a stove, often with new-fangled gadgets such as warming ovens. Unfortunately, it had to be stoked almost continuously with fuel to maintain a proper temperature so that a typical recipe for biscuits read as follows: stoke the stove, get out flour, stoke the stove, wash hands, mix biscuit dough, stoke the stove, wash hands, cut biscuit dough, stoke the stove, wash hands, put biscuits in oven, keep on stoking until the bread is baked and ready for table. And her stock of foodstuffs was enhanced by the goods offered in the rapidly appearing stores and emporiums. Unfortunately, cash was necessary to purchase these items.

People who could afford the new cooking utensils, stoves, and food items found them very convenient. Prepared foods were a particular boon to pioneers. The articles of food offered by the new grocers included staples such as flour and salt, but they also catered to the appetites of migrants hungry for delicacies that they had enjoyed in their former homes. In 1855 the *Iowa Sentinel* (Fairfield, Iowa) advertised a shipment of raisins and figs as well as fresh Baltimore peaches and strawberries. Oysters were particularly esteemed by Iowans, many of whom were former New Englanders and had been brought up on seafoods. In 1857 the *Iowa Sentinel* announced the opening of the "Young America Oyster and Lunch Saloon," which claimed that "its patrons, at all hours, will be served with Oysters in every style, also with Welch Rabbits, Hot Cakes and Coffee, Venison, Steaks, Game, etc." Merchants in interior Iowa also responded to the demand for oysters. In 1861 the *Waterloo Courier* heralded the arrival of a shipment of "Celebrated Baltimore Fresh Oysters," which was rather redundantly guaranteed to be fresh. Hanno Newton noted that a shipment of oysters usually occasioned a series of oyster suppers in the vicinity, a practice which sounds much more like the "civilized" East than the supposedly primitive frontier.[16]

Naturally, the less settled regions of the Iowa frontier did not enjoy such luxuries until after the coming of the railroads in the 1860s and the 1870s. In 1856 Sarah Kenyon's sister Mary mentioned making a meal of "punkin flap jacks" and a few slices of venison, then grumbled that "we don't have anything but 'taters' and punkin here." Even as late as 1869, a newly arrived family of migrants in Clay County subsisted for an entire winter primarily on "sod house soup" made of chunks cut off a "half-of-beef" as needed and mixed with the meager vegetable supply they had brought along.[17]

But whatever their location or circumstances, pioneer women were expected to extend hospitality to friends and strangers alike. Inns and hotels were virtually unknown in the early years and were located only in the towns in the later years of settlement, so anyone traveling had to depend on the sociability of the people along the way. If the latchstring of a cabin or soddie was left hanging on the outside of the door it was a sign that a passerby was welcome to pull up the latchbar and enter anytime, day or night. One observer of frontier society maintained that "the hospitality of the frontier woman is bounded only by their means of affording it." But from some of the contemporary references to guests, it seems that hospitality was sometimes pushed to unreasonable extremes. One sixteen-by-eighteen cabin was reputed to have provided lodging for as many as thirty-two people in one night. Sarah Nossaman remembered that her husband boasted that their cabin could hold as many as there were puncheons in their floor, although on some nights she "thought there were two to a puncheon."[18]

Hospitality was so pervasive on the frontier that its inhabitants, in general, gained a reputation for social equality and its women, in particular, a name for social skills and democratic attitudes.[19] Certainly entertaining guests, no matter how limited the space and fare might be, created additional duties and expense, yet few complaints were heard. May Lacey Crowder commented on her family's attitude towards guests:

> Towns were far apart then and everyone's home was open to any traveler. This was particularly true of our place. People drove for miles to "get to Lacey's" to spend the night. Occasionally a stranger passing through would offer to pay for his accommodations, but by far the greater number were entertained as guests. Father would put the team in the barn and give them feed. The traveler was sent to the house for his meal which mother always seemed glad to get no matter what the hour.[20]

In a similar vein, Emery Bartlett remarked that his mother cared for several boarders plus "numerous visitors who stayed for days or weeks, but no one ever heard her complain."[21]

Surely complaints about the additional workload would have been in order since pioneer women already had more than enough to worry about. One historian of the Iowa frontier concluded that hospitality "was often so general as to impose a serious burden upon the woman as its dispenser."[22] Yet many frontierswomen seemed actually to enjoy having guests in their homes in spite of the extra work for them and the additional strain on their larders. Kitturah Belknap wrote that she was glad her home was located at a crossroads because local preachers often stopped on their way to and from parishioners' homes. She curtained off a small room especially for them and always tried "to keep a little something prepared" to feed them. She expressed pleasure that twice weekly prayer meetings were to be held at her house so she could "see all the neighbors." Belknap's remark is perhaps the key to the relative uncomplaining attitude of pioneer women towards hosting visitors. Most women, confined to their homes for long periods of time, probably looked upon even a chance visitor as a source of entertainment, local news, and momentary relief from everyday routines. For example, Belknap's one observation after a very long evening of cooking for eight people over an open fireplace was, "had a fine time."[23] Like other laborers who worked long hours in one workplace, pioneer women found respite when and where they could.

On the other hand, perhaps frontierswomen just didn't have much time and energy to expend on complaining because their workloads were so extensive and time-consuming. Food processing and preparation, as complex and continuous as they were, only accounted for one segment of the frontierswoman's workday. She was also responsible for domestic commodities manufactured from food by-products, such as soap and lighting facilities. Both required constant attention on her part in order to stockpile the food wastes which in turn would become her raw materials.

Soapmaking involved three separate processes: collecting grease, fat, and tallow from meat; saving wood ashes for lye; and boiling the two together in the correct proportion to create a substance known as soft soap. Collection of grease was a year-long procedure. Drip pans were carefully positioned under spitted meat to catch the drippings, and all leftover grease from frying was put aside. Any nonedible scraps of fat from cuts of meat were also diligently hoarded. By spring, there was usually a sizeable accumulation of waste grease and fat. This was enlarged upon by the addition of scraps of fat saved from the spring butchering of hogs and cattle.

Wood ashes were also collected throughout the year, but these had to be transformed into lye before they were ready to be combined with the grease. Janette Murray described this procedure in detail:

> One neighbor leached lye from wood ashes kept in a barrel. This was perforated in the bottom and set on an inclined board. A circle was chiseled out on the board outside the bottom of the barrel with a groove at the lower edge to let the seeping water run into a wooden pail. This yellow water was the lye. The barrel was kept full of ashes and every once in awhile more water was poured over them.[24]

Soapmaking was done out-of-doors in the spring, with the children joining in. The lye and grease were carefully measured into a large iron kettle, a fire was stoked under the kettle, and the concoction was boiled until the woman judged it to be of the proper consistency. Matilda Peitzke Paul stated, "This had to be watched most of the time to be kept from boiling over. In the meantime the water was being poured into the leach several times a day until the lye was too weak to hold up an egg, for then it was too weak to make soap."[25]

Once the mixture foamed up and had been carefully stirred together, it was poured into crocks or wooden boxes lined with cloth. When it hardened, usually in a day or two, it was cut into "bars" and stored away in kegs, wrapped in hay, or just piled lattice fashion on cellar shelves for use during the coming year. Some women refined the method even further by using pure tallow, rendered from beef fat and molded in pans, to make a whiter soap for dishes and hands, while they used cracklings and scraps to make a darker laundry soap.[26]

Attitudes toward soap making seemed to vary widely. Amelia Murdock Wing remembered it as a "process we enjoyed." Matilda Peitzke Paul, however, rather sourly commented that "it took plenty of work to make it."[27] At any rate, soapmaking apparently continued to be a home function for a good many years for there is little evidence, either in women's sources, or in the newspapers of the time, that soap was manufactured and marketed very widely during the pioneer period.

Since they also lacked kerosene, at least during the early years, pioneer women used ingenuity in providing light in their homes. At first they simply relied on the fireplace to light their homes. As soon as possible this scanty light was supplemented by the easiest type of lighting fixture known on the frontier—the saucer lamp. As its name indicates, it was merely a saucer, usually of wood, filled with some kind of grease with a piece of twisted rag inserted in it as a wick. Margaret E. Archer Murray said that the first lights used by her family were "grease lamps we had a shallow dish first took a soft rad [sic] twisted it then dipped one end in melted lard layed that end up on side of dish pored the melted lard over that then it was ready to light." Similarly, Mary Ellis wrote, "Our light consists of a saucer filled with coons oil with a rag in it." And another pioneer portrayed the family lamp as "a super-annuated saucer, half full of lard, with a strip of cotton goods partly buried in the fat, lighted at the upper end."[28]

By modern standards, it is amazing that pioneers managed to complete all their tasks adequately, let alone efficiently, with such defective lighting. Since evenings and long winter afternoons were crucial work periods for pioneers, it meant that they often mended harness, made nails, carved furniture, processed food, and sewed the family's clothing by the flickering light of fireplaces and saucer lamps. Harriet Bonebright-Closz mentioned in passing that her mother "did much of the family sewing beside the feeble ray of this type of light," while Archer went into a little more detail:

> Mother did all her sewing and knitting by that [saucer light] and the light from the fire place and she sure had a lot of it to do. . . . Mother made all our cloths by hand knit all our stockings and mittens by lamp light.[29]

As soon as they could afford it, most frontierswomen began to produce candles to light their homes. These were of two basic types: the tallow dip and the molded candle, both of which involved some capital investment in supplies. In the case of tallow dips, the tallow itself could be rendered at home from meat fats, but the wicking had to be purchased. Labor, of course, was supplied by women who went through the following procedure once every year:

> She filled the wash boiler with tallow; then, she put wicks over some little round sticks and dipped them in the hot tallow and hung them in a row above the boiler. By the time the last stick was hung up, the first sticks were cool enough to dip again. Thus the work proceeded until the candles were of the right size.[30]

Molded candles required not only the purchase of wicking, but an initial investment in an iron candle mold. Matilda Peitzke Paul recalled that her family had a mold that held one dozen candles. "The wick," she explained, "had to be bought at a store and run through the center of each one after that the tallow was melted and poured into the mold and left till perfectly cold and hard."[31] Murray gave a similar account of the process:

> Pieces of candlewick, cut in proper length, were laid over the sticks across the top of the mold, shaken down, pulled through the small holes at the bottom and tied tightly. The molds were then filled with melted tallow and set outdoors to cool. After heating a moment in the morning, the cream-colored candles could be lifted out.[32]

Most frontierswomen were justifiably proud of their skills. Certainly no frontier homestead could have survived without them. Furthermore, no frontier family would have been clothed if frontierswomen had not fit the manufacture of garments into their already crowded schedules. Somehow, frontierswomen managed to produce both cloth and clothing for their entire family in the limited hours set apart for that specific purpose. During the first years of frontier settlement the manufacture of apparel was both difficult and time-consuming. Since commercially produced yardgoods were not generally marketed as yet, early frontierswomen had literally to begin with plants, such as flax, and with animals, such as sheep, to obtain the fibers that would eventually become thread, then cloth, and finally clothing.

Flax and wool, both standards on the Iowa frontier, required hours of monotonous work before they could be spun into thread. Raw flax was "combed" by throwing the fibers over a hackle and pulling them through its teeth. This hackle was usually made of a wooden base with close-set iron prongs projecting upward from it. A hackle resembled a medieval instrument of torture, or perhaps a bed of nails, and was just as dangerous if a woman was not alert and agile while using it. Wool was not hackled but was carded with a crude currycomb type of instrument. Although not as potentially dangerous as a flax hackle, the carding comb also called for patience and endurance on the part of the woman operating it.

Once the fibers were combed into smooth strands they were spun into thread on a treadle-powered spinning wheel. The spinning wheel occupied a place of honor in many cabins and consumed untold hours of the pioneer woman's time. It was, however, only the second step in an extensive process. Next the thread had to be woven into cloth: flax into linen cloth; wool into woolen cloth; and flax and wool into linsey-woolsey cloth. This cloth was then colored with dyes that women produced themselves from plants such as indigo, red sumac, and various tree leaves. Finally, the cloth was ready to be laboriously handstitched into a finished garment.

Naturally, women got help with these jobs whenever they possibly could, both by inviting in friends to help and by sending the fibers out to a carding machine or the thread to a weaving mill. In 1853, for instance, the *Wapello Intelligencer* advertised a commercial wool carding service in the town of Wapello.[33] But Margaret E. Archer Murray's description indicates that although her mother did get some help she still was responsible for many tiresome tasks herself.

> After shearing was done she washed the fleeces then hand picked the wool to get out the burs and the like often had wool picking invite a few women for the day. After that the wool was sent to the carding machine and made into rolls then mother had to spin it into yarn then have that woven into cloth some for jeans for mens cloths and flannel for us children and apart of the yarn for kniting then she did all the coloring.[34]

Kitturah Belknap's recollections were very much the same. "All this winter I have been spinning flax and tow [coarse, broken fibers of flax] to make some summer clothes," she wrote. "Now the wool must be taken from the sheep's back, washed and picked and sent to the carding machine and made into rolls, then spun, colored and wove ready for next winter." Another year she gave a fuller account:

> I'm the first one to get at the wool (25 fleeces). Will sort it over, take off the poor short wool and put it by to card by hand for comforts. Then sort out the finest for flannels, and the courser [*sic*] for jeans for the men's wear. I find the wool very nice and white but I do hate to sit down alone to pick wool so I will invite about a dozen old ladies in and in a day they will do it all up.[35]

When her wool came home from the carding machine, she was pleased with the nice rolls that were all ready to spin. She planned first to spin her stocking yarn, estimating that she could spin two skeins a day and double and twist it during the evening while her husband read the history of the United States.[36]

Later, Belknap spun thread for the simple dresses which satisfied most women in those years. In 1840 she was elated to get a new calico dress for Sunday and one new homemade dress for everyday. She recalled, "It was cotton warp colored blue and copper and filled with pale blue tow filling so it was striped one way and was almost as nice as gingham." The following year she added a new blue and red plaid flannel dress to her wardrobe. She commented, "I am going to try and make me one dress every year than I can have one for nice and with a clean check apron I would be alright."[37]

Besides their own dresses, women also sewed dresses for the young girls of the family and jeans and cotton shirts for the men and boys. All buttonholes had to be painstakingly worked in by hand to accommodate the hooks, eyes, and buttons that were used for fastening. In addition, warm stockings, mittens, mufflers, and wristlets for all were knitted from wool. Hats were plaited from straw or wild grass gathered in the fields. And sunbonnets were made to extend out over the face approximately four inches using pasteboard slats, a design which Harriet Bonebright-Closz described as such "an obstruction to sight and an impediment to hearing" that most young women let them hang loosely down their backs rather than using them as a protection from the prairie sun as intended."[38]

Although frontierswomen were the primary producers of wearing apparel, they appealed to their families for help whenever possible. When Clara Dodge's husband, Augustus, went to Washington, D.C. in 1848 as Iowa's first senator, she begged him to note the fashions for her and to perhaps buy her something "of his taste" since she felt that she was "here buried as it were." In 1856, Sarah Kenyon enjoined her family to "save all of your old clothes for me as they are just as good as new here and I will dress up my young ones 'right smart.' "[39]

Women also looked to the rapidly proliferating merchants and dry-goods stores to supply them with yard goods and other sewing material. In 1862, Sarah Kenyon said she could buy thin cotton cloth for twenty cents, calico for twenty cents, sheeting for thirty cents, thread for ten cents a spool, but "needles its almost impossible to get."[40] Although she did not give quantities with her prices, her list does signify that these goods were being sold in her area of Plum Creek, Kossuth County, in the north central portion of Iowa by the time of the Civil War.

A survey of some frontier newspapers shows that these goods were widely sold much sooner in areas located along well-traveled routes of settlement and trade. As early as 1836, the *Dubuque Visitor* advertised ready-made clothing and "Calicoes, Ginghams, Muslins, Cambricks, Laces, Ribbands." That fall they featured dry goods, including "Sattinettes, Cassimeres and brodd cloths." In 1837, the *Iowa News,* also in Dubuque, announced "Ready Made Clothing from New York." Later that same month they carried a notice of the opening of a new store which would handle groceries and "Ready Made Clothing of Every Kind" as well as boots and shoes for men, ladies, and children. And in 1844, Dubuque's *Iowa Territorial Gazette and Advertiser* carried ads for "Hats, Hats," "Fashionable Milliner and Dress Maker," "Hats and Bonnets," and "Rich Fancy Goods."[41]

Burlington, also located on the Mississippi River, became another supply center. The *Burlington Daily Hawk-Eye and Telegraph* of the 1850s was filled with commercial notices appealing "to the Ladies." One offered "30 pieces fine linen thread edging," assorted black silk lace edging, lisle and silk gloves, black silk mitts, and kid gloves. A few years later the People's Store offered calicoes, ginghams, silk goods, linens, fancy goods, boots and shoes, with the claim that "The Stock is not, and cannot be surpassed in the West." On the very next page the new Philadelphia Dry Goods and Milliners Emporium advertised that "the best, handsomest and cheapest goods, and the greatest bargains" were to be found in their establishment.[42]

Towns located further from the Mississippi River did their best to compete for the expanding market. In 1854, Mount Pleasant's *Weekly Observer* called for "Ladies! Ladies!! Ladies!!!" to notice new stocks of "Lawn Satin, Silk and Crepe Bonnets of the latest styles," and "Ribbons, Flowers, caps, and every variety in the millinery line." They also offered "Fowler's system of cutting dresses taught in 3 lessons for $3, with model patterns cut to fit the figure for 25 cts." And, like so many other Iowa papers, the *Fairfield Ledger* advertised shops that could sell dresses and millinery at "eastern prices."[43]

Gradually, such goods were offered in the interior portions of Iowa, but it was not a progressive east to west movement. Business development gravitated first to areas along the Mississippi River and second to areas along the Missouri River, leaving central Iowa relatively unserved. This was due in part to the early steamboats that plied both rivers, bringing settlers and trade goods. Commercial trade along the Missouri River (more difficult for steamboats to navigate than the Mississippi), was given an extra boost because of the many migrants who used it as a supply and departure point for overland migration to the Far West. Kanesville (Council Bluffs) was an especially popular staging town. Missouri River region newspapers were thus filled with bills listing supplies, tools, sturdy clothing, wagons, and ferry lines. They also reflected a settled, almost urban population interested in the material aspects of "civilization." A typical issue of the Kanesville *Frontier Guardian* for 1849 proclaimed the availability of "A Large Importation of English and French Dry Goods," "Ladies' Black Gaiters . . . Kid Slippers . . . Polka Slippers," and calico, flannels, ribbons, silk and satin, and laces.[44]

The wide availability and use of these goods does not uphold the stereotype of frontierspeople always dressed in rough homespun and animal-skin clothing. Conditions of grinding poverty on the prairie frontier—at least in pioneer Iowa—were brief and transitory for many frontierspeople. This is demonstrated not only by newspaper advertisements for goods not usually associated with frontier society, but also by the many frontierswomen who developed a taste for fancy needle and craft work of various kinds. By the 1850s and 1860s many Iowa women, supposedly overworked and overburdened, were making wreaths of hair flowers, worsted flowers, and seed flowers for decoration and as recreation. Fancy knitting provided lace edgings, chair tidies, and bedspreads. Crocheted edgings were used on underwear, pillow slips, aprons, and on children's clothes. And some hosiery and mittens were knitted in "featherwork," "shellwork," or "oak leaf" patterns to add to their attractiveness.[45]

That the stereotype does not hold true for Iowa is further indicated by the variety of clothing and the amount of money invested in clothing by a typical young pioneer woman. The sister of Emery Bartlett, an early settler of Grinnell who arrived in 1854 when many people were still living in their wagons, joined him in 1855. Although Grinnell was in the center of the state and could be reached only by stage lines, Eliza Ann Bartlett made the following clothing purchases:[46]

For 1855:

5 yards of cotton cloth	$ .50
3-½ of cotton flannel	.35
A carpet bag	1.00
A pair of gloves	.12-½
11 yards of delane	1.37-½
A pair of gloves	.20
A collar	1.50
2 yards of lawn	1.00
1 yard of lining	.14
1 pair of shoes	1.25
10 yards of berage delane	1.50
10 yards of poplin	.70
1 yard of ribbon	.15
1 hair comb	.15
A mantle	.64

For 1856:

A pair of shoes	$1.50
10 yards of calico	1.25
3 yards of calico	.37
A bonnet	5.00
10 yards of all wool delane	4.40
A pair of kid gloves	1.00
A lawn dress	1.90

For 1857:

A lawn dress	$1.62
A pair of elastics	.20
2-½ of muslin	.87
3-½ of bonnet ribbon	1.22
5 yards of calico	.37

For 1858:

A pair of mitts	$ .70
Hoops	.40
Crape bonnet	1.60
A calico dress	1.60
Another calico dress	1.25
A leather best [sic]	.20

For 1860:

A calico dress	$1.06
A pair of shoes	1.50
A skelaton skirt [sic]	2.00
A veil	.30
Calico dress	1.20
Bonnet ribbon	1.30

Along with dry goods, ready-made clothes, and accessories came another product of technology—the sewing machine. By the 1850s the spinning wheel no longer held the place of honor in most Iowa homes nor was all sewing any longer done by hand. The treadle sewing maching was making its presence felt on many parts of the Iowa frontier. With its variations in design and price, it was to the pioneer housewife what the McCormick reaper was to the pioneer farmer.

An 1855 *Davenport Gazette* advertisement for a Wheeler, Wilson and Company's "Superior Sewing Machine" slightly exaggerated the revolution in the domestic manufacture of clothing: "By the use of these machines very much of that which has been a drudgery becomes but a pleasant task." The *Burlington Daily Hawk-Eye* was flooded with advertisements for the new machines, and within a few month's time in 1859 the following notices were published. Weed's Sewing Machines, a New York based company, now had an agent in Burlington. Raymond's Sewing Machines were double-threaded, cost only twenty-five dollars, and "any person of ordinary intelligence can learn in one hour to use it successfully." And Grover and Baker's Celebrated Family Sewing Machines, now with new styling, priced at only fifty dollars, hemmed, gathered, and stitched better and cheaper than a seamstress.[47]

Advertisements in the *Fairfield Ledger* made similar extravagant claims. Singer and Company's sewing machine offered reduced prices. A forty dollar sewing machine with an adjustable hemmer was the "First-Class Machine in Market." And the Wilcox and Gibbs Sewing Machine, priced between forty dollars and one hundred ten dollars, "will stitch, hem, fell, tuck, cord, bind, braid, quilt and embroider beautifully." Similarly, the *Waterloo Courier* ran illustrated ads of the West and Wilson, the "Woman's Friend," priced from thirty dollars to fifty dollars, and billed the Singer Sewing Machine as the "New Family Sewing Machine."[48]

Sewing machines are frequently mentioned in women's diaries and memoirs. Although the machines were foot-powered and rudimentary by modern standards, many women discovered that they relieved them of hundreds of wearying hours of handstitching. The new machines also made possible the wearing of more complicated fashions. And, young women of the family were able to take over a good share of the family sewing at an earlier age than had been possible when they had to be carefully taught various types of handstitching. A case in point was Alice Money, a young girl who did all the sewing for her family in the 1860s, including muslin undergarments with yards of ruffles and tucks, calico dresses lined and trimmed with more ruffles, tucks, and bias bindings, and shirts and suits for the boys and men. She must have literally treadled hundreds of miles on her family's early model of a Wheeler and Wilson machine, which was said to have "made a noise like a threshing machine and ran almost as hard."[49]

With the aid of these machines, many Iowa frontierswomen attempted to emulate current fashions. They were determined not to become dowdy or outmoded by eastern standards. This was perhaps an attempt on their part to maintain a semblance of civilization in a country that had stripped away so many of their other luxuries and vanities. It caused them to slavishly adopt fashionable fads such as the hoop skirt, the bustle, whalebone corsets, and heavily adorned dresses and bonnets, in spite of the fact that they were neither sensible nor appropriate for most circumstances of frontier living. More than one woman complained about singed dress hems when her hoops carried her skirts into an open fireplace over which she was cooking. Alice Money learned the hard way that hoops could be embarrassing as well as dangerous when she caught hers on a post while going over a stile and hung from the fence trapped in her own fashionable gear. When her beau tried to come to her rescue he caught his foot in the offending hoop and he too became entrapped. It was left to their friends to untangle them, much to everyone's discomfort.[50]

These artifacts of dress cannot be lightly dismissed as ridiculous vanities by women made overly fashion conscious by nineteenth-century standards regarding women's dress. It must be understood that the way women dress reflects what their own society thinks about their position and roles in life. A few twentieth-century examples will clarify this point: women wore slacks for the first time when they became an invaluable source of wartime labor; the flappers of the 1920s sought liberation by binding their chests and cropping their hair to look more like men; professional women of the 1930s and 1940s wore mannish suits with squared-off shoulders; women returning to the home after World War II became sex kittens dressed in baby doll outfits, crinoline petticoats, and spiked heels; and women in the 1970s, more of whom were employed outside the home than in any previous era, enthusiastically adopted the pants suit.

When women are accepted as active, involved people by their own society, the clothes that are acceptable, such as pants, tend to echo those attitudes. When women are seen as docile, passive people by their own society, the clothes that are acceptable, such as awkward hoops and confining corsets tend to echo those particular attitudes. In frontier Iowa a serious paradox was apparent in women's clothing. Women were accepted as active and involved, in practice if not in theory, yet they were still dressing to meet eastern ideals regarding passive, docile women. Iowa frontierswomen dressed restrictively because that was the way nineteenth-century women were "supposed" to dress. This was more than a simple matter of the dictates of fashion; it was a matter of philosophy.

So, while western women were forging out new life-styles, revised concepts of economic importance, and increased demands for political equality, they retained the clothing style of the more settled, more conservative society that had spawned them. In this light, it is not surprising to learn that Iowa frontierswomen did whatever they could, even in a backwoods cabin, to look as much like the fashion plates they so assiduously studied whenever possible. Apparently they were rather successful, for when Frances Dana Gage, a popular writer and lecturer, visited Iowa in 1854 and contributed "Sketches on Iowa" to the *New York Tribune*, she characterized Iowa women as "ladies" who "rustled rich brocades, or flitted in lawns as natural as life."[51]

The fine dresses that Gage so approved rested upon brass or whalebone hoop skirts, the most universal piece of sartorial equipment for women in mid-nineteenth-century America. By the 1850s hoops had become so popular that few women were brave enough to disdain them. Amelia Murdock Wing explained, "To be seen without hoops endangered a woman's standing and she was liable to be called eccentric." Iowa newspaper advertisements indicated that hoops were successfully marketed over most of the state. In 1859, the *Burlington Daily Hawk-Eye* announced a special sale on hoop skirts. A few years later the *Fairfield Ledger* proclaimed "Good News—A full line of Hoop Skirts, Ladies Corsets, white and colored." And by the 1860s many refinements and new designs in hoop skirts were advertised. The *Waterloo Courier* of August 30, 1866, carried this notice:

> New Skirt for 1866! The Great Invention of the Age of Hoop Skirts. J. W. Bradley's New Patent Suplex Elliptic (or double) Spring Skirt . . . seldom bend or break, like the single springs . . . flexibility and comfort . . . in all crowded Assemblies, operas, carriages, railroad cars, church pews, arm chairs. . . . For children, misses and young ladies they are superior to all others.[52]

As hoops became larger, heavier, and more unmanageable, special aids were designed to be worn with them. To hold the outer skirt down over the hoops, a weighted cord was inserted in the bottom of its hem. To hold the hoops and skirt up, a skirt supporter consisting of straps crossing over the shoulders bore their weight.[53]

The bustle was another curious and confining invention. Designed to draw attention to a lady's posterior, it was a bird-cage-like affair which fastened around a woman's waist. The waist itself was supposed to be as narrow as possible and to gain this effect a restraining corset made of whalebone was worn. In 1870, an ad in the *Fairfield Ledger* claimed that "The Best Thing Out is the

Health Corset. . . . They support the entire weight of the under clothing from the shoulder, and for perfection of shape they are without a rival."[54]

The most popular type of dress incorporated three flounces in the skirt, a style which pioneer women often emulated in their calicoes. The outfit was topped off by a bonnet which in the 1860s often featured real stuffed birds, laces, and many ribbons as decoration.[55] Other accessories included gloves, reticules (small handbags), shawls, cloaks, and high-button shoes.

Comments made by Iowa frontierswomen confirm that they wore as many fashionable furbelows as possible, if not for everyday then at least for special events. Thinking back to Newcastle around 1850, Harriet Bonebright-Closz satirically portrayed the petticoats that were the forerunner of hoops.

> Wadded and quilted petticoats undoubtedly were designed for comfort but they were the embodiment of inartistic heaviness and the end of the limit for inefficiency. Instead of serving the purpose of warmth the wearer's nether limbs were half frozen beneath its balloon-like expanse. It had, notwithstanding, one redeeming feature. When outgrown it could be split open and used as a bed-pad or for a horseblanket.[56]

Around 1870 a North Tama woman listed the fashions of the day: "Hoops and great bustles are all the rage. . . . Almost every girl wears curls or frizzes. One day I was walking behind a very gay young lady when her curls fell off among her feet."[57]

A full outfit during this general era often consumed 100 yards of material and weighed as much as fifteen pounds, an obvious impediment to any kind of meaningful activity. Some nineteenth-century women were well aware of this outfit's clumsiness, its possible impairment to health through tight corseting and lacing, and its tendency to make women appear foolish, vain, and indolent. One Iowa woman of the 1850s, Amelia Bloomer, advocated a relatively sensible outfit which had a shortened skirt with long, full "bloomers" coming to the ankles. Although it was a move in the direction of health and sensibility, it was jeered off the streets primarily because of the pants. As Wing noted, "For a female to be seen in pants was considered a disgrace" even in frontier Iowa.[58] So the Bloomer costume, as it was named after Amelia, gained few adherents and gradually disappeared entirely from the fashion scene.

Therefore, Iowa frontierswomen's clothes tended to constrict their activities at the very time they were required to move more freely. As Wing remarked,

> . . . women, with their full skirts over wide hoops showed no more of their lower appendages than the toes of their shoes. In fact the proper term was "lower limbs," and it was even in better taste to act as if women were made in one piece from the waist down![59]

76

Exaggerated standards of nineteenth-century gentility and taste continued to cause problems in a frontier setting. Not only did women have to manipulate their hoop skirts, usually a minimum of three feet wide in diameter at the bottom, through doorways, but they had to learn how to enter, sit, and leave farm wagons gracefully in such cumbersome attire. Janette Murray stated that "When such skirts were spread out on a wagon seat, there was no place for a man to sit."[60]

The care of such clothing was complex and taxing. In an era which predated commercial laundries, dry cleaners, or even washing machines, all apparel had to be handled with the utmost care. Brocades and silks were wrapped in sheets and hung away in spare closets. Most women had at least one "good" dress. This was a black silk which saw her through weddings, funerals, and other special occasions. She would remake it in the latest fashion every four or five years so that it would last most of her lifetime. According to Murray, these and other fancy dresses were made at home or by a local seamstress. "The silk," she explained, "was heavy and rich and the dresses were made with so much lining, crinoline, and boning that they almost stood alone."[61]

Everyday clothing, along with bedding and other linens, had to be washed by hand. On washing day large wooden washtubs were first laboriously filled with water hauled in from the well and heated by the fireplace or stove. A washboard and some soft soap completed the list of necessary equipment. Women then proceeded to rub the clothing back and forth over a convoluted scrub board. When this step was concluded, the garment was hand wrung and hung outside to dry. In inclement weather the wash was hung and draped about the attic, the spare bedroom, or the kitchen to drip on the heads of those working below.

Almost everything, including sheeting, required ironing. This was done with heavy, solid iron flatirons. Several of these were heated in the fireplace or stove while an ironing table was placed nearby. As one iron cooled during use, it was carried back to the source of heat and exchanged for a hot iron. All ruffles, tucks, fluting, and other frills were ironed in with small flatirons made with various types of ridging especially for this purpose. Many garments had to be starched and it took a particularly skillful woman to know just when to remove the iron so that the telltale marks of scorched starch would not be left behind.

Susan Dubell aptly described some of the problems inherent in the ironing process:

> Starching was usually done with wheat-flour starch, but for "fine shirt" bosoms, collars, and cuffs there was "clear starch" which came in lumps, and was very inferior to the laundry starch of today. If it was not cooked properly, there would be trouble in ironing. The starch would stick to the iron, roll up on the clothes, and scorch, worrying the tired, hot, and impa-

tient housewife who toiled back and forth from the stove to change irons. Dresses and petticoats were wide and long, tucked and ruffled. Oh, the ironing.[62]

As Matilda Peitzke Paul mentioned at several points in her memoirs, all of the frontierswoman's duties, from feeding a family through clothing them, "made plenty of work."[63] But on another level, the outcome of her labors also plainly indicated her value as an artisan to a society which judged a person by immediate results rather than by wealth, family name, or social class. Her ability and industry in the manufacture of suitable domestic wares could determine the "comfort level" of her family's existence in frontier Iowa.

The frontierswoman's family depended on her as a kind of paraprofessional in a society which essentially lacked pharmacists, doctors, and morticians. Despite the various promotional claims to the contrary, settlers in Iowa did fall victim to accidents as well as to illnesses which included the prairie itch, fever, ague, and cholera.[64] It was presumed that a frontierswoman would, in addition to all her other capabilities, also become an accomplished herbalist. She gathered herbs in wooded areas at the risk of meeting a deadly rattlesnake or grew them in the "kitchen" garden right outside her own door. After the herbs were picked, they were dried and brewed into medicinal teas, tonics, bitters, or prepared as poultices.

As apothecaries, women were guided not only by the family knowledge that had been passed on to them, but by the recipes for medicine (which often outnumbered the recipes for food) in the receipt books. Some families were fortunate enough to own a "doctor book" that they used for reference. Many herbs that are now ignored by most medical practitioners in our age of antibiotics were pressed into service as medicine. May Lacey Crowder listed a few of the most popular used by her mother in treating her own family as well as the many neighbors who depended on her competence in time of illness.

Many wild plants were used as medicines, most of them steeped and drunk as tea. Among these were "Culver's root" taken "for the liver." The dandelion, both as extract and as wine, was used for the same purpose. Tonics were made from the butterfly weed, sweet flag root, sassafras bark, and boneset. . . . For colds, pennyroyal, prairie balm, and horse mint were popular remedies. Mullen was used externally for pleurisy. . . . Smartweed was used externally for boils. Culeb berries were smoked for catarrh.[65]

Harriet Bonebright-Closz added some others to Crowder's list: "skunk-oil and goose-grease, sulphur and sorghum, rhubarb and butternut pills, boneset and burdock bitters, sassafras and smartwood tea, slippery-elm salve and plaintain poultices."[66]

Home remedies were augmented, when possible, by prepared medicines such as quinine, morphine, and particularly whisky. When Matilda Peitzke

Paul was struck by a poisonous rattlesnake, her affected foot was kept in fresh mud for six hours and she was dosed with whisky. "This one poison," she dryly remarked, "offset another."[67] Bonebright-Closz was especially graphic in her description of the medicinal use of whisky.

> Whisky was the base for all bitters and the vehicle for internal and external application. It was, in fact, an all around remedial rejuvenator . . . it was taken as an eye-opener before breakfast and a victual settler after meals, an exhilarator between them, and as a nightcap at bedtime . . . whisky served in sociability as it did in sickness.[68]

By the 1860s there were also literally hundreds of patent medicines on the market in Iowa, all offering instant relief for any ailment. Looking over the *Waterloo Courier* in the 1860s, for example, one finds the following advertisements inviting the investment of faith and money by sufferers of a variety of ills. For twenty-five cents, Coe's Cough Balsam promised to stop "Tickling in the Throat, Coughs, Influenza, Whooping Cough." Wistar's Balsam of Wild Cherry, billed as "The Consumptive's Friend," would take care of coughs, colds, croup, asthma, influenza, bronchitis, and related problems. Ayer's Sasparilla aimed at "purifying the blood" as well as curing tumors, ulcers, sores, and skin diseases. Dr. Christie's Ague Balsam would end fever and ague. Worm Confections, at twenty-five cents a box, would destroy worms in children thus leaving "their health restored, their lives spared to you." And Leavitt's Great Pile Remedy, an internal vegetable potion, guaranteed "Joy to the Afflicted! A Permanent Cure for this Terrible Disease we now offer to Suffering Humanity."[69]

Clearly, commercially prepared medications were available; whether they were truly efficacious or not is an unanswerable question. If, as Bonebright-Closz believed, whisky was actually the base for many of them, they probably did bring a measure of relief to the sufferer, if not a measure of cure. Whatever their form, medications sometimes were prescribed for a patient by a doctor who possessed dubious medical training. These practitioners used natural medicines, patent medicines, and their own unidentified "doctor's powders." They also used antiquated medical techniques such as bleeding—opening a patient's vein and letting the blood run to remove the harmful spirits from the body. In 1841, for instance, Clara Dodge wrote her husband that she called in a doctor because she was feeling ill. The treatment was to bleed her, then to give her "Calomel and other medicines."[70]

In the preponderancy of cases, however, doctors were too few or too far away to be prevailed upon for their singular brand of medical care. If common preventive medicine, such as the spring doses of sulphur and molasses or the little bag of asafetida (gum resin with a garliclike odor) tied around a person's neck, did not successfully ward off illness then it was up to the women of the family to become doctor and nurse rolled into one.

When Sarah Kenyon's husband became ill with a serious cold, she insisted that "John would have roared if I had not quelled him with morphene." She treated his symptoms by putting "the physic and hoar hound tea to him nice and kept him on water porridge the next day."[71] Mary Ann Davidson had a much more difficult time curing her husband of what she called "that terrible Foe, chills and fever." After two weeks of treatment, he was finally attacked by a "sinking chill" which particularly alarmed her because she had no "doctor's medicine" in the house. She prepared hot teas for him to drink, rubbed his limbs vigorously, and "applied hot flannels wrung out of strong mint tea to his stomach and bowels." She continued to give him ginger tea and in a few days his chills were broken and to her great relief, he gradually regained his strength. When a relative belatedly arrived with provisions, he explained that he had been delayed by his own bout with bilious fever; he also carried the news that their new neighbors would not arrive until spring because they were sick with chills and fever.[72]

These cases indicate that the pioneers were plagued by ailments similar to what is now generally termed "flu" although their remedies differed markedly from current pills and patent medicines. When treatment was not successful, a family often had to face the death of a loved one. Ellen Strang's diary gives a poignant account of her own determined yet unsuccessful treatment of her younger sister for an "Ague chill." Ellen first put mustard poultices on her sister's feet, wrists, and neck and gave her Jamaica Ginger tea once every hour. The next day she tried mustard poultices and by the end of the week sent for a doctor who brought her some "medicine." Ellen continued the Jamaica Ginger tea and various poultices through the next week with only occasional success. By the third week the patient felt better, then had a sudden relapse. Ellen responded by rubbing the child's limbs with whisky, giving her more Jamaica Ginger tea, using mustard water to soak her hands and feet, binding sulphur on the joints of her hands and feet, and feeding her meals of corn meal gruel and flour porridge. She finally gave her quinine measured out on the point of a pen knife every two hours and some "powders" brought by the doctor, but after long weeks of suffering, the little girl died.[73]

THAT women were generally assigned the task of preparing bodies for burial was partly for practical and partly for ideological reasons. Women were in the house most of the hours of the day so they were present to provide constant service. On the ideological level, women were seen as "natural" caretakers of the sick and dead due to the "greater sensibilities" imputed to them by

ELLEN STRANG

nineteenth-century beliefs. Because they were female they were thought to have an inherent wisdom and softness that men lacked. This also at least partially explains why men were normally excluded from childbirth, a mysterious business which was usually handled by the mother-to-be, a female midwife, and perhaps a few female friends or relatives.

Procreation was highly encouraged on the frontier both to aid population growth and to provide future laborers for the family farm or other business. This meant that while the birth rate was dropping somewhat in eastern areas of the United States, it remained relatively high in frontier areas. One scholar believes that ten children as an average size for frontier families is a conservative estimate. There were many cases in Iowa of at least ten children, and as many as sixteen or eighteen, in one family. This tended to lead to a rather relaxed, matter-of-fact attitude regarding childbirth. A typical statement about a first birth was: "There was of course no doctor. No one thought of calling a doctor for so casual a matter."[74]

Although pioneers may have considered childbirth a necessary and natural function, there were of course complications. Both mothers and infants often sickened or died in childbirth or shortly thereafter. Gradually, patent medicines and doctors entered the picture. Cures such as "The Mothers' Companion," a type of liniment, promised help with various problems associated with childbirth and the nursing of a newborn infant.[75] And male doctors, like the increasing numbers of their counterparts in the East, claimed improved expertise in delivery and postnatal care. Unlike midwives who often worked free or for payment in kind, doctors often charged cash payments for their services. In 1868, an Iowa man's diary documented a representative story in a few short lines.

> Feb. 25, 1868—Tacy, my wife, had a new daughter this A.M. at 6-½ o'clock.
> Sat. March 7th—I went to Salem and paid Dr. Siveter $10.00. I had expected him to charge only $5.00.
> Sun. May 3—Baby died![76]

Though it may appear so, frontier families did not look upon the death of a child casually. One family kept their dead child's miniature rocking chair in the living room of their home for forty years after her demise.[77] When Kitturah Belknap's baby died from lung fever, she depicted it as the "first real trial" of her life. When another of her children died, she wrote in her diary:

> I have had to pass thru another season of sorrow. Death has again entered our home. This time it claimed our dear little John for its victim. It was hard for me to give him up but dropsy on the brain ended its work in four short days. . . . We are left again with one baby and I feel that my health is giving way.[78]

Clearly, bearing and rearing children was one of the most important economic functions of frontierswomen, but, as Belknap's comment points out, it was also one of the most physically taxing, often leaving physical evidence of its trials and tribulations on women's bodies. Unfortunately, gynecology was an area of medical practice shrouded in ignorance, superstition, and nineteenth-century standards of "modesty." Variously referred to as female ailments, complaints, weaknesses, diseases, difficulties, and problems, the whole matter was seen as part of woman's lot in life, closely related to her inferiority and dependency on the stronger male who was free from the rigors of childbearing and childcare. Indeed, nineteenth-century women were even encouraged by prevailing cultural norms to appear pallid, frail, and sickly in order to manifest the great "delicacy" which supposedly characterized their gender.[79]

As a result, women were routinely denied reliable information regarding birth control and abortion. When they did dare to take their problems to a doctor, they were discreetly examined swathed in a nightgown, or were asked to describe their symptoms by pointing to a small doll representing a female figure. If treated, they often had to face the ordeal of cauterization of the womb with a hot poker or even a clitoridectomy.[80]

Under the circumstances, it is little wonder that many women turned to mail-order doctors for relief. Characteristic of this trend was Dr. LaCroix of Albany, New York, who advertised his book, *Physiological View of Marriage,* in Iowa newspapers. A bargain at only twenty-five cents, its 250 pages were especially aimed at the ladies "who need a *confidential* medical adviser with regard to any interesting complaints to which their delicate organization renders them liable."[81]

Similarly, many women turned to patent medicines designed for their "ailments," usually composed largely of morphine or liquor. Yellow Dock Sasparilla was advertised as an aid to all "female problems." Henry's Invigorating Cordial maintained that "less suffering, disease and unhappiness among Ladies would exist, were they generally to adopt the use of this Cordial." Dr. Duponco's Golden Periodical Pills for Females claimed to reduce menstrual pain and other "female weaknesses." And Morrell's Electro Magnetic Fluid, a bathing lotion selling for one dollar a bottle, called itself "The Greatest Chemical Wonder of the Age—Electricity in Liquid Form!!" which would cure "Female Weak Back, Spinal Affections, and other Female Diseases."[82]

There is some reason to suspect that many of these medicines were actually designed as abortants. Women who were loath to face the burdens of yet another birth were lured with subtly worded advertisements. For example, James Clarke's Celebrated Female Pills were billed as a "Remedy for Female Difficulties and Obstructions from any cause whatsoever." The ad went on to appeal to "Married Ladies" to whom it promised to "bring on the monthly period with regularity."[83]

It is impossible to know how much damage such medicines may have done. It is more reasonable to think that most of them were relatively ineffective except at bringing in profits for their manufacturers. The number of advertisements and their continuing appearance, however, does indicate that many women rejected both the current social ethic and their own supposed maternalistic natures by attempting to avoid bearing any more children. They frequently sent off their hard-earned coins to buy an ephemeral hope of salvation from their fears.

An interesting footnote to this phenomenon of women's "ailments" is that men were not totally free from similar myths and ignorance regarding their bodies. Books were also published for them offering advice and relief from what might be called "male" complaints. In 1861 a book titled *The Invalid's Medical Confidant* contended that it could cure nervous debility, premature decay, and youthful indiscretions. Another ad appealed to men who had lost confidence: "Manhood! How Lost! How Restored!" Published in a sealed envelope at the reasonable price of six cents, a little booklet promised to steer men on a "proper" and healthy course. If advice failed, there were patent medicines for men too. One advertisement, headed "Manhood," was for Helmbold's Highly Concentrated Fluid Extract of Buchu which would repair "Weakness arising from excessive or early indiscretion."[84]

Advertised products of the day apparently responded to both women's and men's hygenic and sexual problems. In terms of nineteenth-century strictures regarding masculinity, particularly in the physically demanding frontier environment, it was more difficult for society to accept the idea that men had their "ailments" as well. They were expected to plod on, plow or pitchfork in hand, with their independence and strength providing the antithesis to the dependence and weakness of the female of the species.

These ideas about sex roles, which American society is only now beginning to seriously challenge, also underscored the idea that women were to be the primary, if not sole, supervisors of all surviving children. The thinking was that since women were in the home more than men it was again only "natural" that they should have the primary responsibility for child care. But, in Iowa at least, many women left the home to do farm work, carrying their children with them in ingenious ways. Matilda Peitzke Paul hauled up water from the well with her baby tied to her in her apron "to keep her from being trampled on by the thirsty cattle." When she helped her husband with the field work, she took her baby with her and "put her in a large box where she could play." When at home she combined child care with work: "I done all my washing by hand rubbing every garment, and often stood on one foot while rubbing and rocking the baby's cradle with the other foot, to keep her from waking up."[85]

Frontierswomen were the trainers, organizers, and overseers of the family labor force—the children. Therefore, besides their functions as workers and producers, women were also thrust into supervisory positions. As manager of the home, a mother quickly initiated the young children into the tasks of food processing, soapmaking, candlemaking, spinning and weaving, knitting, and the like. While still in their early years both boys and girls were expected to share in these tasks; there is even mention of young Iowa boys taking part in stocking knitting and quilt piecing. But as children advanced in age a division of labor developed, with the boys assuming more of the outdoor chores and the girls more of the indoor ones. It was common for boys to be sent for fuel and water, to help with the planting, to help with the stock, and to work in the fields while the girls continued on with the production of food, soap, candles, and significantly, with the care of the younger children.

Yet these sex role divisions were not absolute; tasks to be done and the available labor supply quite often determined who would undertake what job. The herding of stock was often assigned to boys and girls alike. Children as young as six and seven were sent out to follow the sound of the bell strapped around the lead cow's neck and to persuade the cattle to stop their grazing in order to return home for milking.[86] Matilda Peitzke Paul remembered that as a child she and her brothers and sisters were routinely sent out to find the family cows who wandered at will unrestrained except for the rail-fenced grain fields. She also recalled that she was expected to carry in wood for the cookstove, carry in some of the water, and feed the calves in the morning and evening, in addition to helping with the more traditional household duties. Along with the other younger children, she also worked in the fields dropping corn and potatoes into the rows at planting time while the older children followed along behind covering the holes up with a hoe. Other jobs followed:

> When the corn first came up we had to stay out in the field and chase the black-birds to keep them from digging and eating the corn as fast as it came up. It was our work in spring to pull weeds for the hogs for feed. About the middle of June we used to pick wild strawberries. . . . We often had to watch our cattle to keep them out of other peoples as well as out of our own fields. . . . Before I was old enough to bind grain I helped carry bundles in piles, ready to be shocked up. . . . I often had to get water from a spring and carry it out to the field for drinking for the workers, before I was old enough to do other field work. Later on I helped bind the grain. . . . We children had to go over the whole field and gather up the roots in piles and when they got dry we used them for fuel. . . . After harvest and haying was done we had to dig the potatoes and husk the corn ready for winter.[87]

Paul's detailed listing supports the conclusion that children were considered a valuable supply of labor in their own right during the frontier period. This concept introduces some doubt regarding the image of early marriage on the frontier, for if children were so necessary to the economic survival of the farm would the family be willing to part with them just as they became most valuable as laborers? Unfortunately, no hard data have yet been collected to answer this question for the Iowa frontier, but Blaine T. Williams's study of the frontier family in Texas unearthed census data which indicate that frontier marriage at an early age was largely a myth. According to Williams, "Strong evidence in the data suggests that the frontier family was culture bound with strong sentimental ties and values" as well as economically bound, so most offspring did not marry until sometime during their mid-twenties.[88]

There is some anecdotal evidence in Iowa sources that strongly points to the need for further research on this question of average age at marriage. In the James Duffield family, as a case in point, the eldest son, John, was still at home at age twenty acting as the overseer of the boys of the family and as his father's chief assistant. At the same time, the eldest girl, Maria, at age twenty-two was the overseer of the girls and her mother's chief assistant.[89]

It is true that men continued to outnumber women throughout most of the frontier period and were generally on the lookout for marriageable women. But as long as men or women were already part of a family unit, there was no immediate push to leave it to begin a new one. It was usually to a family's advantage to retain the labor and skills of the offspring as long as possible; it was to the children's advantage to amass experience, capital, and goods to insure a successful start when the time came. Young women profitably used time at home to heighten domestic skills as well as stockpile clothing to carry them through the first, often lean, years of marriage. During a prolonged time with her family, a young woman could build her trousseau, which provided household goods and served as a tangible mark of her domestic talents. It might also help secure her a better "catch" as a mate. So, while there was a demand for marriageable women, marriage did not necessarily occur at an early age.

The complexity of the Iowa frontierswoman's role as domestic producer and as superintendent was further augmented by her participation in what was normally considered "men's work." Because Iowa land was cheap and plentiful, most men felt that "hiring out" their labor was usually less attractive than taking up land for themselves. Those men who did hire out were often temporary, transient, unreliable, or a combination of all three. And since black slavery was not practiced in Iowa, the shortage of labor created a need for women's help in the work of the farm. Women drove teams of plow animals, dropped seed, harvested crops, and did much of the other heavy field work that nineteenth-century mores supposedly prohibited them from doing.

Caroline Phelps helped her trader husband "to pack the skins, as we had no man to help." Matilda Peitzke Paul drove the horses on a reaper during one harvest, and the next year she drove a harvester.[90] And Sarah Kenyon, along with her sister Mary, and her children, did a variety of field jobs including reaping wheat. In 1861 when her husband hired a field hand she told her mother-in-law that things were looking up. "John has hired a man to work for him this Summer," she wrote, "hope I shall not have to dig quite as much out of doors." But when the hired man quit just before the fall corn harvest, she took it philosophically:

> One hired man left just as corn plucking commenced so I shouldered my hoe and have worked out ever since and I guess my services are just as acceptable as his or will be in time to come to the country. . . . I wore a dress with my sunbonnet wrung out in water every few minutes and my dress also wet this was all the clothing . . . I wore.[91]

In one sense, women performing men's work were "gainfully" employed because they helped produce a cash crop and prevented cash being paid to a hired laborer. Yet since no actual cash passed into her hands and because she was laboring within the family unit, the frontierswoman was still not officially considered as gainfully employed. This logic extended to her production of surplus domestic goods such as butter and eggs which were sold outside the home for actual cash. Historian Gilbert Fite maintains that butter was a primary cash product on the farmer's frontier, its income often keeping farms financially afloat during the rocky years.[92] Since women produced butter and other cash products, they brought in actual money to the operation of the homestead.

Margaret Murray remembered that "mother sold Butter Eggs & Beeswax & anything we could spare off the farm in the summer and fall we gatherd Blackberries, wild grapes & anything we raised on the farm that would bring money or exchange for groceries." When her uncle and aunt worked together to build a brick-drying kiln, her aunt realized that she might also use the kiln to dry fruit; the first winter she earned one dollar selling dried peaches. In another case, Kitturah Belknap discovered that she could add a few coins to the savings box intended for their new home by making a few extra pieces of linen for sale while doing her own spinning and weaving.[93]

May Lacey Crowder recalled that her mother was rather successful at producing and selling butter. She took $230 of inheritance money, invested it in milk cows, and from that time on made butter for the market. She packed the butter away in 100-pound tubs and stored it in the cellar until fall when it was hauled to Algona, the nearest market, thirty miles and three days away. The money raised was used for winter clothing and supplies. Finally, hogs were purchased to consume the surplus milk, and hog-raising became the family's principal industry. Crowder states that many frontierswomen not only produced income by selling their produce, but were aware of their economic importance to the family in doing so.

> Frequently enough, while the men were learning to farm, the women and children actually supported the families. They raised chickens and eggs for

the table, raised the vegetables and fruit, and made butter to sell in exchange for things not produced at home. The women were not unaware of this fact and were quite capable of scoring a point on occasion when masculine attitudes became too bumptious.[94]

Many women worked out of their own homes to produce cash income. By taking boarders into their already crowded quarters, women created more work for themselves, but brought in much-needed money. Paul, for instance, had her husband, two baby girls, and a hired man to care for, yet she agreed to board the local teacher for two dollars a week, which she said "helped out a little." When a branch of the Rock Island Railroad cut through the Newtons' farm, they took some of the laborers in to board, which, with the Newtons' five children, created a large household to care for. Emery Bartlett told his children that "for two or three years, with my utmost exertion and strictest economy, I could scarcely tell whether I was gaining or losing and had it not been for the little money my dear wife saved by taking a few boarders, I must certainly have gone under."[95]

Without a doubt, women had economic significance in the settlement of the frontier—a significance that has gone largely unrecognized for many years. Food processing and cooking; extending hospitality to travelers; soap making and candlemaking; spinning, weaving, and sewing; washing and ironing; acting as apothecaries, nurses, doctors, and morticians; rearing and training children; helping with men's work; and generating cash income are significant accomplishments even when performed using modern equipment. Since factories and trained professionals have taken over most of these functions in our own world, it is doubly difficult for us to realize just how much skill and labor was involved. Whether nineteenth-century society or the United States Census Bureau officially recognized it or not, Iowa frontierswomen were indeed "gainfully employed."

CHAPTER FOUR

A *Variety of Heritages*

THE most difficult stereotype to dispel is the one which portrays frontierswomen as white, American, and English-speaking. Scattered bits of evidence—a letter, a diary, or a daguerreotype taken by an itinerant frontier photographer—indicate that frontierswomen came from a variety of cultures. It is known that many foreign-born women participated in settling the American West. Relatively few black women and men settled in frontier regions; their presence was in a few instances recorded—in others it must be inferred. The Exodusters, a group of blacks who fled the South to relocate in Kansas after the Civil War, have received attention from scholars.[1] But such cases of well-documented black migration are, unfortunately, rare. It is reasonable to suppose that some black women accompanied black cowboys to Oklahoma and Texas, black panhandlers to the goldfields, and black soldiers to the plains. On family-farm frontiers, such as Iowa, the 1840 Territorial Census for Iowa reveals a population of 24,256 white males and 18,668 white females as compared to only eighty-one free black males, seventy-two free black females, seven slave males, and eleven slave females.[2]

Although slaves appeared in the 1840 census, Iowa did not legally countenance slavery. The Ordinance of 1787 outlawing slavery in the Northwest Territory applied to Iowa as part of the Louisiana Purchase of 1803; the Missouri Compromise of 1820 declared the territory above latitude 36°30' (except Missouri) to be free. A few early settlers and visitors probably brought slaves into Iowa in defiance of these acts of Congress. In subsequent years, although no black slaves were listed in census enumerations, there was evidence that a few slaves still lived in Iowa, technically held as indentured servants. In 1850, an advertisement in the *Burlington Tri-Weekly Telegraph* posted notice of the escape of one such servant. She was described as black, thirteen or fourteen years of age, with five years left to serve on her indenture. Her owner stated that it was a shame that some "meddling person" had "decoyed" her away as he had intended to return the girl to her family in Maryland. He claimed that "it would be an act of charity to her could she be restored to him"[3]

After 1840, the census recorded blacks but was not consistent in separating black population statistics into male and female, thus ruling out establishing a sense of continuity. Iowa census data indicate that the number of blacks remained small throughout the frontier era.[4]

	1850	1860	1870
Number of blacks to 10,000 whites in Iowa	17	16	48
Total number of blacks in Iowa	333	1,069	5,762

In light of the census figures, it is not surprising that Sarah Kenyon wrote to her family in the East in 1856, "I have not seen a darkey since I have been here."[5]

A decade later the number of freed slaves on the frontier had not increased radically.[6] Although some freed slaves managed to make their way to the frontier after the Civil War, most lacked the mobility, capital, and skills needed for such a venture.[7] Many blacks who entered Iowa after the war did so as contraband brought back by soldiers returning to their homes and farms. May Lacey's father was a representative case. When Alvin Lacey spotted a black man guarding soldiers' bags along the dock in Davenport, Lacey invited the man to return home with him as a farm laborer. May later wrote that he stayed with the family for about a year and a half. She remembered that "he was honest and faithful and idolized the whole family. I was between four and five years old at the time and was a great favorite with Jim, whose admiration I reciprocated."[8]

In the postwar migration from the South, black women were particularly disadvantaged since they had been trained primarily as manual laborers and domestic servants throughout the antebellum period. It would therefore be unrealistic to expect large numbers of freed black women to appear as farmers or wives of farmers. Rather, they were more often hired as domestics, washwomen, and day laborers by frontier families.[9]

The problem in researching black pioneer women in Iowa is twofold. Not only have black women's source materials been neglected, but due to their relatively low numbers in Iowa both before and after the Civil War, black women have been accorded little attention by the historians of the region. Consequently, scholars can only infer the history of black frontierswomen from a study of blacks in general. Events, attitudes, and legislation affecting black men are thus assumed to have affected black women as well.[10] Although black women's history has not necessarily followed an identical course with that of black men, some knowledge of them can be gained through the study of black men on the Iowa frontier.

It is known, for instance, that despite the relatively low numbers of blacks in Iowa, the "Negro question" was an unending source of conflict and discussion in the area. Most of this agitation stemmed from the makeup of the white population in Iowa, rather than from the size of the black population, which hovered around one percent of the total population. As early as 1906, Frank Herriott pointed out that migration from eastern areas to frontier regions did not always flow along parallels of latitude as was commonly believed. Had that been the case, Iowa's population would have been predominantly settled by New Englanders or by their westernized descendants in the Ohio Valley region, most of whom Herriott assumed would have been antislavery in orientation. Instead, in his reading of the census data for the pre–Civil War period in Iowa, Herriott found a large proportion of people he defined as southerners which he believed were proslavery in their views. He observed that New Englanders did not account for quite four per hundred of the population, that the number of southerners was almost six times the number originating east of the Hudson River, and that there were more Virginians than all the New Englanders combined. He concluded,

> . . . Iowa was settled first by sons of the Old Dominion interspersed with the vigor of New England. Upon such a holding much that is inexplicable in Iowa's history becomes easily understandable. We can readily appreciate why Senator Dodge could so confidently proclaim in the senate of 1854 that he and his colleague, General Jones, with the senator from Pennsylvania were the only senators from the north who had voted against the Wilmot Proviso and for the fugitive slave law; and why Governor Grimes found the south half of Iowa so strongly pro-slavery.[11]

Some fifty years after Herriott's study, historian Joel Silbey's research upheld Herriott's conclusions. Silbey identified several streams of migration into Iowa, which created three distinct periods of changing sentiment toward blacks: (1) great support of slavery until 1846, (2) a transition in sentiment until 1854, and (3) the emergence of definite antislavery attitudes in Iowa. Silbey also supposed that southerners were necessarily proslave in their views. He thus tied the first period, that of proslavery thought, to the large influx of southern settlers who dominated both southern Iowa and the first territorial legislature. On the one hand, they feared the competition of cheap black labor, and on the other, declared their paternalism by advocating that keeping blacks in slavery was tantamount to caring for and protecting them. According to Silbey, this kind of thinking met opposition from increasing numbers of migrants to Iowa who had come from free states, Canada, and European countries during the late 1840s and early 1850s. The resulting turmoil in values abated in the mid-1850s, especially after the state constitutional convention of 1857, which reflected the growing antislavery attitudes of the majority of Iowans.[12]

By 1860 Iowa was antislavery, although not abolitionist in outlook. Blacks now numbered 1,069 as compared to 333 in 1850; the increase, however, had not occurred due to overt encouragement by Iowans, for even many of the migrants from the Northeast who opposed slavery found it difficult to accept the personal reality of working and living with blacks. As a result, Iowa opposed slavery, yet at the same time refused to extend full rights and privileges to its own black residents.[13] This dichotomy resulted in ambiguous policies and laws pertaining to blacks in Iowa.

The issue of rights for black men and women in Iowa initially emerged in the sessions of the first territorial legislature of 1838–1839. On June 21, 1839, it passed "An Act to Regulate Blacks and Mulattoes" which required every black to show a certificate of freedom upon entering the territory and to post a bond of $500 to insure his or her good behavior. County governments often quickly passed their own "black laws" which guaranteed the enforcement of the act within their county.[14]

Marion County enacted a code which gave the county commissioners the right to hire out a black who refused or was unable to post bond and to deposit his or her earnings in the county treasury. This law was tested in the mid-1840s when an Illinois farmer moved into Marion County with his freed black wife. After due legal action, the county court ordered that she appear before the court and post the required bond or "be sold to the highest bidder." When she was arrested for failure to appear, she finally posted the bond. Shortly thereafter, she and her husband left the county.

The Marion County case reflected not only the whites' fear of blacks, but their fear of miscegenation as well. In 1840, the Iowa Territorial Legislature had attempted to head off this seeming menace by passing a law prohibiting interracial marriage. In the same session, the legislature also forbade blacks and Native Americans from testifying against whites in court cases. As harsh as these restrictions may seem in an area where settlers were supposedly seeking freedom and democracy, it should be noted that Iowa did not stand alone in her actions. During the 1830s, Ohio, Indiana, Illinois, and Michigan had adopted almost identical statutes. Iowa's physical proximity to Missouri aggravated its fear of engulfment by blacks and, accordingly, increased its willingness to pass restrictive black codes.[15]

That the fear of black inundation was very real to many Iowans was dramatically illustrated by the state constitutional convention of 1844. When a petition was presented to the convention members asking that equal rights for blacks be incorporated in the new constitution, it was referred to a committee. At the same time, the committee was confronted with a proposed provision to prevent black people from settling in Iowa at all. After much discussion about the nature of equality and the ideals of the Declaration of Independence, the committee reported back to the convention that it believed that all people were indeed created equal and that rights were as sacred to blacks as to whites, but that this was only applicable in an abstract state of nature. In the committee's view, the state of society and government was artificial and thus altered the nature of equality. The committee recommended that Iowa refrain from either barring blacks from settlement or giving them equal rights. The granting of equal rights to blacks, it was thought, would only make Iowa a haven for America's black population:

> The policy of other states would drive the whole black population of the Union upon us. The ballot box would fall into their hands and a train of evils would follow that in the opinion of your committee would be incalculable.[16]

The *Iowa Capital Reporter* was quick to voice its approval of the convention's action. "We believe," the editor wrote, that "to have granted the subject of the petition, would not have elevated the blacks in the least, but would have reduced the Anglo-Saxon race to a bare competition with the new partners in the government." The editor concluded with the fervent wish that "this black subject will now rest in Iowa forever."[17]

The state constitution of 1844, having been passed by an all-male convention, embodied what appeared to be a majority opinion regarding rights of black men and women. Slavery was outlawed, but only white males were granted the right of suffrage, holding public office, and serving in the state militia. These same provisions were retained in the consitution of 1846, which became operative when Iowa was admitted to the Union in that year. But within a few years of statehood, some legislators apparently regretted their predecessors' failure to pass a law prohibiting blacks from settling in Iowa. The Third General Assembly of 1851 therefore passed a provision barring blacks from any further settlement in the state, although allowing those already in residence to remain. The assembly's action never passed into law, however, because the editor of the Mount Pleasant *True Democrat,* who was supposed to print the code in order to put it into effect, was antislavery in sentiment and refused to publish it.[18]

In addition to the debate over the "Negro question" in general, there was also much heated discussion over the issue of whether black boys and girls should be educated in Iowa's schools. In 1847, a law passed by the first General Assembly of Iowa limited admittance to the state's schools to white people between ages five and twenty-five. In 1851, Iowa exempted all black property owners from payment of school taxes although there was some indication that some black children were being admitted to local schools despite the exclusion law.[19]

In 1857, a state constitutional convention again debated both the rights and education of black men and women in Iowa. Attitudes toward these issues had not changed noticeably from previous years although a Republican, James W. Grimes, now held the governorship. The convention members still clearly

opposed slavery yet feared the inundation of blacks. They were thrown into
confusion when a proposal to strike the word *white* from the new constitution
was presented.[20] When the Repulicans suggested that the idea be submitted to
the public by means of a referendum, the Democrats opposed such a move on
the basis that the public would surely defeat the measure. The ensuing debate
showed most of the legislators to be fast in their resistance to equal rights for
blacks. This majority included many Republicans who were against the extension of slavery, yet were not committed to black equality. One Democratic
editor summarized the situation: "There is no man of our acquaintance, be his
politics Republican or Democratic, who desires to have negroes come among
us." The majority of the public concurred; when the equal black rights clause
was finally put to a vote, it was soundly defeated by 49,511 to 8,489.[21]

The state constitution of 1857 continued to deny black males access to the
vote, public office, and militia service, although their testimony was now considered acceptable in court.[22] It also gave the state board of education the
authority to determine school regulations. There was an attempt to subvert this
clause in 1858 by an act of the General Assembly establishing separate black
schools. When it was declared unconstitutional, no further reference was made
to racial segregation in Iowa's school laws. It was not until 1868, however, that
a black man brought a school discrimination case on behalf of his daughter to
the Iowa Supreme Court, which ruled that school boards lacked the power to
require separate school attendance due to race.[23] In the same year, the word
white was removed from the suffrage and militia clauses.[24] In 1880 *white* was
finally deleted from the qualification for a seat in the Iowa General Assembly.

In assessing these public policies of Iowa, as well as of other western states,
William L. Katz, author of *The Black West,* has observed, "The black laws
moved westward with the pioneer's wagons." He takes the position that statements made during the 1844 Iowa constitutional convention are examples of
racism:

> We should never consent to open the doors of our beautiful state and in-
> vite him [the black] to settle our lands. . . . The negro not being a party to
> the government, has no right to partake of its privileges. . . . There are
> strong reasons to induce the belief that the two races could not exist in the
> same government upon an equality without discord and violence.

Katz concluded:

> The intrepid pioneers who crossed the western plains carried the virus of
> racism with them. . . . Even the West's vaunted antislavery position was
> largely based not on moral repulsion to an evil institution, or even
> calculated white self-interest—rather it stemmed from hatred and fear of
> blacks as neighbors. Repeatedly and by overwhelming majorities, white
> settlers voted to keep black people from entering their land, voting in their
> elections, testifying in their courts, serving in their militia, or attending
> their schools and churches.[25]

A few white Iowans, however, did devote time, energy, and financial resources to their antislavery or abolitionist beliefs. Joanna Harris Haines, a native of Pennsylvania, recalled that her family members were already staunch abolitionists when they settled in Lee County, Iowa, in 1852. To their dismay, they learned that people sympathetic to slavery were numerous and in control of local politics. Haines remembered, "The intense abolitionism of my parents tended to alienate us and to enhance our sense of loneliness." Moreover, the family found itself out of sympathy with the local churches, who refused either by word or deed to move against the institution of slavery. In spite of local opposition, Haines's father refused to conceal his views, the antislavery meetings held in his home, or his attendance at antislavery conventions. After the family's move to a more productive farm near Grinnell, they became conductors on the Underground Railroad. When the Civil War ended, Haines's brother brought home a young black man whom he intended to educate in the Grinnell school. According to Haines,

> His appearance in the schoolroom precipitated another crisis. Grinnell had a number of New Englanders who were idealists and friends of humanity when thinking of far-away China, Africa, or South Carolina, but their zeal in good works cooled when the actualities came into town and next door.

The protests against the young man's education were abruptly halted when the head of the school firmly upheld his right to an education.[26]

During the prewar years, many other Iowa whites risked fines and imprisonment at the hands of the law or a more violent punishment at the hands of proslave neighbors in order to support the operation of the Underground Railroad across Iowa towards Canada. One young Polk County woman stated that blacks "went through Iowa in meal sacks, under straw, in dry goods boxes—coffins—men in women's clothes, and women in men's clothes." She added that "conversation runs on the great themes of human rights, in the parlor, churches, bar room, stage coaches, and almost everywhere human beings talked." A Fairfield man remembered that his Quaker family entrusted him, although he was only fourteen years old, with the task of "conducting" black fugitives from one "station" to another.[27]

In a few instances, white Iowans also aided and supported black families who were involved in Underground Railroad activities. The Pyles family was one such case. Freed by their owner, a woman, and relocated by her in Keokuk, they began to raise money to buy other members of the family out of slavery. Armed with letters of recommendation from white citizens in Iowa, Charlotta Pyles launched a speaking tour in the East to raise the necessary funds. After her return to Iowa in the mid-1850s, she converted her home into a station on the Underground Railroad and with the aid of white supporters, helped many black slaves on their way to Canada.[28]

Although no formal records or head count was kept due to fear of discovery, the success of the Underground Railroad lines was noted by Abbie Mott Benedict who, while migrating to Iowa by way of Canada in 1855, remarked on the numbers of blacks she saw along the way. "These were," she explained, "ex-slaves from the Southern States who had escaped into Canada via the celebrated Underground Railroad."[29]

But other Iowans did not even consider the situation of blacks until its presence was thrust upon them by the advent of war or some other precipitous situation. Sarah Kenyon, for instance, a New Englander in background, had almost nothing to say to her husband's family back East regarding slavery until October, 1861, when she briefly wrote them, "There is no Secessier about me or rank abolitionism, still now is the time to rid the country of the curse of slavery."[30]

FOUR court cases tested the rights and legal status of black men and women in early Iowa. The first case erupted in Burlington in 1839. It was the initial case to be heard by the Iowa territorial supreme court, which met in the Old Zion Methodist Church with Chief Justice Charles Mason on the bench.[31] The case centered on a black man identified only as Ralph, a slave who came to Dubuque in 1834 with the consent of his master in Missouri. Ralph was to buy his freedom by working in the lead mines, but when he failed to remit the required sum, his master reclaimed Ralph as a slave. Fortunately for Ralph, a Dubuque Abolitionist interfered with his actual seizure and remanded the matter into the hands of the court.

Ralph's case was pled by attorney David Rorer who was southern by birth, a former slaveholder, and an emancipationist since his removal to Burlington in 1836. He argued that since Ralph had been a resident of the Territory of Wisconsin and then of the Iowa Territory at the time of its creation, he was free by the Organic Law of Congress creating Iowa as a free territory. Rorer also referred to the antislavery provisions of the Ordinance of 1787 and the Missouri Compromise. He maintained that Ralph was not a fugitive since he had moved to Iowa with the consent of his master and that if his former owner had a right to any legal action it was to recover the money Ralph had promised to pay him. The plaintiff's counsel argued that Ralph, having failed to fulfill the contract, was a fugitive slave by default and thus liable to return to his master under the fugitive slave law.[32]

After listening to the arguments of both sides, Chief Justice Mason ruled that Ralph's owner had essentially granted him freedom by consenting to Ralph's departure from Missouri and could not impress him back into a state of slavery. Since slavery did not exist in Iowa, Ralph was free by the fact of being allowed by his owner to take up residence in a free territory. Concerning the disputed sum of money owed by Ralph, Mason ruled, "It is a debt which he ought to pay, but for the non-payment of which no man in the Territory can be reduced to slavery."[33] Mason ended his decision with the statement,

> . . . when he [the claimant] applies to our tribunals for the purpose of controlling, as property, that which our laws have declared shall not be property, it is incumbent on them to refuse their co-operation. When in seeking to accomplish his object, he illegally restrains a human being of his liberty, it is proper that the laws, which should extend equal protection to men of all colors and conditions, should exert their remedial interposition. We think therefore, that the petitioner should be discharged from all custody and constraint, and be permitted to go free while he remains under the protection of our laws.[34]

Less than a decade after the Ralph case, a second fugitive slave case made news in Iowa. It involved nine slaves who left their master in Missouri in 1848 and headed towards Salem, Iowa. "Slave-catchers" caught them just as several Salem citizens were guiding them into a hiding place. The citizens demanded that the agents go before the court and prove that the nine blacks in question were indeed slaves. When the agents were unable to prove the slave status of the nine blacks, the judge had no jurisdiction to hold them. Two of the blacks were aided in an immediate escape, an action which so infuriated scores of Missourians that they thoroughly searched Salem for the other blacks. Four were eventually returned to Missouri; three others, a man, woman, and girl, were never accounted for, so it was assumed that they also escaped.

The matter was not yet at an end as Ruel Daggs, the former owner, sued a number of Salem Quakers under the fugitive slave law of 1793 for compensation for the five escaped slaves. In a long summary statement to the jury, Daggs's counsel David Rorer argued that Iowa, now a state, must uphold the United States Constitution and respect the laws of its neighboring states.

> The very subject upon which you are called to decide, is now agitating our country from Washington to the most distant borders. It has been a source of contention among the people of both North and South—of slave-holding and non-slave-holding States. Your verdict will show whether there is just ground for this suspicion, as to us. Whether fanaticism is to be encouraged among us of the North, or the wild and maniac cry of disunion in the South.[35]

Six of the defendants were found guilty and ordered to pay a fine of $2,900, presumably the estimated value of the missing five slaves. The Salem Quakers duly paid the fine with little or no disruption in the operation of their segment of the Underground Railroad.[36]

Shortly after the Daggs case in Salem, the strict Fugitive Slave Law was passed nationwide as part of the Compromise of 1850. This law was to be tested in Iowa in 1855 by a third case, that of a slave named Dick who was a fugitive slave brought to Burlington by a staunch abolitionist actively and publicly involved as a conductor on the Underground Railroad. The progress of the two men through Burlington was halted by slave-catchers from Missouri who declared their intention to return Dick to his master. George Frazee, a young Burlington lawyer and commissioner of the United States District Court for Iowa, watched from his office window in the National Hotel building as a crowd gathered.

> Every man in the crowd who was himself a native of the slave-region, or the son of such a native—and there were many such in Burlington—seemed to be very zealous in his manifestations of sympathy with the slave claimants. . . . And then the sympathy of the northern people in the crowd was scarcely less pronounced. There were probably very few, if any openly acknowledged "abolitionists" among them. But the system to the respectable people of the North seemed inhuman, and was also obnoxious because of its political influence.[37]

As commissioner, it was Frazee's duty to hear the resulting court case. David Rorer appeared as one of Dick's attorneys, but did not have to present an argument in Dick's defense due to the fact that the son of Dick's alleged owner testified that he did not recognize Dick as one of his father's slaves. "As soon as the order of discharge was made," Frazee recalled, "a joyous shout went up from those within the court room, responded to by the crowd without, much more vigorously." He was later told that a thousand people escorted Dick to the ferryboat which started him on his trip to Chicago.[38]

Governor James W. Grimes, who was residing in Burlington at the time, took an intense interest in Dick's case. He wrote his wife who was on a visit in Maine that "I am sorry I am Governor of the State, for although I can and shall prevent the State authorities and officers from interfering in aid of the marshal, yet, if not in office, I am inclined to think I should be a law-breaker." When the Dick case, the first and only to be heard in Iowa under the Fugitive Slave Law of 1850, was resolved, Governor Grimes was relieved that the people of Burlington had been "saved from disgrace." He wrote his wife that he was gratified that opinion had changed so much from the early 1850s when only he and a few others openly opposed the law. "Now I am Governor of the State," he wrote, and "three-fourths of the reading and reflecting people of the county agree with me in my sentiments on the law, and a slave could not be returned from Des Moines County into slavery."[39]

In 1863 there was one last legal attempt to reduce the black population in Iowa. Perhaps alarmed by the Emancipation Proclamation, which some citizens believed would cause Iowa to be overwhelmed by an influx of freed slaves, a group of Polk County residents obtained a notice ordering Archie P. Webb to leave the area under the Code of 1851, which excluded blacks from the state.

The case was heard by thirty-one-year-old John Henry Gray, judge of the Fifth Judicial District Court. In a detailed decision, Gray ruled that the exclusion Code of 1851 was null and void, not because it had never been published in the newspaper as the General Assembly directed, but because it was in violation of the state constitution of 1846, as well as the constitution of 1857, and the United States Constitution, which guaranteed a free black such as Webb the right to reside in Iowa. Gray concluded, "The law under which the plaintiff was arrested is inoperative and void; that the proceedings thereunder were therefore unauthorized, that the plaintiff herein is entitled to his liberty, and that he is hereby discharged from imprisonment."[40]

The *Chicago Tribune* fully supported Gray's judgment. "Thus has ended," it asserted, "a wicked scheme of a gang of semi-traitors to inaugurate a general system of persecution against the free negroes in this State, and to that extent embarrass the execution of the President's Emancipation Proclamation in the Mississippi Valley."[41]

The one consistent theme in each of these cases is the split in sentiment among Iowans towards blacks. The conflicts between the antislave and proslave factions were so acute that they frequently led to arguments and even bloodshed. In 1856, for example, a merchant in Burlington publicly remarked that he thought "a negro as good as himself, or an Irishman, if he behaved himself." The merchant was shot and perhaps would have been killed by the crowd if the police had not fortuitously come to his aid. In the following years, the steamboat *Saracen,* which was docked in Fort Madison, was the scene of a violent fight. A white mate assailed a black with such vehemence that the latter fled the ship, only to be dragged back again by the crew who intended to flog him. When some townspeople, abolitionist in persuasion, attempted to interfere, a fight broke out between the crew and the crowd. The stones and other missiles thrown by the crowd were returned by bullets from the crew, resulting in one death and several injuries.[42]

Even liberal Grinnell had its trouble. Sarah Parker, whose husband was a schoolteacher in town, wrote her mother in 1860 that a Quaker brought four black men to work in Grinnell. As they wished to attend school, their employer consented, but their presence in the schoolroom resulted in a heated town meeting to resolve the question of whether black pupils should attend Grinnell schools. When the "ayes" carried the vote in favor of black attendance, one man shouted, "They shall never enter those doors unless over my dead body." Another exclaimed, "I go with you." Parker was horrified by the violence of the meeting, especially when she and several other women who were graduates of Oberlin "received torrents of abuse." The next morning a mob of whites marched on the school, so alarming the blacks that they armed themselves and prepared to fight. When law officers intervened, the mob took to the streets of Grinnell where riots, secret meetings, and threats were rife. When the mob violence continued the next day, Parker was particularly worried for the safety of her husband who, as head of the school, upheld the blacks' right to attend school. She told her mother,

> Desperate deeds were meditated—men maddened with hate and rage ran through the streets with insulting words ever on their lips. When I bade my husband good morning, I did not know but he would be the first victim of the fury. For he told the mob the day before that if they attempted to touch one of the pupils under his care he should defend him. But we all live—though knives were whetted for hand to hand encounter, guns loaded and pistols made ready.[43]

The incident, which divided the congregation of the church and caused the school to be closed temporarily, was finally resolved in favor of allowing the blacks to attend school in Grinnell.

Instead of lessening such animosities, the Civil War and the Emancipation Proclamation only aggravated them. Thousands of whites, many of them abolitionists, were now faced with the reality of what freedom would mean for them, their families, their towns, and their state. Would freed slaves rush into Iowa? Would cheap black labor threaten white employment and wages? Would interracial marriage, so long feared by many whites, now become a reality? Would black and white children sit on school benches together? The questions were legion and the answers few. Even many of the liberals had not considered the new social problems which emancipation would introduce. The unfortunate results were widespread prejudice, discrimination, and occasionally physical abuse of black men and women.[44]

Clearly, the status of black people in frontier Iowa was ambiguous at best and potentially fatal at worst. Given this situation, it is little wonder that the history of blacks in general and the black frontierswoman in particular has as yet to be uncovered. The reality of limitations in civil rights, in educational opportunities, and in place of residence for black pioneer women in Iowa will become manifest only when their own words and memories are collected, studied, and integrated into the story of all Iowa frontierswomen.

CONDITIONS similar to those faced by blacks, although much less harsh and punitive, were faced by certain segments of Iowa's white population during much of the frontier period. Immigrants from Canada and northern and central European countries disrupted by political conflict, droughts, famines, religious disputes, restrictive land ownership policies, exploding populations, and other problems came to live in pioneer Iowa in hopes of finding a refuge for themselves and providing a happier future for their children.

Foreign-born Iowans do not appear as a separate category in the census until 1850. For that year 2,969 foreign-born persons were counted in Iowa. Their number increased to 106,077 in 1860, and 204,692 ten years later. The foreign-born numbered 1,168 per 10,000 native-born Iowans in 1850; 1,865 per 10,000 in 1860; and 2,069 per 10,000 in 1870.[45] The national origins of the foreign-born were distributed as follows:[46]

	1850	1860	1870
Germany	7,101	35,842	66,162
Sweden	231	1,465	10,796
Norway	361	5,688	17,556
Denmark	19	661	2,827
Netherlands	1,108	2,615	4,513
England	3,785	11,545	18,103
Scotland	712	2,895	5,248
Wales	352	913	1,967
Ireland	4,885	28,072	40,124
Belgium	4	91	650
Switzerland	175	2,519	3,937
France	382	2,421	3,130
Austria	13	2,709	9,457
Hungary			134
Poland		100	178
Russia	41	40	96
Italy	1	30	54
Greece	1	1	1
Canada	1,756	8,313	17,897
Mexico	16	6	14

Many native-born Iowans made favorable mention of "foreigners" in their diaries and memoirs. Amelia Murdock Wing, for instance, retained pleasant memories of a German hired girl, an Austrian farmhand who surprised the family with a Christmas tree lighted with candles, and Hungarian peddlers who carried large packs of trinkets and household utensils over the Iowa prairie. Other Iowans were not so pleased to see the foreign-born enter Iowa and there were occasional outbursts of nativist feeling against them. The foreign-born in general were accused of being clannish, while Irish Catholics were seen as drunkards and brawlers, and Germans were stereotyped as beer drinkers.[47]

There was, however, a generalized expectation that the foreign-born population could and would adjust rapidly to American ways. Therefore, when the subject of their political rights was raised at the 1844 and the 1846 constitutional conventions, a great deal of support emerged for granting the right to vote to male foreign-born settlers. In fact, it is significant that there was much stronger support for granting political rights to the foreign-born males than there was for granting them to women. When completed, both the 1844 and the 1846 constitutions failed to extend full political privileges to foreign-born males, but "foreigners who are residents of this State shall enjoy the same rights, in respect to the possession, enjoyment, and descent of property, as native-born citizens."[48]

By the time of the 1857 constitutional convention, sentiment regarding the foreign-born was somewhat more liberal. Most of the delegates felt that foreign-born males should have the same rights and privileges as other citizens in the state. The major reservation on the part of some convention members was the possible implication for black suffrage if voting rights were extended to the foreign-born. After much discussion, the 1857 constitution retained the wording of previous constitutions giving foreign-born males the right of property, but not of suffrage or holding office.[49]

According to historian Frederick C. Luebke, when the first sizeable numbers of European immigrants reached the United States in the 1840s, many of them chose to settle west of the Appalachian Mountains—in Michigan, Wisconsin, Iowa, and Texas. He has pointed out that most of the immigrants who opted for the frontier were farmers migrating in family units. He found that "if a large number of immigrants entered a community within a short period of time, the likelihood of exciting nativist fears was increased."[50] Despite these nativist tendencies, Luebke believes:

> Ethnic conflict and conscious acts of discrimination were rare on the plains, in contrast to the ethnic conflicts often afflicting industrial and mining communities in the East and parts of the mountainous West. Because cultural differences were ordinarily not great, tolerance was easy; the assimilation process was allowed to proceed at its own pace.[51]

Theodore Saloutos has attempted to assess the impact of the various immigrant groups on agriculture in the United States. He discerns their influence in farm techniques, crops, and rural industries as well as in the more abstract areas of languages, dialects, traditions, and life-styles which they brought to their new homes. His findings reveal that immigrant contributions to agriculture, though numerous, were often undefinable. "Farm techniques, seeds, life styles, and limited quantities of capital," he stated, "brought from the home country and put into American farmlands added to the growth and development of American agriculture." But so did the fact "that the immigrant farmers reinforced the often invoked ideal of the family-sized farm in a society that made it difficult for the family farm to survive."[52]

Perhaps the most important point which Luebke and Saloutos both make is the lack of attention usually paid to immigrant frontiersmen and frontierswomen by historians. In Iowa, the void is not total for some work has been completed on Iowa's foreign-born settlers. As is the case with black frontierswomen, however, little emphasis has been placed on the experience of foreign-born women. Therefore, it is necessary to consider foreign-born settlers as a whole, pointing whenever possible to whatever materials may exist regarding women.

Among Iowa's foreign-born settlers, the Norwegians are the most prominent in terms of historical evidence, although they were not the largest numerically. Because of the efforts of the Norwegian-American Historical Society in Minneapolis, and of Luther College and the Norwegian-American Museum in Decorah, Iowa, both written and material evidence exists relating to the Norwegian pioneer experience in frontier Iowa.

The year 1825 marked the first organized immigration of Norwegians; forty-six Norwegian men and women traveled by ship from Norway to New York. As they learned that the land in their Kendall, New York, settlement was difficult to farm, they eventually moved on to the Fox River valley area of Illinois in 1834. They were gradually joined by more immigrants from the homeland, and their numbers spread into Wisconsin, Minnesota, and Iowa. The first Norwegian settlement in Iowa was located at Sugar Creek in Lee County near Keokuk in 1840. By the late 1840s, Norwegians pushed into northeastern Iowa in search of richer land. Many of these settlers represented internal migration from older Norwegian settlements, such as the one in Illinois, which was rapidly becoming overcrowded. Norwegian colonies were augmented by increasing immigration direct from Norway and they rapidly became the dominant stock in northeast Iowa, especially in Winneshiek County.[53]

The family was the central unit of settlement for the Norwegian pioneers. Strongly cohesive, the Norwegian family typically centered around strong men and women who were determined to improve the lives of family members. The story of Gunda Johnson, a Norwegian woman who in 1854 helped finance a trip to America for herself, her husband and their six children by selling coffee, was not unusual. Some years later, when Gunda's spunky daughter Carrie decided to leave Illinois and accompany her husband in a search for richer land in Iowa, Gunda and her husband packed up once again. They finally settled in Hamilton County, Iowa.[54]

Another example of an energetic woman was a minister's wife, Diderikke Brandt. When Luther College was founded, she took on the formidable task of organizing groups of women who attempted to provide a homelike atmosphere for the all-male student body. The women mended students' clothes, cooked special meals for them, and held open houses and other entertainments in their honor.[55]

The two most complete accounts of Norwegian women on the Iowa frontier are those of Elisabeth Koren and Gro Svendsen. Koren arrived in Decorah in 1853 with her husband who was to become a minister to the Norwegians already settled in the area. In her diary she often took note of the crude living conditions they encountered. "We get a little light from a lead dish in which there are tallow scraps and a little rag for a wick, placed on an overturned salt container," she recorded during her first weeks in the settlement. "The floor consists of unfinished planks, which bob up and down when walked on," she later added. After a few months she concluded, "They are really nature's children, these farmers." Their "rustic manners" amazed her: "I cannot understand why there is not a spittoon, and a mat for wiping the feet. Apparently that is not done here." She marveled at the walls of her cabin, which were "papered with all sorts of newspapers and prints," and was repulsed by one of the men, who before entering the house, "very audibily blew his nose with that nature's handkerchief they customarily use."[56]

Koren deeply felt the lack of time to read, contemplate, and write. She lamented the noise and interruptions of visitors, which often created annoyances in her small house. Many evenings she stayed up later than the others in order to read. At one point she remarked that frequently her "wish to have a cultured person to talk to" became very strong.[57] But even though Koren was dismayed and occasionally depressed by her new surroundings, she never gave up hope for the future. On New Year's Eve of 1853 she made the following notation in her diary:

> Last year I began the new year clad in bobbinet, dancing away with roses in my hair. This year I am sitting here with Vilhelm in this bare room, where tomorrow he is to conduct divine services for all these people who have so long lacked a pastor. Still, this is best.[58]

The 1914 conclusion which she added to the diary before its publication indicated that she considered her hard life also a happy one. "With gratitude I look back on my long life here in this land," she wrote, "and think of the many now dead who received us with so much friendliness and surrounded us with love all our lives."[59]

Gro Svendsen told a similar story of pioneer life in Iowa in the letters she sent back to her family in Norway during the 1860s and 1870s. While still in Norway, she married Ole Svendsen against her parents' protests. They objected to him as a husband for their daughter because he intended to migrate to America, but this did not disturb Gro. As a bride, she moved to Iowa with him in 1862 and soon located on a farm near Estherville where she died in 1878 after the birth of her tenth child.

Like Koren, Svendsen faced the dual difficulty of adjusting to America and to the frontier at the same time. To her, prairie fires were "terrifying": "It is a strange and terrible sight to see all the fields a sea of fire." Snakes also were a source of fear for her. "I am horribly afraid of them," she told her parents, "particularly the rattlesnake." And Native Americans caused her to express a violent prejudice. "I might tell you that the Indian revolt has been somewhat subdued, so we feel much safer, " she wrote in 1862. "It isn't enough to merely subdue them," she added. "I think that not a single one who took part in the revolt should be permitted to live."[60]

She was often terse on the subject of the great amount of work required by frontier living. "We are told," she said, "that the women of America have much leisure time, but I haven't yet met any woman who thought so." When the post–Civil War depression pushed farm prices downward, she became particularly discouraged. She explained to her family that "when the wheat is down to fifty cents a bushel, you will understand that a farmer who has to hire much of his help is not getting on very well." She remarked rather sadly, "Times are not good."[61]

Other Scandinavians who joined the Norwegians in Iowa were the Swedes, who initially settled at New Sweden, Jefferson County, in 1845, and the Danes who settled at Council Bluffs, Pottawattamie County, in 1850. Peter Cassel led the first Swedes to their location in southeastern Iowa.[62] One of the original settlers recalled that in preparation for the trip from Sweden to New Sweden his mother baked a large number of loaves of bread from unbolted rye flour. He explained that the loaves were made as large as a dinner plate "with a hole in the center so they could be strung on a pole and hung up to dry." Here they would become so hard that they would keep for months.

After a difficult journey which exhausted the food supplies the women had prepared, the Swedes found few comforts awaiting them. Nonetheless, Cassel was enthusiastic about the social conditions in Iowa and wrote home praising the freedoms which he encountered. Later immigrants, lured from Sweden by his and other settlers' letters, also saw opportunities in New Sweden. In 1864, Mary Stephenson wrote to her parents in Sweden, "Our new home has many advantages over the old one, and I like it much better." In 1865, she stated, "Oliver [her husband] speaks a great deal of moving to Sweden, but I don't favor it as I have things as good as I could wish. . . . In fact, we have so many things that make for comfort and happiness that, when I compare Sweden with this country, I have no desire to return." In 1868 she advised her parents to join her as she believed they would "spend a happy old age" in Iowa. "I am sure that you will get along better here," she assured them, for "you will not have to grind and cook and bake."[63]

Although many Swedes followed the first immigrants to Iowa, far fewer Danes made the move. Danish immigrants tended to enter the state in the latter part of the 1860s and usually selected homes in the southwestern counties. The best-known Danish pioneer in Iowa was Claus L. Clausen, a minister to a group of Norwegians who led the establishment of the town of St. Ansgar in 1853, in Mitchell County.[64]

Far outnumbering all the Scandinavians were the Germans, who constituted the largest single contingent of foreign-born settlers in Iowa. Many Germans settled in Davenport in the late 1840s after their protest against the lack of civil rights in Germany failed. Because many of these families were wealthy and cultured, the women brought their treasures with them to Iowa. Thus, thin china plates, gold-rimmed cups, mahogany and rosewood furniture, and pianos graced some of the German immigrants' first homes.[65] A pietistic German group settled in the Amanas in the rich farmlands of central eastern Iowa in 1855 in an attempt to find religious and economic freedom for themselves. Many other Germans scattered over the state.

Louisa Sophia H. Gellhorn Boylan's reminiscences give testimony of the average German pioneer woman's life. Her family migrated to Ackley, Iowa in 1868 at the instigation of Louisa's father, Heinrich Gellhorn. Louisa remembered, "Father was very stern and we were afraid of him, but he was always gentle and kind to mother who was a cripple. She was continually knitting and sewing and baking and browning, and in summer working in her garden." Boylan looked back in amazement at the fact that her mother kept the whole family in handknit stockings, two pairs a year for each of the ten family members. Louisa added that her mother "made all our clothes, did all the baking and cooking, and nearly always had a baby at her breast."[66]

Another sizeable group of settlers were the Irish whose most noted community is Emmetsburg in Palo Alto County. Founded in 1856, the town was named after the Irish patriot Robert Emmet by the three Irish speculators who owned it. An account left by an Irish woman who settled in nearby Rodman in 1868 echoes the drudgery of the chores performed by frontierswomen. "Washing was done on a board . . . cooking was done on an iron cook stove . . . we baked all our own bread, baking over 30 loaves a week," she wrote.[67] Her mother's creativity in producing food stuck in her mind:

> . . . when mother would run out of flour she would grind corn, sift it and make a course [sic] Johnny cake . . . . When coffee supply ran low, mother would make coffee from toast made out of real dry bread and crumbled. The coffee was, of course, in bean form and had to be ground and roasted. It was roasted in big pans in the oven.[68]

Her memories also included entertainment consisting of various games as well as dances held in the pioneers' homes. "Stoves," she noted, "were removed from the kitchen for the dance."[69]

English immigration to Iowa was precipitated in part by the advice and instruction of noted Iowa publicist John B. Newhall in his lecture tour of England in 1844. In that same year Newhall published *The British Emigrants' "Hand Book" and Guide to the New States of America, Particularly Illinois, Iowa, and Wisconsin*, which caused some English people to suspect that he was a speculator with large investments in Iowa land.[70] He himself claimed that he was writing for philanthropic purposes only, spurred on by his special qualifications as a longtime resident of the area that became known as Iowa. Newhall touted the "intelligence and correct moral deportment" of Iowa's settlers. He discussed many potential problems of immigrants, but only twice did he address himself to women. Once he mentioned that women occasionally asked him what they would do for tea in America. "The ladies must remember," he replied patronizingly, "that the American ships go to China for Tea, just as the English ships do, and we pay no duty on Sugar, Tea, or Coffee." In his list of possible occupations for "mechanics," "dairymaid" was the only job he noted for women. An earlier handbook, Calvin Colton's *Manual for Emigrants to America,* published in London in 1832, was specifically designed to encourage immigration from England.

In 1849, George Sheppard helped organize a colony of English immigrants who arrived in DeWitt in Clinton County in 1850. One member of his party was pleased with the ease with which Americans were able to earn their living but was displeased with the English response to conditions in America. "The English," Sheppard complained to his father, "make the worst kind of settlers; they grumble and growl at everything—comparing all things with the state of things at home—forgetting that this is an entirely new country, and the one they have left at home is an old one."[71]

This was certainly the case for two young Englishwomen, Lucy and Marianne Rutledge, who made the crossing in 1848. When they arrived at their uncle's home near Davenport, Iowa, "a one-room cabin!" they became angry with their uncle for persuading them to come to such squalid surroundings. Lucy said that they could do nothing but "weep and bemoan" their circumstances. Yet she remembered, "As time passed and we began to make acquaintances, we found our surroundings more congenial than at first appeared." In 1849 Lucy married an Illinois man, William Cooke, and settled in Dubuque. She adjusted so well to the demands of the frontier that in 1852 she willingly accompanied her husband and his family on an overland trip to California in a covered wagon. In four short years she had become such an adept frontierswoman that it was now she who encouraged her husband and her mother-in-law onward despite their complaints and despair.[72]

During the same years in which Lucy Rutledge Cooke made her rapid adjustment to frontier life, many Dutch attempted a similar feat. Led by Peter Henry Scholte to Pella in 1847, the Hollanders brought a distinct culture with them to Iowa.[73] After one Marion County woman got her first look at the Dutch immigrants, she recorded her reaction to them:

> . . . we gazed in wonder at their quaint and unfamiliar appearance. The dress was strange to us. Women were perched on high piles of queer looking chests and boxes and trunks, many of them wearing caps, but no bonnets. Some of the men, and women too, wore wooden shoes.[74]

The trip itself had already disillusioned some of the Dutch women. One Hollander who had been deserted by his wife for the fifth time since leaving their home, feared that she would return to Holland. Scholte's own wife was appalled when she reached their rude log cabin. She threw herself on the bedstead weeping and crying out her disbelief. She partially recovered only when Scholte moved her to a new home in 1848. Here, Leonora Scholte reported, surrounded by the few pieces of Delft China that survived the voyage, she was able to build a life for herself in spite of the rude prairie conditions, which at times seemed to overwhelm her.[75]

Other Dutch women exhibited a wide range of reactions to their new homes. The young bride of a doctor moved into the lovely brick house he had built for her only to be stricken down with cholera and die several weeks later. Another young woman who was forced to move to a primitive log cabin when her husband failed in a business venture was said to be heartbroken; she refused to leave her bed and she, too, soon died. Balancing these tales was the story of yet another young Dutch woman who offered her lace for sale when someone complimented her on its beauty. She quickly knitted more, sold it, and eventually parlayed her business ability into the successful ownership of her own shop. Scholte's daughter Sara married a doctor, bore five children, and lived a long, energetic life filled with philanthropic works.[76]

Janette Murray has written about Scots women, especially in the North Tama area, pointing to their many skills as frontierswomen as well as to the customs retained from the homeland such as serving a hearty barley soup or calling the kitchen the "but" and the parlor the "ben." The Hungarians are remembered particularly for their settlement at New Breda in Decatur County where they unsuccessfully attempted to grow grapes before a large number of them moved on to the warmer climate of southern Texas. Harriet Connor Brown has written about the Swiss in Iowa, who are sometimes associated with a love of learning, especially based on the then-emerging theories of Pestalozzi and Froebel. The Jews, represented in Iowa as early as 1833 by Dubuque grocer Alexander Levi, often started out on the frontier as peddlers bringing goods, gossip, and market information to the rural folk until they raised enough capital to move into urban businesses. The Czechs, often called Bohemians after their homeland of Bohemia, also received brief mention in the diaries and journals of frontierswomen. Many of them settled in Cedar Rapids and later around Sioux City where they were noted for their dancing, religious devotion, and fraternal organizations. The Canadians who migrated to the Middle West were often considered native to America rather than "foreign-born."[77]

Mixed feelings of American-born Iowans towards these various groups generated little or no effort to recruit them as settlers until near the end of the frontier period. Although literally hundreds of "emigrants' manuals" were cranked out by the various towns, counties, land companies, transportation companies, individual promoters, and emigrants' associations (chambers of commerce), few were intended for distribution outside of the United States.

Iowans gradually began appealing to settlers from other countries besides

England. In 1858, for instance, there was talk of reprinting the Dubuque Emigrant Association's handbook for gratuitous distribution in Germany.[78] And in 1859, the Iowa land office of Cook and Sargent in Davenport published *Prairie vs. Bush* promoting 12,000 Iowa acres being offered to Canadians through the company's branch office in Canada:

> Are you Moving to the States? No state is better worth thinking about than Iowa. It has fertile Praire Land, accessible by railroad and steamer. Its climate is healthy; its mineral resources are rich and varied; its water is abundant and pure; its markets are good; it has good schools, good churches, and happy and prosperous homes. If you move at all, go to the West! If you move to the West, go to Iowa! Prairie Land in Northern Iowa at $2.50; in Central Iowa on a line of railroad, at $4.00 or $5.00.[79]

Although there were a few other sporadic attempts to advertise Iowa outside of the United States, the first organized push did not occur until 1870 with the formation of the Iowa Board of Immigration by a group of businesspeople and promoters. The board prepared a pamphlet extolling the virtues of Iowa, which appeared in English, German, Dutch, Danish, and Swedish, although most of the Scandinavian edition was burned in the great Chicago fire. The board also sent agents to posts in Germany, Scandinavia, the British Isles, Belgium, and Holland.[80]

The literature prepared by the Iowa Board of Immigration made a special appeal to potential women settlers. The existence of coeducation in Iowa was stressed as were the discussions of the Iowa General Assembly relating to woman suffrage. "For the information of the ladies especially," one brochure pointed out, "it may be well to state, also, that the last General Assembly of our State took the first step necessary for amending the Constitution so as to confer the right of suffrage upon women."

> Under the laws of Iowa no distinction is now made between the husband and wife in the possession and enjoyment of property. One-third in value of all the real estate of the husband, in case of his death, goes to the wife as her property in fee-simple, if she survives him. The husband inherits one-third of the wife's real estate in the same way, in case he survives her. Each is entitled to the same right of dower in the estate of the other, and a like interest descends to their respective heirs.[81]

Although the topic of blacks in Iowa was studiously avoided by the Board of Immigration, some private entrepreneurs freely assured immigrants that Native Americans, blacks, and outlaws were all but extinct in Iowa. As one speculator phrased it, "The Negro and other disturbing elements are conspicuous only by their absence."[82]

An element that may have been considered disturbing were the Mormons, a people often seen as cliquish, fanatical, and immoral in their practice of polygamy. Partly due to bitter feelings about the Mormons, most of whom were not settlers but migrants traveling Iowa's portion of the Mormon Trail towards Utah, the story of the Iowa portion of the Mormon's hegira has not yet been fully told. Although one scholar has recognized that "Not only did the Mormons mark the first great Iowa route from the Mississippi to the Missouri, but they founded settlements along the way, the first places of permanent habitation in the western half of Iowa," only a few other investigators have researched the lives and contributions of Mormon men and women in relation to Iowa.[83]

Another group needing attention from scholars are the Army women who accompanied their men into Iowa on missions to suppress or relocate Native Americans. Yet others include Chicano and Asian women, women in urban areas, in business, in professions, as homesteaders, as Quakers, and as missionaries. Still other pertinent areas of investigation are women's roles in frontier religion, in frontier art and culture, and in the development of frontier folklore and music.

Rewriting the history of frontierswomen in terms of these many diverse characteristics and concerns demands a rejection of the legendary Anglo-American pioneer woman as a role model, a repudiation which seems not only possible but probable as new ways of looking at women and at groups emerge in contemporary America. As an awareness of women's and minority issues grows, so does the likelihood that significant questions about the influence of women from various backgrounds on frontier society, as well as the impact of frontier society upon them, will be answered.

CHAPTER FIVE

Women in Wartime

W ARS are integral to the image of the American West: wars with Native Americans; internecine warfare between settlers over land, mineral claims, and other riches; and wars to establish satisfactory boundary lines. The Civil War, however, is not typically associated with the frontier experience. It is usually seen as an "eastern" war; that is, a conflict between states located primarily east of the Mississippi River. Opposing camps from the North and the South clashed violently over such issues as states' rights, the centralization of national power, and the abolition of slavery at the same time that most frontier areas were deeply engrossed in problems related to their own physical survival.

During the decades preceding the Civil War much of the West was yet experiencing growth and ferment. Technological developments, including early forms of barbed wire and the six-gun, made the Great Plains begin to look like a viable area for settlement. The vast resources of the Far West had already attracted considerable migration. Migrants brought with them arguments about states' rights and abolitionism. But, when fighting began in 1861, both the sparsely settled Great Plains and the more populous Far West were too physically removed from the scene of the war to become very involved in it. The transcontinental railway, which was to tie the coasts together for better or worse in the postwar years, was not completed until 1869.

Certain trans-Mississippi frontier regions such as Iowa did become involved in the war. Already tied to the national economy by roads and fledgling railways as well as to the national government by statehood, granted in 1846, Iowa found itself deeply embroiled in the Civil War. Although a decade away from the termination of its frontier status by the United States Census Bureau, Iowa had to respond to a war that many Iowa settlers had attempted to escape by westward migration. Paradoxically, their attempt to escape controversy only ensured their participation in its escalation. Settlers who came to Iowa as abolitionists bent on fleeing the creeping evils of slavery found that their sentiments and their support of activities such as the Underground Railway de facto committed them to fighting for the northern cause. Many who had deserted tumultuous or oppressive governments in their former homes felt duty bound to take up arms in a rebellion that seemed to be testing the authority of the national government to which they had given their allegiance.

Whatever their personal reasons, Iowans answered the call for volunteers with great enthusiasm. According to Iowa historian Leland L. Sage,

> Virtually all Iowans, including Democrats, responded with enthusiasm and complete approval . . . . Iowa and Iowans met every call for troops, financial support, and political support for the Union cause ("Mr. Lincoln's War"), with room to spare. All quotas assigned to her throughout the war were met, only one time resorting to the draft, and that in 1864, when the end of the war was in sight![1]

Iowa's attention to the Civil War cast the state in the peculiar position of involvement in a national conflict demanding commitment of human resources, arms, and political consciousness at a time when the state was still trying to deal with internal problems associated with settling a frontier area. An illustration of this contradictory situation was the conflict in northwest Iowa. The Santee Sioux in that region had not yet totally capitulated to the pressures of expanding white population and Iowans who had volunteered to fight in the East and the South found themselves on a tour of "guard duty" in their own state instead. Housed in outposts such as Fort Defiance, they were charged with patrolling the Santee Sioux and keeping them away from white settlers for the duration of the war.[2] Considering the relatively small number of Native Americans left in northwest Iowa by the 1860s, the threat was probably greatly exaggerated. The legacy of fear from the so-called Spirit Lake Massacre of 1857 persuaded people in that area to seek protection from possible recurring Sioux attack. Sarah Kenyon told of the pervasive fear among her neighbors:

> Four and five hundred Indians were camped about 10 or 12 miles from here armed to the teeth without a single squaw or papoose with them. People thought if there was a drafting done they would pitch in and burn and kill . . . but the draft passed over and they departed.[3]

Citizens also feared attack from the soldiers themselves. In 1861, the *Burlington Daily Hawk-Eye* lamented that an "infernal outrage was attempted upon the person of a German woman" by a soldier stationed outside the city. In southern Iowa, people lived with the threat of invasion by confederate supporters from Missouri. According to one source, "There were about as many rebels along the Missouri border as there were Union men . . . our country was very unsafe in those days." Another woman explained, "being quite near the Missouri border, we were somewhat apprehensive of visits from Guerillas who had threatened invasion of our section.'' And indeed, a company of home guards was called out on one occasion in the village she lived in to drive back ''a foraging party of Rebels'' who intended to burn the town and confiscate the townspeople's horses.[4]

Foreboding related to the war was compounded for Iowans by the prevailing frontier conditions that demanded building and maintaining of homesteads, producing domestic goods, clearing land, and planting crops. Since between 72,000 and 76,000 of Iowa's men, or about one-half of the male population of the state, performed some kind of military service during the Civil War, these concerns now fell squarely on the shoulders of many of Iowa's women, most of whom were not crushed by the additional demand upon them, but rose to meet the challenge.[5]

Of course, not all Iowa males who were able to join the war effort elected to do so. Although the state sent more men in proportion to its population than any other state, some men chose not to volunteer their services. And in 1864, when the draft act was used in Iowa to bolster the waning war spirit, some men picked the legal option of paying $300 to hire a substitute. Emery Bartlett was one of these. ''When the war of the rebellion broke out,'' he wrote, ''I never quite felt that it was my duty to enlist, and when our quotas for the townships were assigned us with the privilege of paying a certain amount towards hiring substitutes, I, with others, paid the assessment . . . and thus avoided a draft.''[6]

The practice of hiring substitutes kept some Iowa families intact while it disrupted others. Because someone had to be hired as a substitute, men who otherwise would not have been acceptable soldiers were lured away from their families. Matilda Peitzke Paul recalled that her brother was only seventeen years old when he returned from his tour of duty as a substitute soldier in the summer of 1865. Many years later she described his homecoming:

> One afternoon . . . the stage driver stopped at our door bringing a pale and sick-looking passenger. It was my oldest brother who was returning from the Civil War. He was sick most of the time while in the south . . . and finally was dismissed and brought home sick and unable to sit up. . . . You can hardly imagine with what joy he was greeted. He was very weak and slept most of the time for a long time after coming home. He was too young to be drafted to go to war, but was hired as a substitute by a man who had been drafted.[7]

In some cases, families were literally decimated by the overwhelming fervor of their male members. Joanna Harris Haines remembered that her fifty-eight-year-old abolitionist father joined the famed Iowa ''Greybeard Regiment'' while four of her brothers volunteered for duty. When her youngest brother was drafted, however, her mother obtained his release because she desperately needed his help with the family farm. ''I sympathized with his disappointment," she wrote. She added that "all of the able-bodied men" of Grinnell's Iowa College enlisted, including one Quaker man who, although constrained by his religious beliefs from fighting, served as a nurse in a Sanitary Commission hospital.[8]

The swift departure of so many men compelled many Iowa women to cope with radically altered life-styles. According to Mary Livermore, an agent for the Sanitary Commission traveling through the Midwest, numerous women labored at "planting, cultivating, and harvesting," in addition to their usual duties. But, judging from their extant correspondence, increased workloads were only part of women's wartime troubles. A crushing loneliness, perhaps accentuated by the lack of extended kinship networks and long-term community relationships in frontier Iowa, was a constant theme in war letters. "I do want to see you worse then ever in my life," Mary McCall wrote to her husband Thomas in 1862. In a later letter she pleaded, "Please write often and come home as soon as you can." In another missive she asked, "Do you think you will be home this winter?" And in another, "Please write very often to your wife and son." By the end of the year she had made up her mind to go live near his camp, as so many other wives did, if he were not released soon.[9]

These expressions of loneliness were returned in kind by absent lovers and husbands. "But O how my heart was filled with joy when my 'orderly' placed in my hand a letter from you," a young soldier wrote to his fiancée. "I cannot express the happiness it gives me to receive a letter from the loved ones I have left behind at home."[10] In another camp, J. W. Rice pined for his wife. "Being absent from your dear self, is the only thing I regret in coming here," he wrote her in April, 1863. By January, 1865, he was moved to make this homey statement:

> I have had no letters from you since leaving Arkansas. . . . How do you get along these cold nights? Have you taken a bed fellow yet? I do not see what there is about a Man that a woman should want him for a bed fellow. I have tried it here in the Army and I certainly had rather sleep on a sharp fence rail, on top of a fence ten feet high, than sleep with one, why their legs are all full of coarse stiff hair like a hog, yes a perfect hog and I can't nor won't sleep with one. And I can't believe any woman is an angel that will. I'll freeze every toe off, before I'll take one in to my bed. Well, Men are not all like me, that's the reason you took me in I suppose, I certainly would not object to having a nice quiet snooze with you this January night.[11]

Anxieties about finances also dominated letters which shuttled back and forth between women and men during the war years. Due to infrequent or occasionally nonexistent pay envelopes, many soldiers found that they had little or nothing to contribute to their family's support. Quite often, when they did have a bit of money to send, they learned that there was no safe or reliable mail service. Fretting because he heard nothing of the money he sent to his wife, Rice informed her, "There will be no safety in sending more." Apparently she was able to manage on her own for he later commended her for making good trades: "I must give you credit for your good management. I think when I return home I will let you do the financiering." Similarly, Thomas McCall's money worries were assuaged when his wife assured him that she had money yet and would "spend it carefully."[12]

At home, women were financially squeezed not only by the lack of monetary contributions by their husbands but by rising prices as well. Wartime shortages combined with prolonged hostilities drove commodity prices up, thus creating a difficult market for buyers. Inflated wartime prices aggravated the already limited availability of certain goods in Iowa. Consequently, women who were just beginning to learn to cope with the exigencies of frontier economy were now forced to dredge up every ounce of their ingenuity in order to deal with the wartime economy as well. Caught in the throes of wartime conditions and frontier conditions simultaneously, many Iowa women, bereft of the male members of the family, had to tackle roles and functions for which they had little training or experience.

Their difficulties were often intensified by their own newness to Iowa. Sarah Carr Lacey and her husband had migrated to Iowa with their two infant sons in 1860. In 1861 her third baby was born in a log cabin in Howard County only months after the war began. That third child, E. May Lacey, later wrote that her father, "like most young men of the time, wished to be in the thick of it, but under the circumstances he delayed enlistment, ran the little farm, at odd moments hauled and cut wood, and in other ways prepared for army service later on." In 1862, when May was almost a year old, Sarah agreed to her husband's enlistment in Company I of the Thirty-eighth Iowa Infantry. May later noted:

> The newness of Iowa and the fluidity of its population in 1862 is indicated by the fact that not one of the 104 men of Company I had been born in either Minnesota or Iowa, the States in which the company had been recruited. One-fifth of the company had been born outside the United States, seventeen of them being of British origin.[13]

How did the young wife and mother of three that Alvin Lacey left behind contend with her circumstances? She bought nine cows and by selling butter at the wartime price of sixty cents a pound she produced a reasonable income. Even though she paid high prices for goods, as much as sixty cents a yard for calico for example, she was able to support herself and her children nicely until her husband's return in 1865. But, according to May, "milking cows did not appeal to father; one week from the time he returned there was only one left."[14] Sarah's successful entrepreneurship therefore ended as abruptly as it had begun.

Martha Turner Searle saw her husband enlist early in the war. "Up to that time," she later wrote, "my patriotism had been wholly an untried quality." She responded by renting their house, returning to the family homestead with her baby, and taking a teaching position to support herself and her child. In 1864 her husband sent for her to spend her vacation with him in Memphis where she learned firsthand about anti-Yankee sentiment. When she ventured into the Episcopal church she sat alone. "No one would sit nearer a yankee Captain's wife than was absolutely necessary, always giving me plenty of room to pass out, fearing apparently, that if they touched the hem of my garment, they would be defiled." After witnessing a battle and nursing her husband's resulting injuries, she returned to her school duties until he was released from the service due to disability early in 1865.[15]

Naturally, there were almost as many ways of coping and as many degrees of success as there were "war widows" in Iowa. Women ranged from poor to well-to-do, rural to urban, young to old, childless to mothers of many children, and uneducated to highly educated. The cases of three women, each with slightly different backgrounds and situations, illustrate ways in which life went on on the home front in the absence of husbands and fathers.

Marjorie Ann Rogers was the wife of Dr. Samuel C. Rogers and mother of four children. In 1861 the Rogers family was beginning a third year farming in Tama County, but when the news of the war arrived, Dr. Rogers immediately volunteered his services to the Union Army. Because the doctor was a member of the local board of supervisors, Governor Samuel J. Kirkwood asked him to delay his enlistment in order to recruit and ready other volunteers in the Tama County area. Dr. Rogers worked at this task for almost a year without pay while he attempted to continue farming and prepare his family for his own eventual departure.[16]

During this year, described by Rogers as one "full of mental suffering and anxiety," she gradually took on as many of the family responsibilities as possible in order to free her husband for his war-related duties. Her children were too young to provide much assistance—a girl thirteen, two boys eight and ten, and "baby Anna." But along with their "faithful dog" she grouped them about her and proceeded to deal with the obstacles placed in her path by the accelerating war.

Because her husband was now away from home so much of the time, the bulk of the farm work fell upon her shoulders, relieved only by the help of a hired man one or two days each week. She later remarked, "Young as they were, my little thirteen-year-old girl was my little housekeeper while I worked with the boys . . . and the baby would run all day from one to the other cheering us with her glad prattle, the only one that did not feel the sadness that was in each heart unspoken." Yet, she added, "Do as well as we might, much was neglected; it was impossible to get farm help."

A more serious problem in her view were neighboring Sioux who report-edly were being "tampered with by the rebels." After visits to her home by several of the Sioux whom Rogers presumed to be spies, she began to live in fear: "I apprehended danger all the time, knowing our perfectly helpless condition." She resorted to mixing whisky with some of her husband's morphine to give the interlopers—a subterfuge which she hoped might provide her family with a chance to escape.

At one point, reports of angry Indians reached such a fever pitch that she and the children fled to a neighboring farm. During her night's vigil she heard noises which to her "resembled the patting of moccasined feet on the hard ground." But, she explained, she "did not waken the children; I thought they might as well be massacred as to be scared to death." Near morning a small band of Sioux wearing white blankets was spotted through the rain and fog quite near the house. No attack came, however, and in the morning the surprised sentinels learned that the Sioux were in reality "a large flock of geese" which had "taken shelter close to the house." Rogers and her children returned to their own home, yet the dread which permeated their lives did not lessen, for the rumors continued. Because the whites believed that an Indian attack was imminent, the anxiety they felt was real, whether the threat actually existed or not.

Rogers's worries were further increased by reports of rebel spies in the area. She was certain that one tired, hungry visitor with an odd package of papers strapped across his back was indeed such a spy, but not being able to detain him until a law officer could be notified she regretfully let him go on his way. Rogers later commented, "A few were captured, but they were too shrewd and found too many sympathizing copperheads in loyal Iowa even to be afraid. They were very bold and even impertinent." On another occasion, a "spy" insisted upon staying the night, much to her dismay. As he left in the morning, Marjorie Ann watched his departure with relief. She noticed that "he struck the fence a vigorous blow with his cane, which seemed to be an indication of what was passing in his mind—that he would like to annihilate not only the innocent doves but the whole north."

These eventful months of 1861 passed quickly for Rogers and it was soon time for her husband to report to his position as assistant surgeon to the Thirtieth Iowa Infantry. She rented out the farm and with the help of a friend who had not enlisted only because "she was a woman and too old," Rogers moved her family to the town of Toledo, Iowa. With the move, came a new set of problems which she felt ill equipped to face.

> The fifteen years of our married life passed before me as a beautiful panorama. My husband was all devotion to his family. Our children had been spared us, and we had seen very little trouble, but now he was gone. I was to have all the care and responsibility of the family. . . . Where was all my patriotism, my loyalty, my love of country? It was all gone; it had gone

out with the light and joy of our home and was going farther and farther
from me. . . . I felt so inefficient, so weak, not equal to all that would be
required of me.

After observing the war relief work of a widow who had lost her only son in
the war and the work of a friend who had taken over her husband's classes when
he was killed early in the war, Rogers decided to dispel her own personal
despair by engrossing herself in relief work. As she became active in sanitary
work, supplying bandages and other such supplies to the front, she was
dismayed to learn from her husband's letters that the supplies and parcels
prepared so laboriously by town women were often waylaid by other war traffic
and did not reach the sick Iowa soldiers for whom they were intended. When
Governor Kirkwood called for a convention in Des Moines to decide on a more
efficient plan of action, Rogers was among the delegates. She believed the convention to be crucial to war relief, noting that it was the first convention in Iowa
where men and women came together to discuss such important matters.

After the Des Moines meeting, organization of relief work improved and
Rogers became involved in recruiting additional help from the countryside surrounding Toledo. In the meantime, however, she still had the produce from
the family farm to worry about. Although she lacked experience, she hired a
wagon and team in order to haul the crops to market herself. When the skep-
tical owner of the wagon and team questioned her brother as to her driving
abilities, her brother replied that he "saw other women coming into town every
day, soldiers' wives taking their produce to market, and what they could do I
would not be afraid to undertake."

Against advice, she hauled a full load: "I was not going to be laughed at
because I was a woman—I would take the same as a man." Despite having
some misgivings along the way, she made it safely to town where she was met
with surprise and admiration:

> I had to drive right through the business part of town to my brother's of-
> fice, as he was going to unload for me. It was about dark and the
> gentlemen were waiting for their mail when I drove up. They needed a lit-
> tle surprise and now they had it. One came up and held the horses by the
> head, while another ran in his store for a step ladder, while two others
> came to help me down as I was a woman and accustomed to being waited
> on. I declined their kindness and said I would get down the same as a man
> if I could do a man's work.

Marjorie Ann Rogers made many more successful trips between her farm
and the market, but her canvassing of Tama County for relief workers and war
supplies was not quite as productive. Although she was generally met with
kindness, on some occasions she "would feel ready to faint from being denied
or ordered out of the house with a string of abuse." She said that she had not

counted on refusal or acrimony when she accepted the position: "We were so glad to do everything ourselves we could that we thought everyone else would be when applied to." She uncovered many more Copperheads, both female and male, than she had realized existed, for although public censure kept them relatively quiet in public, they often unleashed antiwar sentiments when asked to contribute help or money.

Undaunted, she continued with her own relief work, particularly support of the State Sanitary Fair at Dubuque and the establishment of an Iowa Orphans' Home. The many women who helped her, often offering a small contribution, which they could ill afford, offset her discouragement with the Copperheads. She recalled:

> It was touching beyond my power to describe the stories of these Iowa women, these mothers, wives, and daughters—their endurance, their hardships, sickness, poverty and deaths, in many families doing the work of the absent father or husband on the farm, saving from his poor salary to pay off a mortgage perhaps or a debt that would soon eat up their home.

She lamented the fact that as the war dragged on, more supplies were demanded at the front although prices were high and goods were in increasingly short supply at home. "Our work for the soldiers," she recalled, "became harder as we had less and less to do with." An additional strain was placed upon the townspeople's meager resources as returning soldiers brought contraband blacks into the region and as the blacks filtered in themselves as refugees. Women formed committees to clothe and feed the black fugitives although it seemed as if the limits of their supplies had already been reached. According to Rogers, many women sacrificed just a bit more because the blacks "must be made to feel they were among friends and welcome to this land of liberty, our own beautiful Iowa."

By 1864, the numbers of returning soldiers in need of medical care and financial aid, the destitute widows, and the homeless orphans in Tama County complicated the problems of the relief workers even more. Then, as weary Toledo citizens were on the brink of exhaustion, rumors of an Indian attack descended upon them. Soldiers home on furlough were dispatched as scouts while panicked families gathered in the courthouse. After spending the night in dread, the townsfolk learned that all was quiet at the nearby reservation and that the trouble stemmed from a few threatening speeches made to frightened whites who carried exaggerated accounts back to Toledo. As Rogers later said, "The people did not have the utmost confidence in Indians anywhere found . . . it needed only a word spoken at the wrong time or in the wrong place to alarm the almost helpless town."

The war took a toll of everyone's energies. Rogers's own strength was at a low ebb when a false report of her husband's death arrived in April, 1865. Her worst fear, she felt, was finally realized: suddenly she was a widow and her children orphans. After eight days of mourning, an amended report reached her with news of Dr. Rogers's "thrilling adventure and escape." Her husband had been spared after all. When the doctor was shortly thereafter discharged, Marjorie Ann Rogers, more fortunate than many, was finally reunited with her husband. Her war work did not end with the declaration of peace. "Mother" Rogers, as she was now known for her extensive relief efforts, continued dispersing sanitary goods to the orphans and widows in need as well as becoming an active backer of the Orphans' Home in Davenport. She soon learned that although her own family survived the war intact, it would take many years to provide for those families that had not. In her later years, she also continued philanthropic endeavors on behalf of women, children, and the aged. Her memoirs of the war years first appeared in 1894; she died at the home of one of her daughters in Grinnell less than a year after their publication.

Mother Rogers's wartime experiences are representative of a relatively privileged class of Iowa women: those who lived in towns comparatively free from the cares of maintaining a farmstead; who had psychological support for themselves, their families, and their activities in the form of neighbors and relatives; and who were relatively free from financial woes. Women in these circumstances were more likely to have the time and stamina to engage in war work that was so crucial to the survival of Iowa's volunteer soldiers. Many other women, however, were so overwhelmed by their own problems that it was all they could do to survive themselves.

Helen Maria Sharp is a touching illustration of the latter. She was first left alone in 1861 when her husband John enlisted as a private in the Second Regiment of the Iowa Volunteer Infantry. After being slightly wounded in the Battle of Shiloh, he was discharged with a physical disability in late 1862. In early 1865 he reenlisted with the Tenth Regiment of the Iowa Volunteer Infantry, marched with Sherman to Richmond, and then went on to Washington, D.C., for the grand review marking the climax of the war. He was mustered out in 1865 and returned to his family.

Helen's barely literate letters to John in 1861–1862 were filled with despair, complaint, and admonitions. She was so completely overwhelmed by the basic concerns of clothing and feeding herself and four children that there was little mention of her neighborhood or her impressions of the war itself in her writing. The letters poignantly chronicle a distressed, hard-pressed woman who frequently blamed her absent husband for many of her miseries.[17]

> . . . we are well in body but i can't say as much about my mind. i can hardly tell you how much trouble i see. you said before you went away that you would do all you could but your generosity overcomes your prudence so that now what my family will do for the winter is more than i can tell. your first payment has gone but 4 or 5 dollars and i expect you will contrive some place for that.

Sharp felt that her husband was lax in caring for his family, particularly because he loaned ill-spared money to others. In fact, she became so distraught about his loans that she implicitly threatened suicide: "It makes me low spirited so that i cant help writeing to you to not for gods sake if you want to save me from getting rid of myself lend your money till you relieve your family." At another point she complained that he had left her with a problem relating to the deed on their farm, an issue she apparently could not resolve because she lacked money to get the deed recorded. "I supposed you had seen about it," she chastised him. "You said i should not have to run around to see to such things," she continued. "I am so near wild now that one drop more trouble would upset my reason for i do not think that i am all right now." In another letter she took him to task again for not providing for her better before he left home. "You said that i would not have anything to see to," she wrote, "but i tell you if i should wait to have someone come and see if i wanted anything i would both freeze and starve for no one comes in the house unless i go beg for it and sometimes not then."

Lack of money is a constant theme throughout Sharp's letters. She continually begged her husband to send her another five or ten dollars, lamented the fact that she was going into debt to stay alive, and protested the difficulty of obtaining local credit. When John did respond by sending money, the mails were so unreliable that the money was sometimes lost or stolen, a situation which caused Sharp to admonish him to be more careful. "Send me some money but be careful how," she told him. "If you send me money dont trust it to mail. It would be safer to send by express."

Financial aid from sources other than her husband seemed initially to be out of Sharp's grasp. She mentioned that she was unable to get any goods from the local volunteer aid society, but she did not explain why. She lacked even ink, stamps, and paper to write to him more often, and she seemed to have no place to turn for help. Rising prices only exacerbated her plight. "Everything is getting higher so it will cost more to live," she stated. Then, on a slight note of optimism, she said, "My shoes have give out so i shall soon be barefooted but it is getting warmer."

By 1862 Sharp finally decided to help herself. She plowed and planted a garden and kept a cow that supplied adequate amounts of milk and butter. She also hired herself out doing washing for other women and stripping cane for molasses. Still, these were evidently barely survival measures for she wrote her husband, "I have to get me a dress and shoes before long. . . . I have so many places to put money i cant think of getting myself any thing."

One of her greatest problems was obtaining enough wood to heat her small home. At first she attempted to chop wood herself, but found it to be too heavy a job in addition to her other tasks.

HELEN MARIA SHARP

> My back hurts me so that i cant stand it to chop hardly at all. i shall have to brake up housekeeping before long. if i was only out of the way folks would take care of my children but to scatter them while im alive is more trouble than i can bare to think about.

In a later missive she mentioned a neighbor cutting some wood for her, but when it ran out she and one of the children tried to resupply themselves: "We most freeze chopping this morning." Finally she traded taking in washing for wood and was thus able to keep a small amount on hand.

Through these trials, Sharp was often lonely. "It is very lonesome," she noted in 1861. By the next year, she wrote her husband that "every week you are gone I am more lonely." And again, "Three years seems a long time . . . it is very lonesome . . . it is so lonely and thare is so many mean men that a woman has to deal with." After her husband was wounded in 1862, she advised him to try for a discharge rather than a furlough even though a discharge would cause him to lose his bonus payment for finishing his full time in the army. "We wont starve if i keep my health," she assured him. "The law is now a soldier must serve 2 years or no bounty so they are keen to give discharges to soldiers they think will be sick long."

Perhaps Sharp was also anxious to remove her husband from the temptations of camp life. In an early letter she warned him,

> . . . i want you to keep out of bad company as much as possible. I know that it is difficult but you know you are not obliged to join them in there wickedness. i want you to be respectible it is in your power.

She later added, "I want you to be carefull of your health and live right so that if you do fall you will fall Zionward and we will try to meet you in heaven if not on earth."

Sharp was especially anxious about her husband's physical and moral well-being because he didn't write often enough to suit her. Every letter she wrote to him contained a command to write her more often, to tell her about daily camp life, and to inform her how he was getting along. Apparently, his lack of communication was one more vexation to her in an already aggravating situation. That she had not agreed with his enlisting in the first place was clear in her statement, "You wanted me to make the children think you done right by going away but i cant teach them that when i know it is not right so i dont teach them anything." She seemed uninterested in the war except to say: "There is great war excitment now. The drafting commences tomorrow. There is some afraid of the Indians but i do not know how it is."

John returned to their farm in Dallas County in 1862, but reenlisted in 1865. When her letters to him resumed, her complaints had not changed much from 1862. The infant she had been nursing then had long since been weaned, but now there was another in its place. Money was still a problem and she persisted in berating John for not writing often enough. Local affairs interested her as little as they had before. She wrote John that people were so upset over the assassination of Lincoln that "them cops [Copperheads] has to cool a little." At another point, she asked him, "Now i hear that some of the tenth had turned cop. What does that mean?"

Wartime prices continued to bedevil her. "It cost so much to live," she complained. "Everything is so high." And when she did have money she felt that her children's needs must come before her own:

> about money i do not suppose you will have much when you get home for i cant save it and starve or go naked. things are so high it costs to live but many things that i could have had i would look at my money and then look at my big children that needed so many things and i would put it in my pocket and take bread and butter and tea.

Through personal sacrifice, she somehow managed to clothe and feed her five children, yet she was still disconsolate because she believed that she could not discipline them effectively. "The children are so hard to manage too," she wrote in 1865, "that i feel as if my trouble was more than i can bare. . . . i have to whop Ira every day."

By July, 1865, when John had not yet returned home, she felt near a breaking point. Her younger son inquired of her, "If he dont come will you git another pa?" Fortunately, she did not have to face such a dilemma because by late summer John finally returned. The Sharps continued to farm in Iowa until sometime after 1870 when they relocated on a farm near Roxbury, Kansas. Despite the tribulations of the war years they both lived long lives; his ended in 1901 and hers in 1905. As far as is known neither of them ever again wrote about their Civil War experiences.

Another wartime woman, Harriet Jane Thompson, managed with difficulty to cope with prolonged loneliness and the attendant problems of a wartime economy. As a young childless wife she temporarily deserted her Iowa home to visit with her husband's family in Pennsylvania. When the war began, William Thompson, a young lawyer embroiled in Republican politics, anti-southern sentiment, and war fever, was determined to enlist despite his wife's reluctance. He helped organize the Twentieth Iowa Volunteer Infantry and was elected Major. After about six months of service, on December 7, 1862, he was severely wounded at the Battle of Prairie Grove in Arkansas. By that time Jane (as she was called by relatives and friends) had returned from Pennsylvania, somewhat against her husband's wishes, to her own family in Marion, Iowa, although she did not have the heart or the funds to return to their own homestead alone.

Her first letters were postmarked Marion, Iowa, a town stirred by excitement at the departure of men for the front, many of them according to Thompson, "feeling pretty well with liquor before they left."[18] Jane herself was experiencing loneliness and anomie, which caused her to beg her husband "Billie" to come home, to consider visiting his parents in Pennsylvania to fill her time, and to vent her jealousy toward a female neighbor who had been to his camp:

> Mrs. Sessions told me that she had a letter from Miss Sessions a few days ago and that you had called on her and that she had been in Camp several times to see you. I felt very much hurt for I thought that if you could spend time to go and see her that you could come home and see me. If I have done anything to keep you away please tell me. I suppose you knew that she was coming home this week. But I shall not call on her for I do not think she is the right kind of a girl to try to win my Husband's affections when she knows I am not present.

Within a few days, however, she had gained enough equanimity to tell him to "stay until you are satisfied." "I am proud," she declared, "to think I have a Husband that wants to fight for his Country."

WILLIAM G. THOMPSON
and HARRIET JANE THOMPSON

Perhaps her change of heart was bolstered by her decision to travel to William's family's home in Pennsylvania for a visit. Her plans for the trip consumed a few days and the journey itself a few more, yet when she arrived she quickly realized that she had carried all her feelings of isolation and abandonment with her. "It is the first thing in the morning and the last thing when I go to bed," she told him, "wondering where you are and if you are well." She began to wonder whether she would be any happier if she had a child, but concluded that "I am very glad now that we never had any [children] for if you should never get home from the war I will have no children to support."

She was soon overcome by homesickness: "I think I am a great baby this time for I am not contented anyplace but I will try and stand it for a little while." Her loneliness was diverted somewhat by caring for her ill mother-in-law. But despite the extra work, Thompson's mind returned to the question of a child. "Do you wish we had a baby?" she asked her husband. "I am very glad now the way things have turned out that we have none," she continued. "For I am lonely enough and feel bad enough without having a baby to think about."

As in Iowa, Thompson was constantly surrounded by war fever. Soldiers drilling, companies being formed, and rumors of the rebels taking Baltimore made her feel as if the war was "coming pretty near home." Patriotism also engulfed her. A young female neighbor, according to Jane, was "quite patriotic" because "she will not have much to do with a young fellow that is able to go to war and will not go." And local women who prepared lint, bandages, and shirts for soldiers at the front invited Thompson to help in the relief work.

Jane was moved to offer a statement of support to her husband:

> It was a great sacrifice to me and to you no doubt for you to leave home and its pleasures to fight for your country and I have not regretted that you went although I spend a great many lonely hours but that is nothing to what it would have been to had you staid at home and been called a coward and another thing your country needed you and why should I object to your going. But I am thankful I did not but instead told you to go. Did I object once? Did I not always say go!

Jane's patriotism ebbed and flowed, for a few days later she enjoined William: "I want you to shoot every rebel you can find and hurry and get this war to a close for this thing of living in excitement all the time is not very pleasant."

Although his family treated her as a daughter, her loneliness persisted as did her pleas that he get a furlough to visit them all in Pennsylvania. Jane added his mother's worsening condition as a reason for William to come home. She told him that "if I did not send you word and she would die before you saw her I should always feel as though I was to blame." But he could not or would not come, although Jane wrote him that "Indeed I am afraid she will drop away sometime when we least expect it."

By fall 1862, as her mother-in-law's health improved, Jane decided it was time for her to go back to her own home in Iowa. She requested her husband's permission: "I hope to hear from you soon telling me I may go home the last of this month or the first of next." Apparently hesitant to have her leave the care of his family, he did not answer his wife's request immediately and she gradually became impatient.

> I am still looking for an answer to my letter about my going home to Iowa, and hope you will not ask me to stay longer than the last of this month or the first of next for I think I will be better contented in Iowa and if I could go to housekeeping I would feel better for I would have my work to think about and I would not have so much time to think about being left alone.

When he still failed to answer, she said, "I think I will start for Iowa by the middle of next month," and then, "I would like to start to Iowa next week to see if I will be any better contented." In the meantime, her father-in-law fell ill, delaying her departure. Her determination to leave remained strong. "I think I will start home as soon as Father gets well," she informed William. "I cannot stay contented here and I do not know as I will feel any better there but I can try it."

Even when her father-in-law directed that he should be buried with a box made of two-inch plank, she remarked to William, "I hope you will tell me I may go to housekeeping when I get home." When he replied that she should remain with his parents until he could send her some money, she declared that she would borrow from his brother since her small purchases had consumed her money. "My patriotism is nearly all exhausted," she admitted. "I always like to do as you want me to but indeed, dear William, I cannot this time." As the health of her father-in-law began to improve, there was little to hold her and by November she was back in Marion, Iowa, with her own family.

Of course Jane Thompson was no happier in Iowa than she had been in Pennsylvania and she moaned, "This thing of living alone is awful." She went to visit the house that she and her husband had lived in and thought of moving back there, but did not stay long for it gave her "such awful feelings." She now decided that she must visit him for Christmas, to lessen her depression. "I am perfectly disheartened," she confessed. "I do not want to live long if I have got to live this way."

She attempted to fill her time as best she could. She helped with chores, read extensively, tried to keep her husband posted on bits of political news at home, learned to play all the new war songs on the piano, and did some relief work, although she refused to join a society "for they always end in a fuss." One great advantage of her quiet life-style, as she saw it, was not having to ask William for money. "I will get along some way, for I shall not go anyplace and will not need anything," she assured him. In another note she added, "Now

William, do not give yourself one bit of trouble about me for I am fixed just as comfortable as I can be. . . . I do not need any money." And again later she comforted him, "Now do not worry about me because you cannot send me money."

In the meantime, Thompson did not give up the idea of joining her husband for Christmas and persisted in raising the issue with him. In early December, however, she learned that he had been wounded. Although shocked and concerned, she inquired, "Did you think of me when you went into battle?" She was far from displeased when his wound brought him home on furlough for several months.

Like Maria Sharp, Thompson was not only happy to see her husband, but she was pleased to have him removed from the evils of camp life, especially the temptation to drink. Shortly after he left she advised: "I am younger than you and whenever we were at home if I said anything to you about drinking you did not like it and thought you knew when to drink and when not but please do not get in the habit. . . . You are just as apt to get in that habit as anyone." Later she commented that she was glad that he was enjoying himself "but hope it is not in forming bad habits . . . . I cannot help but feel uneasy for there are quite a number in the Regiment . . . that does like liquor . . . and I know when you are at home you can most always take a drink along." In another letter she repeats her caution about drink.

> I heard about Carskaddon being drunk and gambling. I have felt uneasy not that you are anything like him. But you had always told me they could not get any liquor in camp and I felt easy with that. Since I came here [Pennsylvania] I have heard what a bad place it was for drinking and gambling and I hope you will not indulge in anything of this kind and hardly think you will.

One of the reasons Thompson was glad to have her husband home was clearly personal. She wrote him what was on her mind in relatively unequivocal terms:

> I have very pleasant times with you in my dreams, and it worries me a great deal for I never done such a thing as to dream every night but I have not missed a night since I left you. . . . Do you not think of our bed at home when you lay down on your cot? . . . Do you think you would push me away now if I was where I could kiss you? . . . Do you ever wish you had me for a bedfellow? I have wished you were here more than once when I would get ready for bed. But I feel in hopes that we can have that privilege before long, don't you?

At another point, she added, "Oh, how I wish I could sleep with you tonight. . . . But I can only dream of being with you and that is very pleasant for

HARRIET JANE THOMPSON

I see you every night in my dreams." And then again she asked, "Do you ever wish when it comes night you were with me?"

Her dreams of William's final homecoming were not realized until May 1864, when he was allowed to resign due to continued problems with his 1862 injury. At that time, he resumed the practice of law in Marion and Jane bore their first child who, unhappily, died in infancy. Jane eventually gave birth to a second child, while William fulfilled his political ambitions through election to the United States Congress in 1879. He was appointed judge of the Eighteenth Judicial District in 1894. Jane died in 1897, William in 1911, and their son John in 1962.

The experience of Rogers, Sharp, and Thompson forms a composite view of the tribulations borne by many Iowa women during the Civil War. The full story, of course, is not only how they bore up under stress, but what Iowa women contributed to the war effort. The preceding three cases give evidence that women by and large kept the farms, family businesses, families, and schools functioning while a major portion of the male population was involved in war operations of some sort. Only one of the three women, Marjorie Ann Rogers, indicated that she was also active in the sanitary commissions, organized to send war supplies to the front, which were quite effective and widespread in Iowa.

WHEN the war began, many Iowa women were quick to see that Iowa volunteer soldiers would need more clothing, blankets, food, and other goods than the federal government could possibly mobilize on such short notice. Small groups of women banded together across Iowa in ladies' aid societies, sanitary commissions, and benevolent societies where they stitched clothing, rolled bandages, prepared and preserved foodstuffs, and packed boxes to be shipped to the front. In addition, they frequently held charity bazaars where they sold their homemade foods and other items to raise money for the purchase of items they could not produce themselves.

Although statistics are not available, there is little doubt that numbers of Iowa women participated in these groups and that untold amounts of supplies were produced or purchased. However, because women of the Civil War era were not experienced in organizational and business techniques, they soon discovered that they faced major problems in coordinating efforts between groups and in distributing their produce to Iowa soldiers. When Ann E. Harlan, wife of Iowa Senator James Harlan, went into the field with sanitary goods and aides to distribute them, she was appalled at the waste of the materials sent by "patriotic ladies all over the land."[19] Clothing left lying on the ground after one use for want of people to wash it, wagons of goods left to rot on the roadsides because of misrouting or inability to move through lines of troops and munitions, and the excess of goods in one hospital while another was doing without were all too common problems.

In Iowa the city of Keokuk fast became the hub of sanitary operations, with all its attendant dilemmas. On the Mississippi River at the southeastern-most tip of Iowa, Keokuk was a crucial departure point for both troops and supplies as well as a center for disabled soldiers, corpses, and disconcerting war news. Accordingly, its people were called upon to provide as much time and material as possible in order to alleviate the chaos and destruction that swirled about them.

One woman in particular, Annie Turner Wittenmyer, distinguished herself through benevolent undertakings. She had migrated to Keokuk in 1850 with her husband, William, a merchant of relative wealth much her senior. During the decade before the war, Annie Wittenmyer was active in establishing a free private school for poor children and in helping found a local church. When the Civil War broke out she was a widow in her mid-thirties living quietly with her one surviving child, a son who was too young for service in the war. She watched three of her four brothers, the fourth being physically disabled, leave in rapid succession to support the Union cause.

Wittenmyer, like countless other Iowans, had a personal interest in the state's volunteers. She soon joined with neighbors and friends to roll bandages, sew clothing, and package footstuffs for the troops. Since there was no parent charity organization, such as the Red Cross, to channel and direct these groups, the results of their efforts were haphazard at best. The women themselves soon

ANNIE TURNER WITTENMYER

realized that they needed more organization so they formed the Soldiers' Aid Society of Keokuk with Wittenmyer as executive secretary. In her new position she went into the field, sometimes at her own expense and sometimes at the expense of the society, to send back firsthand reports of conditions and needs.

Her field reports helped the women to more efficiently decide what types of supplies should be sent and where, and soon women from all over Iowa were contacting Wittenmyer asking her to take charge of the products of their sanitary societies. Since a comprehensive effort was clearly needed, in August of 1861 the Keokuk Aid Society appealed to the women of Iowa to come together in a statewide organization. A short time later, however, Governor Samuel J. Kirkwood appointed thirteen male Iowans as members of the Army Sanitary Commission for the State of Iowa, a group which was to supply Iowa troops just as the United States Sanitary Commission supplied Union troops.

Many women felt that their efforts were unrecognized and undercut by the establishment of this new all-male group who now sent out its own circulars and appeals calling for contributions from Iowans. Others were totally confused, thinking that the two groups were working together or that Wittenmyer represented the governor's group. At about this time Wittenmyer sent back another report that made it clear how imperative it was to have an efficient sanitary organization.

> That there should be a lack of such hospital furniture and stores as the government proposes to supply, may be a matter of surprise to some, but when we take into consideration that the Government, at the commencement of this war, was almost in a state of disorganization, and that within the compass of a few months, a vast military campaign has been set on foot, involving millions of dollars, and the health and comfort of hundreds of thousands of men, and that the Government has had to contend with an injured credit and hordes of dishonest army contractors, there is little cause to wonder that her supplies are not bountiful.[20]

She called for bed clothes, sheets and blankets, socks, slippers, towels, lint, bandages, jellies, fruits, and other delicacies. She also suggested that two or more female nurses be sent to each Iowa regiment to aid in caring for the wounded men.[21] But due to inexperience, the overwhelming pressures of the situation, and undercurrents of political jealousies, the various Iowa sanitary organizations could not blend themselves together into one smoothly functioning group.

Early in 1862, Wittenmyer, still on her rounds of field hospitals, came upon her youngest brother refusing a breakfast tray that held "a tin cup full of black, strong coffee, beside it . . . a leaden looking tin platter, on which was a piece of fried fat bacon, swimming in its own grease, and a slice of bread."[22] It was this scene that caused her to recognize the urgent need to establish diet kitchens throughout the army hospitals to serve nourishing meals to men desperately in need of proper nutrition. She added this crusade to her other efforts, and by September 1862 her work was recognized by her appointment as one of the state sanitary agents for Iowa.

In 1863 she added yet another cause, the founding of a home for soldiers' orphans, to her already long list. An appeal from 480 soldiers in southern hospitals inspired her efforts:

> We are grateful for all the kindness shown us. We appreciate your noble charity, which reaches us in camp—in the hospital and on the battle field—but we prefer you should forget us, and leave us to struggle with our fate as best we may—if you will but look after our wives and children, our mothers and sisters, who are dependent upon us for support. A severe winter is before them and we are rent with anxiety as we remember their slender resources and our meager and irregular pay. Succor them, and withhold your charity from us.[23]

Although Wittenmyer was successful in founding two homes to meet the pressing need of caring for soldiers' orphans, she found herself more and more embroiled in politics to raise support for these institutions. The diary of her aide, Mary E. Shelton, is filled with accounts of the letters to be written, speeches to be given, and politicians to be contacted. At one point Shelton remarked, "Mrs. Wittenmyer addressed the General Assembly and succeeded charmingly" in convincing them of the usefulness of orphans' homes.[24]

On other occasions Wittenmyer was seen in a less favorable light. There were charges leveled against her for misusing public funds, for selling goods for profit, and for misallocating goods, none of which were ever proven. She also found herself in conflict with other women involved in hospital work. Wittenmyer's clash with Dorothea Dix, for example, was later described by a Civil War nurse, Amanda Shelton Stewart.

> Mrs. Wittenmyer and Miss Dix had opposite views as to the kind of women who should be employed in the hospital work. The latter selected elderly, homely, women on the theory that female nurses should not be too attractive. That many of her nurses were comely, despite their years, was due to the fact that the supply of ill-favored women was so small that it could not equal the demand. . . . Age and ugliness were not among Mrs. Wittenmyer's requirements. She expected us to be capable and discreet and to dress like home folks.[25]

Stewart went on to say that women nurses were received in most field hospitals with "hostile reluctance." According to her, the women "bore hardships as good soldiers and won recognition" in caring not only for the wounded men but for the many wives who had to be housed and fed as they flocked to the hospitals to be near their husbands.[26]

Unfortunately, the friction continued. In late 1863, Wittenmyer was elected president of the Iowa State Sanitary Commission by a convention held in Muscatine. Only a month later, another convention met at Des Moines, largely at the instigation of Ann Harlan, herself an active participant in relief efforts, and formed a rival group called the Iowa Sanitary Commission which was unfriendly to Wittenmyer. In 1864, after a move to oust her as a state sanitary agent, Wittenmyer resigned her post to spend all her time and energy on the diet kitchen system, funded now by the United States Christian Commission. She continued in this capacity until the end of the war. General Ulysses S. Grant said of her, "No soldier on the firing line gave more heroic service than she rendered."[27]

Nearly thirty years after the war, when Wittenmyer was finally persuaded to write her memoirs, she made no mention of conflict or dissension. She wrote,

> I was loyally and generously sustained by the women of Iowa; was elected by the Iowa Legislature sanitary agent of the State; was commissioned by Iowa's grand old war governor, Samuel J. Kirkwood; was furnished by Secretary Stanton with a pass to all parts of the field, and government transportation for myself and supplies. . . . I had also the co-operation of the Sanitary and Christian Commissions, and the chief medical officers and government officials, so that I had unusual facilities for doing good.[28]

Although she charitably omitted any reference to her detractors, many people were aware of the complaints against her. Newspapers were quick to publish reports of antagonisms and freely interjected their own editorial opinions. Yet in the long run, Wittenmyer's work attracted more favorable publicity to women's efforts than bad. Combined with the endeavors of the many women working all over the state, her labors brought increasing recognition to the achievements of Iowa women in producing wartime supplies.

Unfortunately, the history of the many other Iowa women besides Wittenmyer and Harlan who engaged in relief work has yet to be written. Amelia Bloomer of Council Bluffs, known for her editorship of a temperance journal called *The Lily* and her advocacy of the Bloomer costume, was one of the more notable figures to actively participate in soldiers' aid. There were many others of lesser fame as well. One of these was Mary A. Weare Ely, whose husband was appointed surgeon with the Twenty-fourth Iowa Regiment. Ely organized a soldiers' aid society in her home in Cedar Rapids and served as its president for the duration of the war. She represented Iowa at several sanitary fairs in Chicago and after the war became a tireless worker on behalf of the Iowa Soldiers' Orphans' Home.[29]

The numbers of such women were so great and their influence so widespread that Iowa newspapers, whose reports at the beginning of the war told little or nothing of women's benevolent ventures, gradually began to regularly carry announcements and reports of various ladies' soldiers' aid society meetings. An 1863 benefit concert in Burlington was reported as having raised $160, a sum larger than expected. "The ladies . . . not only deserved the gratitude of the soldiers," the *Hawk-Eye* stated, "but the thanks of the community for a very pleasant evening's entertainment, which we hope will be repeated on some future occasion." In the following year, the paper reported that Burlington women had arranged a scheme to board and lodge indigent soldiers in a local boardinghouse.[30]

Iowa newspapers paid special attention to the sanitary fairs. As public festivals, these fund-raising fairs had great success in other states. In 1864 Iowa, too, planned a large sanitary fair in Dubuque. An organization called the Northern Iowa Sanitary Fair appealed to Iowans and citizens in neighboring states for support, assistance, and contributions. The fair combined booths, displays, prizes, and evening entertainments to stimulate interest in the war work. After running for eight days in June 1864, the Northern Iowa Sanitary Fair turned over $50,000 to the United States Sanitary Commission as well as distributing many unsold goods to local agencies.

Other similar fairs followed, including the Iowa Central Fair at Muscatine and the Southern Iowa Fair at Burlington, both held in September 1864. And it must be remembered that although recognition and large-scale organization came only near the end of the war, many local aid societies had been holding similar events for several years—bazaars, dinners, concerts, dances, and innumerable types of entertainment staged on the local level to raise funds, supplies, or both. The proceeds were used not only to help soldiers at the front, but also to aid returning veterans, soldiers' widows, orphans, and others put in need by the war.[31]

IOWA women quickly learned to manage a frontier society and a wartime society with remarkable results. While it is possible to say, therefore, that the contribution of Iowa women, both at home and at the front, was significant, it is almost impossible to assess the impact of the war years on the women themselves. Clearly, several nineteenth-century idealized beliefs concerning the status and position of women in society were destroyed or at least badly tarnished. During the war years, women performed work, carried out responsibilities, and made decisions in the formerly male realm without great impairment to their health, mental capacities, or nervous systems. The argument that they were incapable of assuming "men's work" without serious damage to themselves was becoming anachronistic. Even though many women retreated into their homes, relinquishing many of their wartime responsibilities, they did so armed with the knowledge that homemaking was not their only "lot" in life.

At the same time, Iowa women were becoming increasingly aware of disillusionment emanating from eastern feminists who had put aside the cause of women's rights to work for abolition during the war years. These women were disappointed that their toil and sacrifice was not rewarded at the end of the war by formal recognition of their civil and political rights. When these women were told by congressmen as well as abolitionist reformers such as Frederick Douglass that it was the "Negro's hour" and that their pleas for equality would have to wait until an undetermined later time, they reacted at first with dismay, then with militancy. One outcome of their dissatisfaction with this aspect of the war's conclusion was the conviction held by many that the only way to implement an improved situation for American women was by achieving suffrage for themselves. Suffragism, a cause barely articulated before the Civil War, became widely viewed as a panacea in postwar years.

CHAPTER SIX

Strong-Minded Women

N O W, in those days," wrote Amelia Murdock Wing, referring to the mid-nineteenth century, "a woman who had very decided opinions of her own was frequently sneeringly called by some men 'a strong-minded woman.' "[1] This epithet was applied to an increasing number of women who, even in the era preceding the Civil War, spoke out forcefully on a wide range of topics. Many of them actively sought improved educational opportunities, worked at a variety of paid jobs and professions, and began to evince an interest in women's rights, suffragism, and feminism.

The appearance of strong-minded women on the Iowa family-farm frontier was contradictory to the stereotypic tradition of women confined to their homes. The model of domesticity—an obedient, passive, docile, and quiet wife—was metamorphosing. The reality of life on the Iowa frontier fostered the very characteristics which led to strong-mindedness. Although they may have paid lip service to the nineteenth-century ideal of a "proper lady," most Iowa frontierswomen were too deeply immersed in a system of economic partnership with men to really believe in it or practice it. As historian Robert F. Berkhofer points out, the frontier often presented this kind of paradox, for while "the Westerners . . . possessed one conception of society," they usually "erected quite another."[2] The paradox certainly applied to frontierswomen. Sharing in the conquering of the frontier helped women dispel the image of their weak-mindedness, so highly touted as an innate part of their nature.

Like many of their progressive sisters back East, it didn't take long for many Iowa women to recognize that their most immediate "escape route" from the farm was through the local school. Although this escape was temporary, since most female teachers shortly married and became farm wives, education was seen as the most accessible deliverance from what one girl called the "drudgery" of farm work.

Most of the year meant drudgery on the farms, and school was a relief from hard work. We were looking forward to the time when we could leave the farm and do something else, preferably in a town or city, so there was a good deal of speculation the first day of school as to how much help the teacher was likely to be as a stepping-stone to our ambition.[3]

Education had been denied most American women in the past due to the supposedly inferior capacity of their alleged small brains and the "sheltered" nature of their lives, but such specious arguments were slowly losing credence. It was becoming increasingly difficult to interpret equal education for women as potentially dangerous because so many reformers were tactfully pointing out that education could only help make women better wives and mothers, more sage advisors to their husbands, and wiser teachers of the children they might bear and raise. "Without knowledge," said a frontier newspaper, "no wife is truly a wife—no mother truly a mother." The education of wives and mothers "will only render them more worthy of the name." The courageous male writer concluded on a polemical note: "Even should it [education] never serve any such purpose, I say that women have a right to claim it."[4]

The drive for improved educational opportunities received additional impetus on the frontier by the fact that women were already equal in so many other areas of life. Social historian Louis B. Wright describes the situation succinctly. "It was," he said, "hard to explain to a pioneer woman who could endure the toil and hardships of trail or field that she was physically incapable of enduring the strain of a masculine education."[5]

"To the Iowa pioneers," historian Ruth Gallaher explains, equal education "was the natural and only possible plan for the primitive schools" since the pioneer "boys and girls worked and played together on the prairies."[6] In Iowa, when the boys headed for the one-room schoolhouse, they were frequently accompanied by their sisters. In fact, it was frequently the sisters who remained in school while their brothers were kept home to help with the heavy field work. As a result, neither equal education for women nor coeducation were ever contestable issues in Iowa. Education was an integral part of a lifestyle in which both men and women were significant participants.

By modern standards the early Iowa schoolhouse was a limited resource at best. Matilda Peitzke Paul remembered that she first attended school in an old log "Still House."

For seats there were long benches placed on three sides of the room. Had no desks or table to write on, instead had a slanting shelf across one side of the room attached to the wall. When occasion came to use a desk we turned and faced the wall while writing or working arithmetic. We got our drinking water for the school from a spring about a quarter of a mile away.

It was considered a favor to go after water consequently we changed off. When the water came our teacher would let us pass it, first to teacher then to pupils, all drinking out of the same long-handled tin dipper.[7]

Because the building could not adequately protect its inhabitants from Iowa's winds and snow, Paul's school moved to the small back room of a neighbor's log house during the winter term. By the mid-1860s her family bought a farm near Riceville, Iowa and for the first time she attended school in a real schoolhouse. Her memories of her years there were fond ones.

Nothing so thrilling but we learned a little and always had plenty of fun. . . . Our teachers had very little education and schools were not graded, but usually started at the front of our book at the beginning of every term and went as far as we could, then start all over again at the beginning of next term. Stood up in a row when we spelled and some teachers gave a prize to the one who left off head most times. . . . We played many games at school, such as Pussy wants a Corner, Pull Away—I am on Dickies Land—Ring around the Rosie—Needles Eye—Drop Handkerchief—Poison and other games. It still thrills me when I think of it. Often in the winter we slid on frozen ponds and slid down hill and snow balled each other.[8]

Margaret Archer Murray's recollections of her school in the 1860s were much the same as Paul's. "We had a log school house," she stated, "with wood heated stove and had to carry drinking water from a farm well about ¼ miles away." She recalled that she was able to attend only the summer term until she was ten or eleven years old because she "couldent wade deep snow in winter time." After traveling the two and a half miles to her school she sat on puncheon benches with no backs and no desks; once a day she went to the teacher's large table in the front of the room to write in her copy book. "Our studies," she later said, "were reading writing spelling and a little arithmatic."[9]

May Lacey Crowder's first school was the upstairs loft of her own family's cabin. It accommodated a long bench and desk made by her father where seven pupils and a teacher studied under its steeply sloped roof. Crowder attended regularly, but her two brothers came only when they were not busy in the fields. She wryly commented that "Fred, oftener than Frank, had to be at work, but I was seldom asked, or permitted, to lose a day of school."[10] By 1874 a first school building was constructed:

The interior was a simple oblong, wainscotted about three feet above the floor and plastered above that and overhead. . . . A partition near one end formed an entrance hall where we left our wraps and lunches. During recess and noon hour, when the weather was too cold to go outside, we used to play there. . . . On Friday afternoons following the recess there was usually a program of recitations and a spelling match to close the day.[11]

These pioneer schools, although crude and rudimentary, served to awaken pioneer children's minds. In order not to interfere with the requisite for children's labor at planting and harvest time, the schools conducted two terms a year, summer and winter. The teacher was supplied with whatever equipment the community could afford, usually a blackboard but sometimes even a globe or maps. The students were expected to bring their own slates or copybooks as well as whatever textbooks their families owned. The level of instruction was strictly individualized. It was based on the student's competency in the books he or she presented to the teacher on the first day of school as well as on the teacher's own preparation.

Considering these limitations, it was remarkable that many frontier schools offered as much as they did. In 1861, Ellen Strang noted that she and her brother studied "McGuffeys fifth reader, McGuffeys spelling book, Rays Arithmetic second and third part, Pinneo's Grammar, Michels Geography and practice writing." In addition, she captured the honor of being "editress" of the school's semimonthly paper and signed up for a "Geography School" in the evenings at "$1.00 for a schollar" for twelve evenings.[12]

With relatively simple curriculum and school activities, the rural schools awakened many students' interest in securing some type of secondary education for themselves. In frontier days, secondary education was the province of private academies. They were established and operated by individuals, by farmers or tradespeople interested in education, or by members of a religious denomination concerned with the education of its youth. Also called seminaries, lyceums, institutes, societies, even colleges, these academies were sometimes limited to males, sometimes to females, but in Iowa they were primarily coeducational.[13]

THE 1840 census, taken only a few years after the first white settlers pushed into Iowa, recorded no universities or colleges and only two academies and grammar schools (with a total of fifty students) in existence.[14] One of these was the Dubuque Seminary, a secular coeducational institution, created by the territorial legislature in 1838. It was in all likelihood one of the schools referred to in "Plumbe's Sketches" when, in lauding the attractions of Dubuque to potential settlers, John Plumbe, Jr., pointed out that Dubuque of 1839 boasted both "a classical School, and a Ladies' Academy."[15] The abundant early references to Dubuque's academies suggest that there was a great deal of interest and activity in education in the area.

As early as 1838 the *Iowa News* (Dubuque) advertised the DuBuque Academy run by Mrs. Louisa King. Her notice promised that "either sex" could get a "good English education" and that in addition, "in the female department, the various branches of useful and ornamental needle work will be taught, and instructions given on the Piano Forte." In that same year, the *Iowa News* also ran an ad for the weekly DuBuque Lyceum, which was then meeting every Tuesday. A few years later a detailed advertisement in the *Iowa Territorial Gazette and Advertiser* explained that a particular denominational school under the patronage of Bishop Loras taught by local "sisters" cost $100 for board and tuition "including bed, bedding and washing," with an additional one dollar fee for fuel. An 1850s guidebook emphasized the excellence of the Dubuque Female Institute established in 1853 under the patronage of Miss Catharine Beecher as well as a "ladies' " college at Davenport. Beecher visited Dubuque sometime in the early 1850s with the idea of setting up a school for girls. Her efforts brought about erection of a building in 1852 and instruction began in 1854. Unfortunately, however, this school failed in 1858 due to lack of endowment. Yet in that same year, one Iowa promoter was so taken with the "Dubuque Female College . . . a beautiful edifice . . . in a prosperous condition," that he was moved to state in rather extravagant terms that Iowa was the home of the "most liberal school system of any State in the Union."[16]

Dubuque was not the only Iowa town infected with the fever to establish schools. Although most of their institutions were shortlived and unremarked, towns were proud of those they produced. In 1853 the founding of the Iowa Female Collegiate Institute in Iowa City was accompanied by a typically flowery, optimistic address attendant to such occasions in that era. The speaker, Dr. Charles O. Waters, pointed out that like Mount Holyoke, which had "already done much to bless the world by making American mothers worthy of the name," the Iowa Female Institute believed in "sending forth the females of our land fully prepared to accomplish the grand and lofty mission of their sex." He reminded his audience that since "the future destinies of our Republic" depended upon the characters of sisters, wives, and mothers, the school would cast its "mite into the great stream of moral influence." He concluded that not only would this be "an Institution which shall impress pure and ennobling influences upon the minds of the young females of Iowa" but that it would also "mould the character of those who will control the destinies and direct the influences of this great country."[17]

Despite the lofty rhetoric issued at the Iowa Female Institute's founding, the school lasted only two years. Its main supporter, a member of the Odd Fellows' Lodge which had conceived the school in 1853 and commenced building it in 1855, died in 1856. The Collegiate Institute died with him just as the Mechanics' Mutual Aid Association school had disappeared some years earlier. Organized in 1841, the Mechanics' school had started out strong by laying a cornerstone in 1842, opening a female department in 1843, and instituting a male department later that same year. Although its "usual cost," three dollars a session, was not exorbitant, the Mechanics' school died shortly, perhaps smothered by the welter of other schools springing up around it.[18]

A random scanning of the newspapers in the southeastern portion of Iowa between the late 1830s and the end of the frontier period in 1870 indicates a proliferation of interest in the various types of secondary schools during this period. As early as 1839, for example, the *Hawk-Eye and Iowa Patriot* (Burlington) advertised the Select School for Young Ladies which offered orthography, reading, writing, and sewing at a fee of $1.50 per month while all "higher branches" cost two dollars per month. In 1845, the Monticello Female Seminary advertised twenty-four weeks of instruction for sixty dollars for board, tuition, fuel, and "incidentals."[19] In 1849 Catharine Beecher spoke in support of her institution in Dubuque. She drew an "immense crowd" and engendered a great deal of enthusiasm. Later that year a High School for Young Ladies, offering instruction in French, drawing, fancy work, and music for three dollars to five dollars per month, was announced. It was, of course, not Beecher's plan. She was more interested in a practical education which would train young women in the domestic arts and provide female teachers to the rural schools where instructors with even minimal training in the basics were badly needed.

Despite Beecher's speeches throughout the Midwest, most schools continued to concern themselves at least in part with the "female accomplishments." In 1850 the Select School for Young Ladies claimed that "in addition to English branches, instructions will be given in the French and Spanish languages, with Drawing, Music and Painting." In 1857 the Keokuk Female College stated that it afforded to "young ladies the best facilities for an extensive education and thorough mental discipline," all at six dollars a month for the primary department, eight dollars a month for the advanced department, with a mere one dollar for "incidentals." By 1859 the Mount Ida Female College in Davenport proudly advertised its sophisticated curriculum: "Model School for Misses, An Academic department preparatory to entering the Collegiate, A Collegiate course, An Ornamental department, extra." By 1860 the Fairfield Female Seminary had added Greek and Latin, a branch of its program that accepted both males and females but in which only females could "board."[20] In 1866 the *Hawk-Eye* carried an announcement for Iowa College's fall term which prominently announced the Ladies Department and Ladies Boarding House. In 1866 the Mount Pleasant Female Seminary ran a large advertisement for its fall term, and in 1869 the Birmingham Academy for Males and Females held out the inducement of "a thorough preparation for business life, for teaching or entering any of our various colleges."

Of all the schools mentioned, the Mount Pleasant Female Seminary was one of the more eminent female seminaries. It had a music department and a painting teacher in addition to its regular curriculum. The school practiced coeducation. "Gentlemen and ladies, boys and girls, are taught in the same classes, because this is God's plan, and any other is faulty and mischievous."

While they were at school, Mount Pleasant's women students' lives were rigidly, if not despotically, controlled. Jewelry and ornate dresses were confiscated, candy was seized as "contraband," personal funds could be spent only on books, personal reading was limited to one hour per week, church attendance was compulsory, and fathers and brothers were the only men allowed to communicate with the female students. By 1879, it, like so many of the other academies, closed its doors due to a steady decline in enrollment.[21]

Other short-lived schools for women in frontier Iowa were Lyons Female College, founded in 1859 in Lyons (Clinton County) and Saint Agatha's Seminary, founded in 1864 in Iowa City. Most of these institutions offered a continually changing variety of courses to their students, probably in an attempt to attract as many scholars as possible. Schools that stressed the "accomplishments" such as singing, embroidery, and French more than any other part of the curriculum probably fell into the category of "finishing schools"; those that stressed the "English branches" usually emphasized English grammar and other practical skills designed to make the pupil a conscientious and employable citizen; a few schools incorporated "collegiate branches" into their programs. Fee schedules were fairly consistent among the schools. In 1854, the Young Ladies' Seminary of Davenport charged the following fees: common English branches, five dollars for a term (eleven weeks); mathematics and natural sciences, an additional two dollars; Latin, French, and German, an additional four dollars; and music, an additional ten dollars. In that same year a school for boys advertised tuition rates of three dollars for an eleven-week term in the primary branch which included spelling, reading, writing, and arithmetic, and four dollars for an eleven-week term which covered grammar, geography, history, and philosophy. Similarly, in 1858 the "Grinnell School" charged seventy-five cents per month for primary studies, one dollar per month for advanced studies, and one dollar twenty-five cents per month for the classics. Extras at Grinnell included French at one dollar per month, piano music at ten dollars for twelve weeks, and a fee for the use of the school's instruments at two dollars for the twelve weeks. In 1859 the Burlington Female Institute offered orthography, reading, and writing for four dollars per ten-week term; English grammar, modern geography, United States history, and arithmetic for five dollars; higher English and Latin for six dollars; and lessons in music and the pianoforte simply "extra."[22]

Although the fees appear ridiculously low in terms of today's inflated economy, many Iowa families had to work long and hard to eke out a four dollar or five dollar tuition fee as well as money for books and supplies. Sarah Gillespie Huftalen recalled,

> These pupils were the children of pioneer parents in Iowa and grandchildren of pioneers in New York and Michigan and from them they had learned to live frugally. Textbooks were appreciated and were accepted as

rewards. My mother raised turkeys and "took in sewing" so that my brother and I might each have a set of schoolbooks.[23]

The fact that many people worked hard to foster the growth of secondary education in the early settlements in Iowa suggests that education was esteemed by the area's settlers. In Keokuk in 1857 a letter to the newspaper expressed the opinion "that a permanent, well-endowed and well-conducted Seminary, where our daughters may be trained as extensively and as thoroughly as anywhere else in the country, is a great desideratum in our city, all intelligent persons, we presume, are agreed."[24] The Waterloo Female Seminary, with headmistress Anna Field, a graduate of Mount Holyoke Female Seminary, received support from the editor of the *Waterloo Courier*. "We cannot do too much to encourage such institutions in our midst." On a private level as well, aspiring women students received encouragement. Ann Eliza Peck spent much of the time that she and James Harlan were courting reciting to him from "mental science and other advanced studies" not included in the course she pursued at school. Rather than being taken aback, he was supportive and "formed a very flattering opinion of her capacity."[25]

Although many early Iowans evidently supported a young woman's right to gain some type of secondary education, their feelings were more ambivalent toward a college education for women. Many people stubbornly clung to the old belief that women's minds were too frail, their brains too small in size, and their bodies too weak to withstand the rigors of a college education.[26] At the same time, others realized that the changing times demanded new skills from women.

> If women conduct our great charities, they must hold public meetings; if they hold public meetings, they must know the rules of deliberative bodies. . . . Our civilization produces a large class of women to whom the traditional limits are cruelty, and the old formulas inapplicable. . . . Give her a chance—a fair field and no favor! Let old paths widen and new avenues unlock their rusted and creaking gates.[27]

When the first state-supported university in Iowa opened its doors in 1856, it made little attempt to bar women from admission. The 1856 catalog of the State University of Iowa recorded 124 students in attendance, eighty-three of them male and forty-one female. The university included a preparatory department designed "to fit the student for some of the Departments in the University," such as departments of ancient languages, modern languages, intellectual philosophy, moral philosophy, history, natural history, mathematics, natural philosophy, chemistry, and a normal school to train teachers. By 1858 the university's board of trustees faced the possibility of having to close the university due to lack of adequate funding. Part of the retrenchment program was the elimination of women students, but after a heated debate on the value of retaining them, the preparatory and normal departments remained open—with a substantial number of owmen in attendance.[28]

During the next few years the State University of Iowa awarded several degrees to women. In the process, the board of trustees learned that no moral decline resulted from higher coeducation as so many people had feared it would. To their surprise, coeducation actually seemed to foster decorum and sedateness among the student body. Women students sustained the university through the Civil War years while the young men, who might have been enrolled, were engaged in war-related duties. By 1868–1869 the trustees suggested expanded course offerings "for the ladies" and the board of regents appropriated $1,000 for a boardinghouse for women students.[29]

During these same years plans were progressing for a second state college, Iowa State College, to be located in Ames. That women students would be admitted to this institution was not questioned. When the first president, Adonijah S. Welch, gave an address to the student body in 1870, he made it clear that the college aimed to include practical skills in the education of women.

> [Women] can never become accomplished and thoroughly educated . . . without a knowledge of conducting every household occupation, with system, intelligence, and womanly grace. The most alarming feature of educating our girls is the almost total disregard of these branches, known as the useful and practical, that will prepare them for the proper discharge of the best and noblest duties of rational and intelligent women.[30]

Every student at Iowa State was required to work two and a half hours per day. In the case of women students, this meant that they were arranged in "squads" in the dining room, kitchen, laundry, and bakery on a rotating basis designed to involve them in every task.

In 1872, Mary B. Welch, the president's wife, began teaching classes in domestic science at Iowa State. The course "Domestic Economy," which began modestly in a basement experimental kitchen, quickly attracted many women students to Iowa State. By the time the Normal School in Cedar Falls opened in 1876, few people were surprised that women students outnumbered men who enrolled for the course in teacher training.[31]

Private colleges were also founded during the frontier period. One of the more important of these was the Congregationalists' Iowa College, incorporated by the city of Davenport in 1847 and first offering instruction in 1848. Relations were not always smooth between the temperance-abolitionist oriented college and citizens of the boisterous river town. When the city of Davenport built a street through the campus in the late 1850s, the college trustees decided that it was time to find a more compatible location for their school. A merger was arranged with Josiah B. Grinnell's "university" in 1859 with classes actually beginning in 1861. Most of the males in the first class left for war duty; women formed the bulk of the student body and kept the school going during the lean war years.[32]

The war retarded the development of the physical plant of the college in Grinnell. Originally two separate buildings were planned, one for men and one for women, located at least a quarter mile apart. Since the women's building was completed at the same time that the Civil War started and funds dried up, it was used by the whole college for several years. Iowa College, or Grinnell College as it was later known, boasted a woman principal named Sarah Parker until the late 1860s. In 1867, the college granted its first Bachelor of Science degree to a woman graduate. Other pre–Civil War colleges included Dubuque University (1852), Wartburg College in Waverly (1852), Central College in Pella (1854), Cornell College in Mt. Vernon (1850), Coe College in Cedar Rapids (1851), and Simpson College in Indianola (1860).[33]

How women would apply their degrees or use the knowledge acquired during a few terms at a secondary school or university was a complex question. In mid-nineteenth-century Iowa, marriage was still the be-all and end-all of any young woman's life. Insofar as education fitted her for her roles as wife and mother, it was considered salutary. What a woman was to do with the portion of her education which did not have domestic applications was not quite so clear-cut. Certain paid positions, such as clerking in a dry-goods store or working as a seamstress, were acceptable as stopgaps between girlhood and marriage, possible employment for a woman who had to help support her family, or for a widow. Of course the primary profession open to women and considered "socially acceptable" for them was teaching.

Accordingly, bright young Iowa women flocked to the teaching profession. An early chronicler of Iowa history, Benjamin Gue, said that as academies and colleges afforded women educational opportunities, many "farm girls began to crowd out the ancient men teachers who had long ruled with the birch rod." He remarked that the "self-reliant teacher was usually some ambitious daughter of a pioneer farmer." Another writer remembered a woman teacher near Fort Madison in 1834 as the "first lady teacher in Iowa" who "opened her school after the men had engrossed the business for some four years." In his opinion she was the first of a host of women who "so completely elbowed" men out of their places in the schoolroom.[34]

May Lacey Crowder recalled that as a young girl in a rural schoolhouse her highest ambition was to qualify as a teacher. She later attended a month-long teacher's institute, which was a training session, and at age fifteen embarked upon her teaching career. Alice Money Lawrence worked for her father as a shepherd at a dollar and half per week to pay for one term at Albion Seminary. She then added more study at Marshall Seminary in Marshalltown to her credentials and was assigned her first teaching job in Grundy County in 1869.[35]

In the mid-nineteenth century, American men in the East and the West were quickly learning that they could make more money and be assured of employment more days of the year in a factory job or farming a piece of land than they could teaching. They left the rapidly increasing number of schoolrooms, thus creating a void which young women were happy to fill. These women usually considered it a welcome opportunity to be employed several months in the summer and several months in the winter, even though they worked for lower wages than men. Since most of these women taught for only several months to a few years, then married and left to raise their own children, a constant turnover was created so that there were usually enough vacant teaching positions for the young women so anxious to fill them.

There were exceptions to this general trend. After her marriage, Druscilla Allen Stoddard continued to teach and in 1858 was appointed head of the Woman's Department at Iowa Central College in Pella. Eleanor Gordon, who dropped out of Iowa State after one year's work due to financial problems, taught country schools, remained single, and continued to educate herself through night courses. In the early 1870s she despaired because to her "the outlook for the ambitious American young woman was dreary enough." But she pushed on with her own work, maintaining that she did not have to marry: "I had two hands, a brain of my own. No one should dictate as to ways and means." Her dedication was rewarded with her election to the assistant principalship of Centerville High School and her eventual election to the principalship of the Humboldt Public Schools.[36]

In looking back over the conditions faced by frontier teachers, it is not difficult to understand why many of them were not too reluctant to give up teaching for marriage. In the mid-1860s, Mary E. Shelton made the following diary notation: "How long I can endure this teaching I cannot tell. Oh it is hard, hard. . . . Two months I have been teaching and outside of the schoolroom they have passed delightfully."[37] Since Shelton had just returned from service as a Civil War nurse, her laments on the grueling routine in the schoolroom raise questions about how the rigors of teaching compared to wartime nursing duty. Maintaining discipline called for fortitude and great energy. Mary S. Ellis wondered how she would handle the farm boys during winter session she was to teach in 1857. "What shall I do with the big boys this winter," she wrote to her in-laws back East. "They have never had a woman teacher and such a thing is scarcely thought of in the winter here."[38] Alice Money Lawrence expressed a similar concern to her sister during her first teaching job in 1869:

> You ask if I like teaching. Oh, yes, the teaching part but not the discipline. I had to keep all my scholars but one in at recess today, and I had to whip one boy—the first punishment of that kind that has been necessary.[39]

Another teacher, Ellen Strang, did not have trouble with her pupils, but her home chores claimed much of her energy before she even got to the schoolroom. "Got up at quarter past four," she wrote in 1867. "Made the beads [*sic*], picked up the clothes to wash, switched out and comed my hair. After breakfast worked at sundries. Got to school in good season schollars all there before 9 o'clock."[40] In another case, the school itself was the difficulty.

> The desks were in all stages of demoralization. The dictionary had been used for a billiard ball until it was a handful of shreds and patches. The few scattered bits of plaster, which still adherred to the wall, furnished small protection from the keen northwest winds that played hide and seek though a thousand crevices. The snow drifted in through the roof.[41]

A frontier teacher's salary compensated little for such problems in spite of the fact that smaller sums of money had greater buying power in the nineteenth century than they do today. One account listed teachers' wages in 1836 as a dollar fifty per week for female teachers and twelve dollars per month for male teachers, plus board and room.[42] In 1863, Ellen Strang mentioned a young woman teacher who was to receive twenty-six dollars per month plus her board. An 1865 record noted that the average pay for male teachers was about six dollars per week and that of female teachers was about five dollars per week. While it was true that most teachers' salaries were supplemented by board with the pupils' families, one of Alice Money Lawrence's experiences with board illustrates that these living arrangements were not always desirable. She found her boarding place dirty and learned to her dismay that her hostess could not cook. Breakfast every morning consisted of bread and an egg fried in lard, which Alice slipped to the small boy of the family. She spent as much time as possible at the schoolhouse reading, preparing for class, and writing letters to her sister. Alice Briggs Olmstead also disliked her boarding place. She did not mind boarding with the "front room family" in a two-family, two-room cabin, but she objected to some of the family's customs and chose to live at home and walk the five miles to school each day. On the other hand, Arozina Perkins found herself in a favorable room and board situation in 1849 in Fort Des Moines. She lived with a family of four in a three-room house, yet they turned the entire parlor over to her. She was also pleased with the food served to her. "The diet too just suits me," she wrote her brother, "for we have plenty of corn bread, mush, and milk." However, she did not like the teaching conditions and soon moved on to Fairfield to take up another teaching position.[43]

In spite of the problems and inconveniences, most women teachers felt that the advantages of the job outweighed the disadvantages. They received a cash wage (albeit less than a man would receive), they could help support their family or contribute to a brother's—sometimes a sister's—education, they were free from the unceasing demands of farm work, they could expand their own horizons through books and new acquaintances, and they could help children become more effective adults in a rapidly changing world. The public responded favorably to woman's emerging role of shaping the nation's youth. In 1855, when the *Eddyville Free Press* reported on the "closing Examinations and Exhibitions" of Mount Pleasant High School and Female Seminary, the article stressed that "the more of such exercises the better, for the times eminently demand vigorous, and effective thinkers and speakers."[44] Comments like this indicate that people were increasingly beginning to question the image of docile and weak women.

The territorial census records of Iowa offer clues to women branching out into occupations other than teaching. Although the early census rolls did not count people by occupation, they did list heads of households by name thus making it possible to determine that many households headed by women existed. In these cases, however, the source of support for the household as well as the woman's marital status were usually not specified. The 1836 listing for Mrs. R. Mallett with a household of three males and four females in Dubuque County gives no hint whether she was a widow, whether she supported the household, or whether the three males were elder sons who lived at home and supported the family (perhaps with their wives, which would account for the three females besides Mallett listed). One atypical listing specified a *Widow* Lowry with three males and three females in her household in Des Moines County; support of the household is not recorded. Another unusual listing named Matilda Dickinson in Dubuque County. She was apparently one of the few who lived alone; there is no information on her age or whether she was employed outside the home. She may have been a prostitute who plied her trade in her home. Another curious annotation was Mary McBride, with a household of four females; apparently one or more of the females supported this family.[45]

In the 1856 *Burlington Business Directory*, employed women were listed with marital titles. The only three jobs listed for women were: milliner, dressmaker, and midwife. The criteria for listing women in these occupations are not explained in the directory; it is not known if they were heads of households or owned property. It is therefore impossible to judge the extent to which they might have fairly represented the bulk of Burlington's female population.[46]

By the mid-1860s many of the business directories were becoming elaborate and detailed. The *Iowa State Gazeteer* for 1865 lists the category "Dress Makers," which mentions a total of twenty-four women dressmakers and one company. Two complete pages list "Milliners and Dealers in Millinery Goods," the majority of which were women. Under "Music Teachers," both women and men are listed, as is the case for "Restaurants." Only two other categories name women: "Stocking Manufacturers" claims one woman, Louisa Walther of Burlington, and "Vineyards" claims a Mrs. Disque of Burlington.[47]

In 1840, Isaac Galland's *Iowa Emigrant* listed state officials from the governor on down the line of power. Near the bottom, the name Ruth Kerr appears as a "laborer" at the Sauk and Fox agency. All the other names on the list were clearly male or were indeterminate due to the use of initials in place of a first name. An 1874 history of Polk County records the existence of a Mrs. Barton, who was apparently the only physician in the area until 1853. The story of Elizabeth H. Shearer Jones is told in a history of Cedar Rapids. Jones completed her education in 1844 and decided to move to Iowa to earn her own living and "carve out her fortune." Instead, she married a minister, but passed her aspirations on to her daughter who became a physician and a professor at Wellesley. Dr. Margaret V. Clark practiced in Waterloo, and Emily C. Stebbins became the first woman notary public in Iowa, commissioned in New Hampton in 1855. And Lucy Earle was the first postmistress of Muscatine during the 1860s.[48]

In 1900 one Iowa citizen recalled two women of Clinton County: Mary E. Spencer, who became the first female clerk in the Iowa legislature in 1870, and J. Ellen Foster, who

> . . . at an early day broke into the carefully guarded ranks of the legal fraternity, to the great disgust of some of the ancient fossils who had long stood guard on the outer walls of the moss covered fortress of "precedents." She not only practiced law, but she mounted the stump and told the men how to vote, while they fairly held their breath at her audacity.[49]

Unfortunately, only occasionally do the sources reveal a more detailed account of an employed frontierswoman. In Amelia Murdock Wing's reminiscences of her family's life in Clayton County during the 1850s and 1860s, not only does she describe her own career as a teacher, but she frequently speaks of her sister, Marian Murdock, who graduated from the Unitarian Theological Seminary in Meadville, Pennsylvania, and took up a pastorate in Humboldt, Iowa. While Marian initiated literary clubs and other cultural activities in Humboldt, she also developed a talent for preaching which brought her invitations to serve as a guest minister in neighboring towns and states. In passing, Wing also mentions a woman who wrote literary pieces for the county newspaper, another who filed on a homestead in the Dakotas, a woman railroad station agent who kept the station windows "full of Indian candlesticks and those fragile pink and white orchids," and Dr. Margaret Clark of Humboldt.[50]

If the record is incomplete concerning the ordinary achievers, it is more filled out in regard to the extraordinary women who have claimed attention for their accomplishments. One of these was Alice French, better known by her pen name of "Octave Thanet." Born in 1850 in Massachusetts, she emigrated with her parents to Davenport in 1857. Early in her life she displayed a flair for writing stories, a talent which she eventually parlayed into a reputation as one of the best authors of fiction in the West. Her most memorable works include *Knitters in the Sun, Otto the Knight, Stories of a Western Town,* and *Expiation.* Less well known was Pauline Given Swalm, a native of Wapello County, who graduated from Iowa College of Grinnell around 1870. An accomplished writer, she spent her professional life working as an editor, a newspaper reporter, and a public speaker. Rebecca Harrington Smith of Farmington wrote under the pseudonyms "An American Lady" and "Kate Harrington." She contributed many articles to newspapers and magazines as well as a response to *Uncle Tom's Cabin* titled *Emma Bartlett,* published in 1856. In the 1860s she turned to teaching school in Farmington, Keokuk, and Fort Madison. In that capacity she developed unique methods of instruction which she disseminated in a series of spellers, readers, stencil pictures, and teacher's manuals called the "Pollard Series," Pollard being her husband's name.[51]

Because writing was becoming acceptable work for women in the midnineteenth century, some women channeled their talents in that direction. Others were beginning to enter the professions. One such woman was Arabella Babb Mansfield of Mount Pleasant. Born in Des Moines County in 1846, she moved with her family to Mount Pleasant after her father's accidental death in 1850. In 1868 she married John M. Mansfield, a professor she met while attending Iowa Wesleyan University. She began her study of law in 1867 by "reading" in a law office in Mount Pleasant, a task which she continued after her marriage and which culminated in her successfully passing the Iowa bar exam in 1869. One of her examiners complimented her highly at the time of her examination:

> Your committee takes unusual pleasure in recommending the admission of Mrs. Mansfield, not only because she is the first lady who has applied for this authority in this state, but because in her examination she has given the very best rebuke possible to the imputation that ladies cannot qualify for the practice of law.[52]

Arabella Babb Mansfield was the first woman to be admitted to the bar in the United States; however, she never practiced law. Instead, she immersed herself alongside her husband in the academic world. Mansfield served Iowa Wesleyan for some years as Professor of English; then in 1881 she moved with her husband to DePauw University in Indiana where she held various academic posts, including that of Professor of History. She died in 1911 at age sixty-five, unremarked in her own lifetime as the nation's first licensed woman lawyer.[53]

Although professional achievements by women did not receive much at-

ARABELLA BABB MANSFIELD

tention, there *was* growing support for the idea that women should learn an employable skill. In 1872, the Estherville *Northern Vindicator* ran the following item:

> The great curse of woman is her dependence and helplessness. And these are caused mainly by her having no trade or profession by which she may earn a livelihood and be independent. . . . But this is far from being the prevalent opinion today. The common idea is that it is not woman's place to do any kind of work except unremunerative household drudgery. . . . We do not say that women should not cook or do housework, but we do say they should be allowed the same latitude of choice of the diversified labor of our country that men have.[54]

As paradoxical as this advice might seem, considering nineteenth-century values, the *Vindicator* did not stand alone. More and more voices were joining the chorus that supported occupations and interests outside the home for women. In 1884, the editor of the *Annals of Iowa* asked Dr. Jennie McCowen, a medical doctor, to examine the 1880 Iowa Census for signs of employed women. She discovered,

> . . . over eighty thousand women are at work at various gainful occupations. Women have money invested in almost every kind of industry and business enterprise in the State, and inquiry reveals an unexpected number of women managing business enterprises of various kinds.[55]

On a deeper level, McCowen's findings show the significant economic and philosophical changes regarding "women's sphere" which had occurred since the first white woman entered the Iowa region in 1828. Given the dramatic changes in attitudes towards women, it is not surprising that many Iowans took an active part in the emerging American women's rights movement as early as the 1850s.

WOMEN'S RIGHTS were publicly defined as an issue in the United States by the first women's rights convention held in Seneca Falls, New York in 1848. It was an event anticipated by Lucretia Mott and Elizabeth Cady Stanton since their rejection as full-fledged members of the World Antislavery Convention in London in 1840. When the Seneca Falls meeting drew a crowd of hundreds including a large number of men, Mott and Stanton were surprised and gratified. The convention issued a statement of rights based on the Declaration of Independence and even went so far as to declare women's right to the ballot box. Although the efforts of the Seneca Falls meeting met with unsparing ridicule in the public press, the conference seemed to put its finger on the sore and swollen pulse of many dissatisfied women who began organizing their own women's rights conventions during the next few years.

By the 1850s the actions of the primarily urban, eastern, middle- and upper-class movement were beginning to reverberate in frontier Iowa. In 1850 the *Burlington Hawk-Eye* ran a poem titled "Woman's Rights" which turned out to be a disclaimer of the issue.

> It is her right to watch beside
> The bed of sickness and pain;
> . . . . to train her sons
> So they may Senate chambers grace—
> . . . to be admired
> By every generous, manly heart,
>
> . . .
> What would she more, than to perform,
> On earth, life's holiest, sweetest tasks:
> When you a perfect woman find,
> No other rights than these, she asks.[56]

Similarly, in 1853 at the opening of the Iowa Female Collegiate Institute in Iowa City another tradition-bound poem accompanied the ceremony. Although the author declared in a patronizing tone that he "would essay t'uphold your modern sex, Espouse their right," he decried women's rights conventions. To him, they were "a novel riot! Of dames indignant and of mad reformers . . . Conventions called, astound the other gender." He invoked a stereotype when he concluded that women's true power and influence lay in their love and gentleness like the scion of all women, George Washington's sainted mother.[57]

Antifeminist sentiments such as these could not stem the growing tide of interest in "the woman question" as the era so often termed it. By the mid-1850s, suffrage agitation began in Iowa. In 1854, Frances Dana Gage, a women's rights advocate from Ohio, made a well-received lecture tour on behalf of woman suffrage through southern Iowa. In 1855 temperance reformer and suffragist Amelia Bloomer settled in Council Bluffs. In 1857, the Iowa State Teachers Association passed a resolution in favor of woman suffrage. And in 1858 a lyceum program in Keokuk County debated the question of equal rights for women.[58]

Increasing attention accorded women's rights in the 1850s may have seemed sudden and even capricious to many Iowans, but the roots of the women's rights issue extended back to the beginning of the colonization of North America. When the first settlers arrived, they brought their value systems with them: English ideas about what to eat, how to dress, and what constituted a proper house. English common law traditions influenced attitudes regarding the actions and status of women in the new society. Derived primarily from the legal writings of Sir William Blackstone, the delineation of legal restrictions on colonial American women was based on the concept of "civil death." Under this code, women could not sign contracts or own property, and had no right to their own earnings or to the guardianship of their own children. When a woman married she passed from her father's hands to her husband's. In the words of the law, a married couple became one, that one being the husband. The husband was to protect, support, and be responsible for certain debts and crimes of his wife, but he also totally controlled her and could even legally beat her for various infringements of marital rules.

The seeming harshness of civil death was modified somewhat, as were so many of the other ideas of the first settlers, by the demands of their new environment. Since Colonial America encompassed pioneer conditions, women by necessity had to run family businesses, make decisions, and handle money. Many Colonial women were thus afforded a certain degree of independence, which softened the sharp edges of the English common law traditions governing their behavior.

As American society prospered and became "civilized," its practices and ideals more closely resembled its European models. Among other trappings of civilization, civil death was strengthened in the early 1800s. But when the Industrial Revolution created leisured, wealthy, educated middle and upper classes, women soon discovered that they were articulate and intelligent enough to pinpoint the problems that civil death created for them. They had the time and energy to bring demands for some change in the system. The first feminists, then, were not the thousands of women flocking into the new factories; they were the middle- and upper-class women who were aware of and worried about issues such as the family property which passed from their fathers to their husbands with no thought or provision for the women's welfare. Yet when they attempted to speak about their legitimate concerns, or to approach a legislator to request reform, they were rebuked for leaving "women's sphere." Out of these actions and reactions the first women's rights movement in the United States burst forth.

In most of the western territories, the women's movement took on its own peculiar complexion. As in the thirteen original colonies, literal survival—more than civil death—consumed the energy and attention of early settlers. Certain western law codes reflected woman's importance to that survival and her contributions to molding society. In Iowa the first revisions of English common law began in 1840 when the territorial legislature declared that a married woman would be permitted to release her own dower rights (the property she brought to a marriage) and transfer her real estate by conveyance executed by herself and her husband. In 1851 Iowa women were granted the legal right to control their property.[59]

In the opinion of writer-lecturer Frances Dana Gage, the founders of Iowa "must have been more just than common men, or they would not at first have secured the property rights of the wife, and made her the joint guardian, with her husband, of her children." She concluded that Iowa was "the most moral and progressive, as well as the best-improved State, of its age, in all our country."[60] Ruth Gallaher agrees with Gage's opinion. According to her, legal rights came relatively early and without great bitterness in Iowa because,

> Pioneer life fostered independence and equality. Women who settled here have been, for the most part, intelligent and educated, while the lawmakers and judges have been responsive to the demand for reform when once their attention has been called to unjust treatment of women.[61]

Although both of these assessments seem slightly tinged by overstatement, social legislation concerning Iowa women was relatively liberal. In the area of divorce, for instance, laws and court decisions were as favorable to women as to men, while in the eastern states women like Frances Wright, Scottish-born author and lecturer, and Frances Kemble, English-born actress and author, lost both their property and children to their husbands in divorce actions. In Iowa, the first divorce legislation was passed by the legislative assembly of the Territory of Iowa, which met in 1838 and 1839. It delineated four causes for divorce: impotency, extreme cruelty, adultery, or willful desertion for one year. In 1842 and 1843 the assembly revised the divorce code to include four more grounds for divorce: bigamy, commission of a felony or infamous crime, habitual drunkenness after marriage, and personal indignities. The next major revision, the code of 1851, broadened the eighth cause for divorce to read "cannot live in peace and happiness." Perhaps the assembly found this wording too liberal in practice, for in its revision of 1860 the eighth cause was removed entirely and desertion was changed to two years.[62]

The Iowa legislature stayed out of the actual granting of divorces, leaving that task to circuit courts or the state supreme court. In 1844 the Iowa Constitution stated, "No divorce shall be granted by the legislature"; restated in the State Constitution of 1846: "No divorce shall be granted by the General Assembly"; and again in the 1857 constitution: "No divorce shall be granted by the General Assembly."[63] These provisions probably gave women greater access to divorce actions. Since the all-male legislature was generally not approachable by women during this era, especially on matters pertaining to divorce, the circuit and supreme courts may have offered them an authority that would listen.

Many women's rights advocates were committed to taking action against social problems, especially those that indirectly plagued women, such as "Demon Rum." Not only did many women consider it a pernicious evil which could have deleterious effects on anyone who drank to excess, they saw clearly that it threatened their source of support (their husbands). Without healthy husbands capable of working, many women found themselves stranded economically with a family to raise in a society that offered little in the way of vocational training, jobs, or charitable programs. According to Eleanor Flexner, women were concerned with temperance because

> . . . the law placed married women so much at the mercy of their husbands. What might be a moral injustice if the latter was a sober citizen became sheer tragedy if he were a heavy drinker who consumed not only his own earnings but his wife's, and reduced her and her children to destitution. . . . A combination of idleness, boredom, and misfortune could make a man the bane instead of the mainstay of his family, while his wife would have no legal redress.[64]

(Courtesy of the Everett D. Graff Collection, the Newberry Library, Chicago)

In response to their altruism as well as to their fears of destitution, many Iowa women, beginning in the 1840s and 1850s, banded together in temperance associations. A typical broadside of one of these early temperance unions carried a pictorial interpretation of women's role in temperance reform. Printed in Muscatine in 1850 for the Bloomington Union No. 1 of the Daughters of Temperance, it pictured a woman with her foot implanted firmly on a serpent while her one hand poured the contents of a jug of wine on the ground and the other hand held aloft a staff surmounted by a liberty cap.[65]

Temperance reform in the United States sprang from the ideals of the American Revolution, the medical lectures of Dr. Benjamin Rush in Philadelphia, and the reform fervor of the Jacksonian Era. It peaked around 1855 when thirteen states included alcohol prohibitory laws in their statutes, then receded during the Civil War period when abolitionism, armed warfare, and postwar reconstruction assumed center stage. By the 1870s, temperance reform reappeared with new vigor, first with the founding of the Prohibition party and then with the creation of the Woman's Christian Temperance Union. The WCTU was organized in Cleveland in 1874 with former Iowan Annie Wittenmyer as president and a young, newly converted temperance worker, Frances Willard, as its secretary. Shortly, Iowa's loosely organized temperance bands, unions, and societies aligned themselves with the WCTU. Not only were many WCTU locals established throughout Iowa, but the Benedict Home for "erring women" was created to help those women who fell prey to the poisonous effects of alcohol.[66] In the latter part of the nineteenth century, the WCTU became a comprehensive women's organization that worked for the education of women, social reform in many diverse areas, and suffragism.

IOWA WOMEN were attuned to issues other than social legislation and social problems. In 1854, when the Iowa State Agricultural Society announced its sponsorship of the first Iowa State Fair, several women complained bitterly that there were no prizes offered for "female equestrians." The president of the society responded by offering "a fine gold watch to the boldest and most graceful female equestrian who would enter for the prize." Ten competitors entered the contest and according to one fair-goer, they "attracted the greatest interest of any thing at the Fair."[67] Perhaps these women attracted such great attention partly because of the pomp and gallantry surrounding their competition:

> The ladies were mounted on fine horses, dressed in the most splendid style, each attended by a cavalier, and their first appearance on the fair grounds seemed to call forth the admiration of every body present. The committee directed, in order to test their skill, that each lady, accompanied by her cavalier, should in a gentle gait ride once around the circle, when the cavalier was to retire into the center, and then each lady could ride four times around the track at any speed she might choose.[68]

Spirits ran so high that the women were requested to return and exhibit their skills again the next day before a final decision could be made by the committee of judges. When the gold watch was awarded to one young woman, the judges' choice did not meet with the crowd's approval. A spectator reported, "Spontaneously as if by concert, men sprung up in all quarters of the field." In a few minutes $165 was collected, plus six months' tuition and board pledged for a Miss Hodges, the crowd's favorite.[69]

As pressing or exciting as these women's causes were to many Iowans, they did not seem to have much noticeable impact upon women's civil rights. Despite small victories in certain areas, the women's movement had not made any revolutionary gains by the time the Civil War broke out. During the war years the immediate problems of supplying the troops and emancipating the slaves pushed the campaign for women's rights into the background for even the most committed feminists. But when the war finally ended and feminists realized that women's rights were not to be an integral part of black rights as they had supposed, they pursued the cause of women's rights with vengeance. Some of these women, notably Elizabeth Cady Stanton, had already taken the position that the means to ameliorate women's lack of rights was through suffrage. Now, due to the Civil War debacle, more and more women began to view gaining the vote as the answer to their problems. Suffrage, they realized, was the key to political clout. Thus, by the late 1860s woman suffrage became the rallying cry, the organizing principle, and the panacea for the postwar women's rights movement in the United States.

The course of woman suffrage in Iowa, as in many other western states, had been influenced to some extent by ideas current in eastern states about the status of women. Frequently these influences from the East insinuated themselves into western regions and tended to erode women's freedoms. Woman suffrage was not considered during Iowa's constitutional convention in 1846. According to Ruth Gallaher, "the demand for 'women's rights' was just becoming articulate and the suggestion that women should vote and hold office was frankly ridiculed." By 1857, when the present constitution replaced the 1846 document, it too mandated that only "every white male citizen of the United States" who was twenty-one years old and a resident of Iowa for six months could vote within the state.[70]

After the Civil War a number of groups began calling for a reconsideration of the suffrage provision. Iowa suffragists, strengthened by disillusionment over the lack of a woman suffrage provision in the Fourteenth Amendment, looked to the Iowa legislature for redress. In addition, many Democrats, perhaps with an eye to bedeviling the Republicans then in power, supported a women's rights amendment to the Iowa Constitution. Probably most difficult to resist of all the pressure groups were the wives and daughters of the Republican members of the Iowa General Assembly who sought the right of suffrage for themselves.

When the Eleventh General Assembly convened in 1866 its members were confronted with demands for woman suffrage. In early January, the senate defeated a woman suffrage bill proposed by James Crookham of Oskaloosa. But by the end of January, the house approved a resolution stating that "the

Committee on Constitutional Amendments be instructed to inquire into the expediency of striking out the word 'male' where it occurs in the Constitution in relation to franchise.''[71] In mid-March, while the resolution was still in committee, twenty-six Iowa women submitted a petition to the house asking for a suffrage amendment to the Iowa Constitution which argued that women

> . . . represent nearly one half of the entire population of the State, and also one-half of its stability, intelligence, and virtue; that they are counted in the basis of representation, yet are governed and taxed without their consent, and punished for violation of law without judge or jury; and claiming further, that life, liberty, and property, are uncertain so long as the ballot, the only weapon of self-protection, is not in the hands of every citizen.[72]

The women's pleas went unheeded, for the next day the committee on constitutional amendments recommended to the house that it defeat the woman suffrage provision because the committee asserted that ''the substance thereof is the law now.'' House members were apparently satisfied to accept the committee's conclusions verbatim for they did not argue the falsity of the committee's phrase, ''is the law now.'' The woman suffrage issue received no further consideration from the Eleventh General Assembly. Suffrage for women was denied by the Iowa legislature just as it was denied by state legislatures in the East as well as in England. Although the activities and speeches of national women's rights advocates were reported by the Iowa press, especially by the *Burlington Hawk-Eye* whose editor was a firm proponent of woman suffrage, the General Assembly was too embroiled in the black suffrage issue to take much notice.[73]

The General Assembly's failure to approve woman suffrage in 1866 seemed to encourage increasing numbers of public debates on the issue by various organizations throughout Iowa. Both men and women turned out in large numbers to hear fiery lectures delivered by noted feminist speakers such as Anna Dickinson during 1866 and 1867. Pressure was renewed on the Twelfth General Assembly in 1868. On January 23, 1868, the house once again took up the suffrage question. After some discussion, Benjamin F. Murray of Winterset recommended that an earlier motion giving the right of suffrage to ''all men in the State of Iowa irrespective of race or color'' be amended by striking out the word ''men'' and replacing it with the words ''all persons of the age of 21 and upwards.''[74] After further discussion, the house referred the woman suffrage issue to the committee on constitutional amendments. When the committee stalled on taking any action, on March 31 William G. Wilson of Davis County introduced another woman suffrage resolution derived from the Declaration of Independence. Its text was a dramatic entreaty to the recalcitrant legislators.

> WHEREAS, We hold these truths to be self evident, that all men are created equal, and endowed by their Creator with certain inalienable

rights, that to secure these rights governments are instituted deriving their just powers from the consent of the governed; and,
WHEREAS, We believe "men," in the memorable document from which we quote, refers to the whole human race, regardless of nationality, or sex; and,
WHEREAS, We recognize the fact, that as a general principle, taxation and representation should be co-extensive; and,
WHEREAS, It is a fact that women are compelled to give allegiance, and pay taxes, to a government, in the enactment of whose laws, they have been, and still are, denied a voice, Therefore,
Be it resolved as the sense of this House, That steps should be taken looking towards a change in the constitution of this State so as to allow women the right of franchise, for the proper use of which, her quick perception, strong intellect, and above all, her high sense of right and justice, have proven her so well qualified.[75]

Being fully cognizant that his resolution would be sent to the committee on constitutional amendments, Wilson concluded his statement with the request that "the committee to whom this resolution must be referred . . . be instructed to report upon the same at an early day."[76]

Within a week, the committee reported back to the house that the majority of its members favored adoption of the woman suffrage resolution.[77] But for some unexplained reason, the committee's recommendaton was not put to a vote of the house. Perhaps it was once again overshadowed by the cause of black suffrage, which passed the General Assembly of Iowa on March 31, 1868, the same day that Wilson presented his woman suffrage resolution. Black male suffrage was approved by Iowa's male voters at the polls on November 3, 1868. Suffragists were not overly discouraged by this turn of events; rather they increased their efforts to have the word *male* removed from the Iowa Constitution as the word *black* had just been deleted.

Many Iowa women now began publicly to contribute to the increasingly vehement drive for woman suffrage. Annie N. Savery was the first Des Moines woman to admit in public that she would like to vote. She was joined on Iowa lecture platforms by Mattie Griffith, a young Mount Pleasant teacher, Mary A. Beavers, a former Civil War nurse, Arabella Babb Mansfield, the nation's first woman admitted to the bar, Alice Bird, an 1869 graduate of Iowa Wesleyan College, Nettie Sanford, author of a history of Marshall County, Mary Darwin, a particularly effective speaker from Burlington, and Mary E. Shelton, former Civil War nurse.[78]

During these years, nationally known suffragists such as Elizabeth Cady Stanton and Susan B. Anthony toured the Midwest in an effort to rally support for the suffrage crusade. After hearing a moving lecture by Stanton and Anthony in Galena, Illinois, a group of Dubuque women decided to organize an Iowa woman suffrage organization. In 1869 a call for a meeting was issued by Henrietta E. Wilson, Mary Newbury Adams, Laura G. Robinson, Lucy C.

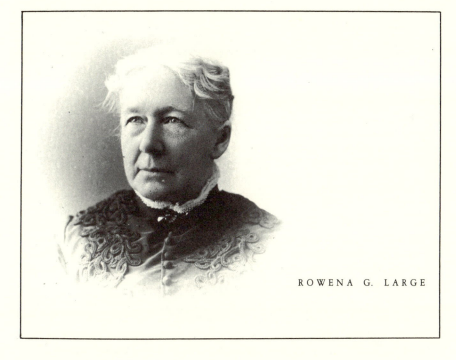

ROWENA G. LARGE

Graves, Rowena Guthrie Large, and Edna Snell. All of the women were wives of socially prominent Dubuque businessmen with the exception of Snell who was a teacher in Dubuque. They formed the Northern Iowa Woman Suffrage Association, which was met with combined excitement, interest, and ridicule from the citizens of Dubuque. Undeterred by public censure, the members of the association launched a suffrage crusade in the hope that their example would soon be followed in other towns across Iowa. This expectation went unfulfilled, but the fledgling Dubuque organization was given a major shot in the arm by a lyceum appearance by Stanton in 1869.[79]

For many Iowans, the cause of women's rights was still no more than a nonsensical passing fashion of the day. Jokes were told, cartoons printed, and one enterprising merchant even used the leader, "A Woman's Rights Meeting," to bring attention to his boot and shoe ad. But for others, it was a matter of the utmost importance, which demanded immediate action. As Gallaher explains, the "division of opinion was not between men and women, but between the progressives and conservatives of both sexes." As the debate intensified, the two factions rapidly multiplied their arguments for or against woman suffrage. The prosuffrage people argued that equal suffrage: (1) was socially just; (2) was of benefit to women whose effectiveness in professional endeavors depended on having a voice in government; (3) was of benefit to the nation since women would be able to vote on social issues, such as the family and labor problems, on which they were "natural" experts; (4) would abolish the moral double standard; (5) was advocated by the great statesmen of the times; (6) would socialize one-half of the human race; and (7) would make woman man's equal not in every respect, but only within her own limitations. The antisuffragists claimed that women (1) were naturally inferior, too emotional, and lacking the physical strength necessary to wield authority; (2) should stay in their sphere of the home; (3) were already represented by men who would effectively reform any wrongs against women; (4) were already taking jobs from men; (5) would become men's rivals and thus ruin the institutions of marriage and the family; (6) would be degraded by entering polling places; (7) would vote as their husbands and other males told them to; (8) should be silent according to scriptural command; (9) would dominate men and make them inferior; and (10) did not want to vote anyway. Moreover, the antis added, woman suffrage would destroy chivalry and open the question of black female suffrage.[80]

Although there obviously was no shortage of arguments, two of the "pro" positions were particularly popular with suffrage proponents. One was the "justice" argument; it was fair, just, and democratic to give female as well as male citizens the vote. The other was the "expediency" argument; give women the vote and they will clean up legislation as well as attracting the "right" kinds of people to the state. These two approaches persuaded large numbers of people to at least consider the idea of woman suffrage, so that by the time the Thirteenth Iowa General Assembly convened in 1870, it looked to many suffragists like the battle of woman suffrage was all but won.

An early house action indicated that progress was indeed occurring. For the first time in its history the Iowa House of Representatives appointed a woman, Mary E. Spencer of Clinton County, as clerk. Not only was she the first woman to hold the position, but she was to receive the same pay as a male clerk for her labors. Her name was put in nomination by a Republican who declared, "The State of Iowa, firmly attached as she is to the Car of Progress, cannot afford to be behind her sister States in the rights of woman." Although the scant fourteen Democrats in the House declared their gallantry and cast their votes for her to make the appointment unanimous, they facetiously nominated a second woman for another position, an action which created some laughter as well as some serious question as to whether women belonged in government at all.[81]

The legislators were forgiven their sport, and feminists throughout Iowa hailed Spencer's appointment as a milestone signifying progress for the state's women. They were similarly pleased when on January 20, 1870, the house resolved that the following evening Matilda Fletcher of Council Bluffs, a professional lyceum lecturer, would address legislators and other officials on the topic of woman suffrage in the Hall of the House.[82] Just a few days before her appearance, minority leader of the house John Irish proposed that a committee on constitutional amendments be appointed and be asked to report "a joint resolution amending the Constitution so as to confer on women the right to vote and hold office in Iowa." After some debate, this motion was amended to ask the committee to inquire into the expediency of giving women the vote, a proposal which passed by a large majority. The committee's report was issued on March 22 and it said, "It is inexpedient for the General Assembly to take any steps toward a change in the Constitution of the State so as to allow women the right of suffrage." A minority report stated that they *did* find it expedient to amend the Iowa Constitution to allow women the right to vote. Following some heated interchanges, a motion was made to postpone the house vote on the woman suffrage question until March 29, 1870.[83]

When the appointed day arrived the gallery and hallways were jammed, primarily with women. John Green of Davenport presented a long and eloquent address attempting to persuade the house to vote to substitute the minority report for the majority report. "We know the shackle and the slave of the past. Give to woman the ballot and Iowa will crown her loyalty by proclaiming in the truest and broadest sense, 'Liberty throughout the land and to all the people thereof.' " After Green's conclusion, a majority of the house members agreed to consider the minority report. The proceedings following this action included some light bantering, a great deal of intense debate, and high tension on the part of both participants and observers. When the vote was called, the house voted fifty-two to thirty-three for a joint resolution giving women the right to vote and to hold office in Iowa. The elated crowd in the galleries demonstrated its approval with resounding applause.[84]

The next day, March 30, the joint resolution was passed on to the senate.

> Mr. President—I herewith transmit a joint resolution which has been agreed to by the House of Representatives, providing for amendment to the constitution so as to allow women to vote, and rendering them eligible to seats in the General Assembly. The concurrence of the honorable Senate is respectfully asked.

When the resolution was read by the clerk, Mary E. Spencer, she received a standing ovation from the senators. There was little debate since many senators felt that the time had come to refer the issue to the voters of Iowa. The resolution passed the senate by thirty-two to eleven. Again the crowd roared approval of the legislators' action.[85]

Most suffragists were now convinced that the 1872 Iowa General Assembly would quickly give the resolution its required second approval. They thus believed that all that was necessary to insure the actual passage of woman suffrage in the state was to create a favorable climate of opinion among the male citizens who would be voting in the referendum. Towards this end many Iowa

MARY A. LIVERMORE

women swung into action on behalf of the resolution. Speakers and writers renewed their efforts, but many suffragists saw organization as the key to success.

The first organizing convention, held in Mount Pleasant in June, 1870, attracted the curious as well as those committed to the cause of woman suffrage. The convention's intense efforts produced the Iowa Woman Suffrage Association with membership open to all, regardless of race, color, or gender. The association gradually attracted the backing of articulate suffragists across the state and received additional aid when the lecture season brought three nationally known suffragist speakers to Iowa. In 1870 and 1871, Lucy Stone, Susan B. Anthony, and Mary Livermore presented their views on woman suffrage to audiences ranging from hostile, to tolerant, to enthusiastic. By the time Livermore ended her 1871 tour, she was convinced that Iowa would be the first state to pass woman suffrage because its women as a whole were "superior to the women of any other state."[86]

Unfortunately, the suffrage movement was increasingly plagued by internecine conflict, the taint of association with "free love" doctrines, and a growing public suspicion that woman suffrage could lead to social revolution and the demise of the family. Widely publicized in the early 1870s, the problems in the movement were nationwide and tended to adversely affect the Iowa suffrage crusade. By the time the Fourteenth General Assembly came into session in 1872, many Republican leaders considered woman suffrage a dead issue, or at least one that should be postponed until sufficient interest and faith in it was revived. John Irish and John Green, both former advocates of the issue, appeared to have been scared off by its free love association in the public mind. When Irish did introduce a woman suffrage motion, it was quickly defeated by the house. This proved to be the opening gambit in a long series of seesaw moves between the house and senate, indefinite postponements of woman suffrage resolutions, and finally one unsuccessful woman suffrage referendum to the voters in 1916. After a promising start, Iowa's suffrage movement lost its momentum in compromise and indecision. The state that was predicted to be first in the woman suffrage column did not allow its women to vote until 1920 when the Nineteenth Amendment was added to the United States Constitution, granting the right of suffrage to all women in the nation.

DESPITE its less than triumphant conclusion, the early Iowa woman suffrage movement spawned leaders whose talent and energy deserve notice. Most of them were pioneers on two fronts simultaneously; they settled in Iowa when it was still considered part of the American frontier and they were in the forefront of the campaign for equal rights for women. None of them were native-born Iowans, yet they, like so many other Iowa pioneers, found fertile ground to pursue their goals.

One of the lesser known of these early suffragists, Martha Coonley Callanan, was born in New York in 1826. She married James Callanan, a lawyer and a New York native, in 1846. Due to his business interests, the Callanans relocated in Des Moines in 1863 where they both became active in temperance and other social reform organizations. Since she had no children, Martha devoted many hours to causes such as the Benedict Home and the Des Moines Home for the Aged. She was one of the few suffragists in Iowa who owned substantial property of her own and thus had funds to donate to the cause of woman suffrage. She also opened her elegant Des Moines home as a headquarters for local suffrage leaders and activities. In 1870 she was one of the founders of the Iowa Equal Suffrage Association and later served several terms as its president. Because she preferred the pen to the public platform she edited and published the *Woman's Standard* rather than taking to the lecture circuit as did so many of her cosuffragists. When she died in 1901 she was far from being famous, yet her work on behalf on equal suffrage in Iowa would long be remembered.[87]

Mary Newbury Adams was another of the early Iowa feminists. Born in

MARY   NEWBURY   ADAMS

MARTHA   COONLEY   CALLANAN

Peru, Indiana in 1837, her girlhood included an above average education since her father was a proponent of equal education for women. Mary moved with her family to Dubuque in 1853, then in 1856 became a student at the Troy Female Seminary in Troy, New York. She had already agreed to marry a Dubuque attorney, Austin Adams, but only after her year at Troy was completed. Austin, like Mary's father, was a supporter of women's education so he was willing to wait for her, believing that she was "laying the foundation for a happier life." Mary's year at Troy was spent vacillating between a growing awareness that male students were treated in a different manner from female students and a sense of gratitude that she was getting a better education than most women. After her graduation in 1857, she married Austin and by the following year she bore the first of their five children. Being a mother was another ambivalent situation for Adams. She continued her course of study and reading in hopes of helping her children, yet she was often discouraged because child care consumed so much of her time and energy. In 1860 she wrote her sister, "Of all pitiable women, next to an old maid, is a childless wife. It is a great incentive for improvement to be a mother." In 1861 she added, "It is the easyest [*sic*] thing in the world for a mother to feel she is a mere drudge (at least it is for me). But when I look within I see that it is just the discipline a woman needs."[88]

In 1867 Adams launched a speaking career and organized a study club for Dubuque women in 1868. The following year she was hired by the *Dubuque Times* to cover the woman suffrage meeting at Galena, Illinois, which featured Stanton and Anthony. Although her first impulse was to present arguments against suffrage, she admitted that "my pail full of arguments is getting emptied and the pail for arguments for [suffrage] is filling up." She was a founder of the subsequent Northern Iowa Suffrage Association of Dubuque, but her full commitment to suffragism took years to develop. In the meantime, she continued speaking and writing on behalf of women as well as supporting the organization of women's clubs. By the time of her death in Dubuque in 1901 she had opened new paths for exploration by the women of younger generations.[89]

A better-known Iowa suffrage leader was Annie N. Savery. Born in London in 1831, she came to America with her parents while still a young child. Unlike Adams, her girlhood was marked by only a few years of common school education. In 1854 she married an inveterate speculator, James C. Savery of New York. The following year the couple settled in Des Moines and began a careening course of speculation and investment. Riding the crest of prosperity

ANNIE N. SAVERY

in the 1860s, James promoted the Hotel Savery in Des Moines and aided the settlement of immigrants to Iowa. Because they had no children, Annie was free to travel with her husband on his many business trips in the United States and Europe. She designed a course of self-study which she pursued conscientiously.[90]

In 1868 Savery alienated some of her admirers by delivering the first pro-suffrage address in Des Moines. She was one of the founders of the Iowa Equal Suffrage Association in 1870 and became a primary spokesperson for the Iowa movement by 1871. Savery abruptly lost her credibility when she refused to denounce free love advocate Victoria Woodhull, a champion of sexual freedom and birth control. After the woman suffrage amendment failed the house in 1872, at least partly as a result of the free love scandal, Iowa suffragists rejected any further aid from Savery. Although she continued her interest in women's rights for the rest of her life, she now channeled her energy into her other concerns, including free public education, the welfare of the poor and underprivileged, the Des Moines Library Association, and conditions in the Polk County Jail. When she died in 1891 many of her friends and acquaintances eulogized at great length her good works and pleasant spirit.[91]

The most noted early suffragist in Iowa was Amelia Bloomer. Born Amelia Jenks in New York in 1818, the daughter of a clothier, her education was limited to a few terms in township schools. In 1840 she married Dexter Bloomer, a lawyer in Seneca Falls, New York, where the couple took up residence. In 1848 Amelia attended the Seneca Falls Convention out of curiosity, but felt that the sentiments expressed were too radical for her taste. Six months later, Bloomer took a groundbreaking step of her own by beginning publication of *The Lily,* a temperance journal. Elizabeth Cady Stanton soon noticed Bloomer and her journal. She wooed Amelia to the cause of suffragism, and *The Lily* became the first newspaper in the United States to print women's rights literature.[92]

In 1851 Bloomer and *The Lily* were catapulted into the national limelight because of her adoption of a combination of skirt and trousers. The outfit was named for Bloomer due to her early and continued advocacy of it. She wore bloomers when she and her husband moved to Ohio in 1853 and then to the river community of Council Bluffs, Iowa, in 1855. En route to Iowa, the Bloomers traveled in a stagecoach with several other passengers, including the infamous Kit Carson. Amelia commented later that she saw nothing remarkable about him except his clothing; perhaps, if given the opportunity, he would have said the same of her.[93]

Since she had left *The Lily* behind her, Bloomer now threw herself into the reform of the ragged frontier town which was her new home. She lectured on temperance and women's enfranchisement thus becoming the only woman in Iowa before the Civil War to speak publicly on women's rights. When the Civil War broke out, Bloomer formed the Council Bluffs Soldiers' Aid Society, using

AMELIA BLOOMER

her own home as a headquarters. During the war years she exchanged her Bloomer costume for the more fashionable hoop skirt, but retained her liberal ideas. Increasingly, as the war ended and the decade waned, she spoke out on the subject of women's rights. In 1870 she helped found the Iowa Woman's Suffrage Association and served as its second president. During the following years she continued her writing on behalf of woman suffrage and contributed the chapter on Iowa for Stanton and Anthony's *History of Women's Suffrage*. Charles R. Tuttle, an early writer on Iowa and Bloomer's contemporary, described her as "a woman of decided views on temperance, slavery and other questions." He added that she was in the front rank of the Iowa suffrage movement and that both the Bloomers were highly respected for their contributions to their adopted state and town. Bloomer died in 1894 in her Council Bluffs home. A year after her death, her husband Dexter, always supportive of her work, published the *Life and Writings of Amelia Bloomer* in her memory.[94]

Although Bloomer is the most familiar name from the early years of the Iowa women's rights crusade, there were many others who swelled the ranks of suffragists. When studies of Iowa suffragists become more complete, it will be interesting to compare other suffragists' characteristics with those of Callanan, Savery, Adams, and Bloomer. These four women were born east of the Mississippi, were well educated (even if self-educated), had supportive husbands, and in three of the four cases, were childless. In addition, all four were middle- or upper-class women with wealth, leisure time, and expectations of involvement in social reformism. Since this profile roughly conforms to that of national suffrage leaders such as Elizabeth Cady Stanton, Lucretia Mott, and Lucy Stone, one might extrapolate that the lesser-known suffragists had similar characteristics. With the field of state and local history rapidly gaining ascendancy, the geneologists hard at work in the various archives across Iowa, and women's history becoming a substantial area of endeavor, it is entirely possible that the kind of woman who worked for woman suffrage may be more accurately identified and more thoroughly understood within the lifetime of the present generation.

Clearly, a measure of "strong-mindedness" was the one characteristic that all suffragists shared. By the same token, it was a quality found in those women who fought for improved education, moved into Iowa classrooms as teachers, and pushed into a variety of paid jobs. As twentieth-century women think about prominent early strong-minded women, the impulse may be to congratulate them for broadening women's perspectives at a time when cultural norms mitigated against any expansion of "women's sphere." Certainly congratulations are in order, but in the process of extending them, it is necessary to remember the thousands of ordinary women who confined their labor and accomplishments to their own homes. The women who stayed at home helped maintain the families and farms of Iowa and certainly theirs was an achievement which, in its own way, also required strong-mindedness.

CHAPTER SEVEN

Myths and Realities

THE underlying theme of this study has been an attempt to penetrate the myths and legends surrounding Iowa frontierswomen. A realistic and balanced picture of their daily lives emerges from the sources, but stereotypes are elusive amorphous concepts—difficult to dissect and even more troublesome to dispel. Rather than admit the less-than-colorful dailiness of frontierswomen's lives, twentieth-century Americans have found it easier to cling to the dramatic, sentimental portrayal of pioneer women presented by writers such as Hamlin Garland. Presenting his own mother's life on the Middle Border as representative of pioneer women, he wrote that she was burdened with a "grinding weight of drudgery, enduring a life centered around a "rude little cabin" and desperate poverty. According to Garland, this pathetic woman followed her husband to each new homestead "without complaining word" in spite of the "bitter pangs of doubt and unrest which strike through the woman's heart when called upon to leave her snug, safe fire for a ruder cabin in a strange land."[1]

Disclosing aspects of frontierswomen's lives, other than the brutal ones revealed by Garland, demands recognition that pioneer women are deserving of serious study. It also requires the collection and thorough examination of their source materials, although such use of women's resources is fraught with problems.

Because women customarily spent so much of their time in traditional roles behind hut or cabin walls, the source materials they left behind are usually of a personal, individualized nature. There is little in the way of public records, newspaper accounts, or census data directly related to women. What remains are the artifacts discarded by pioneer women—bits of material culture such as cream skimmers or candle molds. Such items are just beginning to be viewed as valuable tools by historians. If the historian is fortunate enough to resurrect some of the personal papers of frontierswomen, he or she may find that reading them objectively is an almost impossible task. Do letters from women on the frontier represent their true feelings about their makeshift homes, or were the letters intended to elicit sympathy, respect, or urge a move to the West by the home folks? Are reminiscences and memoirs reliable, or are they colored by the glow of passing time to a burnished hue that does not match reality? Did diaries and daybooks record anything of "note," or were they filled to the point of tedium with daily domestic routines—and if so, what does that in itself tell the historian about the writer's life?

As complex as these questions are, they represent only a superficial level of inquiry. One must also ask whether or not nineteenth-century frontierswomen accurately reflected upon their own lives or were they so accepting of a taxing social system that they were unaware and thus unable to adequately articulate the way they felt about the harshness and the limitations of their environment? Did women's running commentaries on the difficulty of men's tasks indicate that women had been socialized to think of their own labor as only supplementary? Or did women genuinely feel sympathetic with the demanding lot of their men?

In addition, frontiersmen's sources must be critically examined in relation to women's lives. Does the fact that men had little to say about women, children, and domestic affairs indicate their unconcern or disdain of them, or does it simply demonstrate that the culture pressured men to be more involved with the accepted "manly" pursuits of business and finance? Or does it only suggest that men were out of the home so much that they were not as cognizant of the nature of women's chores as women were of men's? It is known that at least some men seemed to recognize the crucial role of women's labor in subduing the frontier. At an old settlers' association meeting in Louisa County in 1860, one man noted that "Man has too long monopolized the entire attention of history and of the world. Men occupy themselves in celebrating and perpetuating the deeds and heroic action of men, while those of women are unmentioned and forgotten." But perhaps this was just a sop, for as another male "old settler" tellingly remarked to the women present, "Although not recognized as members of our organization, you are not forgotten."[2]

Complicating these impediments to interpretation are the distorted media images of the last hundred years. Dime novels, newspapers, radio, and television have presented their audiences with the drama and color or the pathos and hardship that they expected of the West. The media representations of frontier life have become so institutionalized that they now form what one historian has called a "collective mythology."[3] How does a scholar who has matured in a country steeped in such mythology discard it in order to enhance his or her own objectivity towards the western experience? Clearly, the questions arising from frontierswomen's source materials are legion and the answers few. Two characteristics of frontierswomen that have been assumed to be archetypal—debilitating loneliness and overwhelming fear of Indians—particularly prove to be at odds with reality. First, in considering the loneliness of frontierswomen, the generalized nature of a statement such as, "Isolation and loneliness was the portion of the border woman," must be recognized.[4] It, or a remark much like it, so frequently accompanies a sketch of frontierswomen that it has become trite. Indeed, woman after woman did lament the fact that she did not see another white woman for months at a time after migrating westward. Scores of women sorrowed endlessly over the loss of their friends and relatives; others spent many tearful hours as a result of their solitude.[5]

Such complaints tell only part of the story. In Iowa such grievances were usually short-lived because most pioneers, desirous of companionship and the safety of numbers, settled loosely structured neighborhoods. One Iowa woman, Jessie Newcomb, admitted that "after the first two years things were not quite so bad." Even during her first year on the Iowa frontier another woman "did not feel the least lonely or homesick," and yet another cogently noted, "Not homesick much."[6]

Towns, stage routes, and eventually railroads followed lines of settlement, so that few frontierspeople were truly isolated for very long.[7] One woman described the rapidly changing landscape in Iowa before the Civil War.

> We saw the country change almost overnight, it seemed, from raw, un-broken prairie to a settled community with schools and churches. We saw the coming of the railroad, the building of roads and bridges, and the growth of a nearby county seat from a scraggly village to a thriving, up-to-date town with all the improvements of a city.[8]

Another woman who arrived in Iowa in 1835 offered a similar obervation: "The summer of 1837 we raised considerable grain, our health was good and we prospered finally." A decade later, she added the comment that "nothing of importance occurred save that the country was fast improving and settling up . . . all was peace and tranquility in our little home."[9]

Since women were more likely to be tied to their homes, they were less likely than men to be affected by rapid changes in transportation and other technological advancements. Yet, many women managed to create domestic, women-centered activities to relieve their seclusion. Quiltings provided a com-bination social-work event. Other women organized farmers' wives' societies to create an "opportunity for discussing informally those things pertaining to the duties of a farmer's wife, and a relief from the routine and monotony of such a life." And others formed literary societies to add sociability to their lives while "improving" their minds at the same time. Social activities provided a focal point for many women. Mary J. Mason, daughter of Chief Justice Charles Mason, frequently attended the many balls, circuses, and masquerades held in her home city of Burlington. Virginia Ivins of Keokuk retained pleasant memories of sleighing on the river ice, parties in elegant homes, and dancing

174

"the night away" at fancy dress balls.[10] Even many country women were not necessarily cut off from society. One of these rural women recalled,

> For years after moving to the country I still took part in various activities in town. I often drove to Lue's [her sister] and to my parents' home. In fact I was away in the afternoon almost daily. Marion [her husband] always inquired at noon if I had plans to go. If so, he harnessed a horse and left it hitched to buggy all ready for me.[11]

Another rural woman believed that social life in her area was actually fostered by the slow pace of country living. People "took time for all day visits and the few social gatherings were all the more enjoyed for being held so seldom." She added that in one sense even the difficulties of frontier life aided the pioneers' social interaction for the "hardships they endured together bound them with ties of sympathy and understanding."[12]

Religion formed the basis for social cohesion in many pioneer communities. Camp meetings were well attended, drawing people who pitched tents and remained as long as two or three weeks to participate in the various activities. Formal churches were organized very rapidly in most areas. Congregations first met in the local schoolhouse and later erected a simple log structure shared by several denominations until each could afford its own individual building. Churches sponsored "socials" which involved both good fellowship and bounteous food. They also supported Sunday schools, prayer meetings, singing schools, and musical groups, all of which were regularly attended by the congregation. Wedding ceremonies were often accompanied by a celebration or a raucous charivari which "enlivened the neighborhood until morning" with the noise of "cow-bells, whistles, horse-fiddles, and drumming on tin pans."[13]

Other social gatherings revolved around the settlers' own homes. Log-rollings to clear the land, house-raisings to build a dwelling, and house-warmings to celebrate a home's completion all called for feasting, dancing, and games. Cards, checkers, songfests, or a Saturday night dance in someone's cabin to the music of the local fiddler also brought friends and neighbors together. And affairs such as apple-parings, husking bees, and harvest days, although demanding women's labor in preparing meals and other refreshments, "gave the farmer's wife an opportunity to exchange ideas with her neighbors, gave her a change of surroundings and scenes and an opporunity to form lifelong friendships."[14]

Christmas was another time of festivity for Iowa pioneers. Although the presents were frequently as simple as a pair of handmade wristlets, frontier people appreciated the day of leisure to share some time with their families as well as to enjoy the inevitable feast.[15] As Matilda Peitzke Paul portrayed the pioneers' Christmas,

The pioneer enjoyed life much better and had many more good times than people do now and were so much more appreciative than now. Christmas was always a day of great joy. We always got one present which cost from five to ten cents also got a little candy and an apple.[16]

For many years Paul treasured "a little tin pail about the size of a ½ pint cup" which she received one Christmas. "It was painted green," she recalled, "with the word Girl painted on it in yellow. . . . I can still feel the joy I had when I looked at it and to know it was mine."[17]

The Fourth of July was another recognized occasion for conviviality. For some Iowans it meant an elaborate dinner and ball, such as the one held at the Roe House in Fort Madison in 1859. For others it signified impromptu toasts, local orators, singing, and colorful parades. For still others, it brought lemonade, firecrackers, and horse racing. For the very lucky, the Fourth was sometimes even attended by "Fire Works! Fire Works! Confectionary, Nuts, Cigars, and everything else with which to Celebrate the Glorious 4th of July."[18] But for most pioneers, the Fourth was probably much like the one described by a young German woman:

Father took us to the grove where the crowd was gathered to hear the Declaration of Independence read, band music played, and "My Country Tis of Thee" sung. Then we had a fine lunch from the basket we carried with us and mother and I stayed in the grove and visited with some German women while father took Anna [her sister] to a dance pavilion.[19]

As the Iowa frontier became more settled, a variety of professional entertainments appeared to augment social events and festivities. In 1885, a new dancing school opened in Burlington offering instruction in popular dances such as quadrilles, waltzes, and fancy dances including the Hornpipe and Highland Fling. Later that same year in Burlington a "Grand Balloon Ascension and Exhibition of Fire Works" was accompanied by a contest of "Female Equestrianship."[20]

One of the more exotic amusements was the circus. Many circuses ventured across the Mississippi River into Iowa in the mid-1850s. For fifty cents for a box seat or twenty-five cents for a "pit" seat, one could view the "Grand Olympic Arena and North American Circus" in Davenport in 1855. It was shortly followed by another circus in Burlington, which offered "The Unrivalled Female Equestrian" as its leading attraction. Within the year another circus appeared in Burlington with an Indian exhibition. By the early 1860s, Waterloo was the scene of a "multicerial Combination Circus! and Homohippocal Amphitheatre!" which featured "Madamoiselle Ida—The Fairy Equestrianne." A few years later a Fairfield circus promised "A Magnificent Array of Unparalleled Novelties," and another advertised a display of "Wild Animals and Rare Birds." By 1868 "Yankee Robinson's Consolidated Shows" attempted to out-dazzle all its competitors with a "Mass Meeting of all the Rare Specimens of Zoology from both Hemispheres" combined with a "Ballet of Beautiful Ladies, and Other Artistes, which will Completely Revolutionize the Programme."[21]

After Matilda Peitzke Paul attended one of these traveling circuses in Riceville in 1868, she characterized it as "one great event." She and her brothers and sisters almost missed the main show since they lacked the money to buy tickets, but when they hung around the doorway longingly, a kind door-tender invited them inside to see the show. She declared that they "felt well repaid for our trip by seeing an elephant, camel, bear and monkey," all admittedly rather strange sights to early Iowans.[22]

Elaborate and splashy shows on the Iowa prairie during the mid-nineteenth century were welcome entertainments, but some pioneers cherished fonder memories of homey pursuits such as spelling bees or lyceums at the local school. Camaraderie among neighbors and family was a continuing source of contentment. As one woman said, "Sometimes I had to make a bed in the kitchen when company stayed overnight, but although we were crowded, we were all well and happy so it didn't make much difference." Other Iowans thought family times were the best. "There was nothing," one Iowa woman wrote, "which gave us more joy than the long winter evenings when we would all gather around the fire—mother knitting, father reading aloud, and we children cracking nuts."[23]

When Frances Dana Gage visited Iowa in 1854 she surveyed the situation of frontierswomen and quickly dismissed any notions about their being downcast due to isolation. "Not one—not one desponding wife or mother did we find," she reported, "not one willing to go back and live in the old States."[24] A resident of the state confirmed Gage's assessment, writing to her husband's family in 1856:

> I have not been homesick or felt so awfully as I have heard folks tell of who come out here people as a general thing clothe the west with to much romance I take it its not all gold that shines anywhere I thought this was the best place for a poor man to get a living with nothing but his hands to help himself with and I think so now. I can't say I like the west as well as I do New England yet I think it is better for me to be here.[25]

It appears, then, that feelings of isolation and loneliness are relative. If some of us record that we are lonely in our high-rise, industralized, technological world of the 1980s, will historians someday praise our fortitude in surviving such a harsh world, or will they pity us our cruel situation? And if they should take either of these positions, would they be accurate in their interpretation? Clearly, they would face the same problems that today's historians confront in attempting to assess the position of nineteenth-century frontierswomen. Pinpointing the tenor and character of frontierswomen's attitudes toward Native Americans is as elusive as judging their degree of loneliness. The myth is that white women feared and hated Native Americans; that they were raped and carried off by Native Americans in vast numbers; and that they always chose to return to their homes rather than to remain with their captors.

Convictions like these were originally presented to an already prejudiced American public by means of captivity narratives. These were usually based on fact, laced rather liberally with fiction, and sold for profit to an audience thirsty for what Roy H. Pearce calls "penny dreadfuls." They almost always involve the odyssey of a courageous soul torn from civilization who prevails over primitive evil and is eventually restored once again to civilization. In women's captivity narratives, the odyssey is translated into a saga of abduction, rape, and escape; a thrilling story that was meant to titillate Americans of the nineteenth century while venting their hatred of Native Americans.[26]

Here again, the few scholars who have looked beyond captivity narratives have unearthed significant, but seemingly contradictory, views of Native Americans by white women. One scholar argues that white women were socialized by nineteenth-century civilization into seeing Indians as primitive, savage, and dirty. Because society relegated women to the position of "civilizers" they had no choice but to visualize Native Americans as "representative of an alien and depraved culture, decidedly inferior to their own." As guardians of public morality, women were given to understand one basic fact before they left their eastern homes—"The American Indian is a savage." Once on the frontier, women described the Native Americans they encountered as filthy, foolish, degraded; in all ways a "symbol of defeat and failure," the antithesis of the white female, who embodied progress and success.[27]

Researcher Dawn L. Gherman maintained that all white women did *not* see themselves as civilizers and Native Americans as primitive savages. To the contrary, she believed that many women actually had a streak of "wildness" in their makeup which caused them to occasionally long for the natural, the free, and the unrestrained qualities which they perceived in the lives of Native Americans.[28] If indeed she was on the right track in her assertion that some women fantasized themselves as "white squaws," it might be a threatening concept for many Americans to consider, given their anti-Indian attitude.

As with the traditions regarding the loneliness of women on the frontier, such intricacies of interpretation exiist that frontierswomen's true feelings towards Native Americans are difficult to detect. In Iowa, only hints are present as to the day-by-day working relationship between white settlers and indigenous peoples. It is true that there were some actual outbreaks of violence when Indian groups attempted to resist white encroachment on their lands. Black Hawk is famous, or infamous, depending on one's perspective, for leading his people in an ill-fated resistance movement against the whites in 1831. The Sauk and the Fox, pressured by their restriction to a small land area, carried on internecine warfare in the 1840s which not only diminished their own numbers, but also largely destroyed the peaceful Winnebago who were placed on the so-called neutral ground between them. And the starving Wahpeton Sioux will long be remembered for their depredation of the white settlement at Spirit Lake in 1857.[29]

But more illuminating are the numerous occasions on which white Iowans panicked as a result of unfounded rumors of Indian attacks. Although the area was actually cleared of its native inhabitants rapidly and with little trouble to the whites, the settlers still harbored inordinate fears of uprisings. Fort Dodge was closed in 1853 after only three quiet years of protecting settlers from Indians, yet frequent alarms were still sounded in the region. Author Ruth S. Beitz points out that "reports of some Indian attacks were greatly exaggerated, but the danger seemed real enough to send the settlers scurrying into stoutly built homes for protection." In another western county in the mid-1850s, the appearance of two hungry Cherokee caused an all-night guard to be posted, the members of which almost shot a wandering cow in their panic.[30]

After the much-publicized "massacre" at Spirit Lake, rumors increased in frequency and intensity. Beitz reported that in 1857 "the rumor that a band of warlike red men was coming caused some families . . . to drive from Ida Grove to take shelter at Benjamin Dobson's and Mason's Grove, where they 'forted up.' " In 1858, other false reports spurred the formation of the Iowa Frontier Guard in Iowa's lake region.[31]

On hearing of the New Ulm, Minnesota, clash between white settlers and displaced Indians in 1862, northwestern Iowa reached a fever pitch of excitement and fear. Federal aid was granted, troops were sent, and blockhouses such as Fort Defiance were built in response to the settlers' demands for protection from the supposedly impending attacks. The building of a Sioux City fort, hastily begun on the strength of a scare story, was discontinued when no attack materialized. The stockade, never completed, was finally sold as building timbers and firewood.[32]

Iowans were also quick to abandon their homes in the face of hysterical reports. In April 1857, a group of families left their homes on the Little Sioux River when one of their number told them that "Indians are up on the Des Moines River and are going to come down to kill us." After camping out overnight, they went on to Sac City where they sent out spies "to see if there were any Indians around." Sighting no Indians, they finally realized that they had deserted their homes for no reason.[33] In 1858, a group of Webster City settlers similarly fled their homes:

> With the terror of the Spirit Lake massacre vividly in mind mother and we children hastily grabbed a few belongings, packed a basket of food, and

father took us in the wagon to Webster City. From there a regular train of
wagons, loaded mostly with women and children, started for Boonesboro.
Father returned to our home, determined to defend it.

When the party was compelled to stop for the night, they formed their wagons
into a circle, built a fire, and "everybody sat up and talked all night." By the
following morning "messengers came bearing the good news that the alarm
was false, and so the whole company turned around and reached home that
night, tired but safe."[34]

These unfounded rumors continued well into the 1870s. When one Pennsylvania family moved to Webster City in 1875 they did so with trepidation.
Because of the stories they had heard about Indian raids in Iowa, they determined that three hollow logs would be placed in their front yard, one to hide
each member of the family. About the same time, a young man in the Ackley
area roused his sleeping neighbors with the cry, "Wild Indians." The next
morning it was discovered that the "Indians" were in truth only a hired man
carrying a huge featherbed through the late night shadows.[35]

Beyond the apparent fright, other reactions of Iowa pioneer women to
Native Americans during Iowa's frontier years are difficult to ascertain. Dis-
counting popularized accounts such as Abbie Gardner-Sharp's *The Spirit Lake
Massacre and the Captivity of Miss Abbie Gardner,* women's remarks about
Native Americans are fragmentary, yet their general tone is revealing.

Caroline Phelps, a newly married young woman who moved to southeastern Iowa in the 1830s with her husband in order to trade with the Indians, frequently complained that many of them drank to excess. She did not mention
that they were violent towards whites when drunk, but only that they were aggravating and troublesome. Although they would sometimes "fight wretch-
edly" among themselves when drinking, Phelps wrote, "I never was very much
afraid of them." On the other hand, Phelps also took note of the many Indian
women who befriended her; the Indian doctor who treated her young
daughter; the Indian ceremonies, dances, and parades which she attended; and
the grief her family felt when their Indian helper was killed in an accident. On
his death, she wrote,

> We felt his loss very much, my children cryed for poor John as we called
> him, as much as though he had been a relative. He was their friend truly
> they missed his singing, he used to fix a drum and then sing and drum and
> have them and the little papooses dance.[36]

When Phelps found certain aspects of Native American culture distasteful,
she seemed to deal with them in a stoic manner. At one point she found the
odor disagreeable around her home because it was near an Indian burial site
which had corpses placed upon the ground. "One day we was eating dinner,"
she recalled, "our doors all open and in came our big dog with a dead indians

arm and a hand, right into the house, I took the tongs to take it back to where it belonged." Another time, she sheltered some Indian children until their drunken parents were sober enough to resume cooking and caring for them.[37]

Unlike Phelps, most Iowa women had only brief dealings with their Native American neighbors. A Rodman woman in the mid-1840s said that she could remember groups of them traveling through and camping in the region, but never causing the settlers any difficulty. A Marshall County woman in the late 1840s had a somewhat more detailed story to recount. She and her husband traded food and incidentals regularly with local Indians, one of whom physically attacked her husband over a trade disagreement. Although the altercation ended with little serious damage to either party, she felt rather depressed about the incident until a large group of his people came to her cabin to apologize for his behavior. According to her, "they spoke very indignantly of the Indian who had so badly misused us, and said he was a bad Indian, and often quarreled and fought with his own people." Her recollection was that "most of them treated us kindly as long as they stayed there" in spite of several other quarrels between her family and the tribespeople.[38]

Several women had personal interchanges with Iowa Indians. One received a proposal of marriage from the son of a "powerful Indian chieftain," who in her words "was willing to give up his wickiup and adopt the ways of a white man if necessary, to win his suit." A relative of hers related another turn of events involving a young woman named Viola who

> . . . used to play with a little Indian girl who asked her to stay for supper one day. She was going to until the old Indian Grandmother heard about it and got up and went over to the pot of food cooking on the stove—lifted the lid and spit in it! Viola ran out the door and didn't stop until she got home! She never asked to eat there again![39]

During the 1860s a young German woman watched Indians roam the woods around her family's home and camp in tents in the fields between settlers' houses. She was pleased when her Aunt Liza "would come and take us to this Indian village and the squaws gave us beads which we treasured greatly." She also remembered "a very nice Indian" who visited her family and "spoke English very well." Another of her memories centered on "a young buck" who would follow her and other family members in the cornfield as they harvested corn and would amuse them by singing to them in a "monotone" and "rather weird" way.[40]

By the 1870s and 1880s, Native Americans were no more than stories or pictures in books for many Iowa women. One in particular remembered her grandmother's likeness of Black Hawk, a figure that to her seemed to belong to "ancient history." She was amazed that there were still a few people living in Burlington "who had actually seen him in the flesh." She mused, "It makes me realize how immature is our American civilization when I think that, although I, myself, never saw an Indian in my childhood except under a circus tent, there were residents of my home town who had known Iowa when only the so-called savages lived there.''[41]

CLEARLY, the comments cited by early Iowa women belie the usual representation of frontierswomen as perpetual enemies of Native Americans. Certainly some women were negative in their views. As one stated, although she ''had no neighbors nor company save a straggling land hunter, or the native Indians, the latter were seldom if ever very welcome visitors'' as far as she was concerned. Yet other women demonstrated a more balanced perspective. One woman who migrated to Iowa in 1854 and survived many Indian ''scares,'' commented simply, ''Have seen a great many Indians and they used to dance their war dance in our house, but they never offered to harm us in any way.''[42]

The examination of these two assumed traits of frontierswomen— loneliness and fear of Native Americans—demonstrates that for every one myth about women, there are several levels of reality. By testing the myths against the conditions on one specific frontier, in this case the Iowa frontier, it is apparent that there are many perceptions of frontierswomen's reality. Despite the usual interpretations of their lives, they did not all resist the westward trek, suffer on the trail, and harbor bitterness against their menfolk. They did not all wither in body and spirit in the demanding surroundings they encountered. They did not all feel exploited by the huge amounts of time and energy required to subdue the prairie. Rather, many frontierswomen looked with favor upon the idea of a western relocation, triumphed over the many challenges presented by the new environment, and prevailed over the additional difficulties imposed by wartime conditions or separation from established homes. Their reactions were as varied as the women themselves. As this study demonstrates, the Iowa frontier evoked a wide range of reactions from frontierswomen rather than generalized, stereotypical ones. To fully understand the lives, concerns, and emotions of frontierswomen, the serious student must continually raise the question, where does myth end and reality begin?

NOTES

ABBREVIATIONS
AI   *The Annals of Iowa*
IJH   *Iowa Journal of History*
IJHP   *Iowa Journal of History and Politics*
ISHD-HS   Iowa State Historical Department, Division of the Historical Society
ISHD-MA   Iowa State Historical Department, Division of Museum and Archives
ISU   Iowa State University
PAL   *The Palimpsest*
UI   The University of Iowa

INTRODUCTION

1. Frederick Jackson Turner, *The Frontier in American History* (New York: Holt, Rinehart and Winston, 1962), 4.

2. George F. Parker, *The American Pioneer and His Story* (Iowa City: State Historical Society, 1922), 3.

3. T. A. Larson, "Women's Role in the American West," *Montana: the Magazine of Western History* 34 (Summer 1974): 4.

4. Ibid.

5. Karen Gregg, "American Women in College History Texts: A Content Analysis," *Illinois Journal of Education* 43 (March-April 1972): 10.

6. Glenda Riley, "Is Clio Still Sexist? Women's History in Recent American History Texts," *Teaching History: A Journal of Methods*, vol. 1, no. 1 (Spring 1976): 15.

7. Ray and Victoria Ginger, "Feminist and Family History: Some Pitfalls," *Labor History* 12 (Fall 1971): 617.

8. Donald V. Gawronski, *History: Meaning and Method* (Glenview, Illinois: Scott, Foresman and Company, 1975), 94–95.

9. Brett Harvey Vuolo, "Pioneer Diaries: The Untold Story of the West," *Ms.*, vol. 3, no. 11 (May 1975): 36.

10. Glenda Riley, "Images of the Frontierswoman: Iowa as a Case Study," *The Western Historical Quarterly*, vol. 8, no. 2 (April 1977): 189–202.

11. Leland L. Sage, *A History of Iowa* (Ames: Iowa State University Press, 1974), 92; Thomas D. Clark, *The Great American Frontier: A Story of Western Pioneering* (Indianapolis: Bobbs-Merrill, 1975), 324–26.

12. *Census of Iowa*, 1880, 200–201.

13. Ibid.

14. Michael Conzen, "Local Migration Systems in Nineteenth-Century Iowa," *Geographical Review* 64 (July 1974): 360.

15. Mary Newbury Adams to her aunt, 1854, Austin Adams Family Papers, Special Collections, ISU Library, Ames, Iowa.

CHAPTER ONE

1. *Eddyville Free Press*, April 16, 1855.

2. Diary of Mary Alice Shutes, 1862, ISHD-MA, Des Moines.

3. Allan G. Bogue, *From Prairie to Corn Belt: Farming on the Illinois and Iowa Prairies in the Nineteenth Century* (Chicago: Quadrangle Books, 1968), 14–16; Frank Herriott, "Whence Came the Pioneers of Iowa?" AI, 3rd ser. 7 (April and July 1906): 372–73; Joel H. Silbey, "Proslavery Sentiment in Iowa," IJHP, vol. 55, no. 4 (October 1957): 289–92; and Morton M. Rosenberg, *Iowa on the Eve of the Civil War: A Decade of Frontier Politics* (Norman: University of Oklahoma Press, 1972), 14–19.

4. Bogue, *From Prairie to Corn Belt,* 22; Ray Allen Billington, *Westward Expansion: A History of the American Frontier,* 3rd ed. (New York: Macmillan, 1967), 5; John Mack Faragher, *Women and Men on the Overland Trail* (New Haven: Yale University Press, 1979), 18.

5. Margaret E. Archer Murray, "Memoir of the William Archer Family," AI, 3rd ser. 39 (Summer 1968): 357–71; Sarah Welch Nossaman, "Pioneering at Bonaparte and near Pella," AI, 3rd ser. 13 (October 1922): 441–46; May Lacey Crowder, "Pioneer Life in Palo Alto County," IJHP 46 (April 1948): 156–61; Abbie Mott Benedict, "My Early Days in Iowa," AI, 3rd ser. 17 (July 1930): 323–31; David T. Nelson, ed., *The Diary of Elisabeth Koren, 1853–1855* (Minneapolis: Norwegian-American Historical Association, 1955), ix; Diary of Eliza Ann McAuley Egbert, 1852, California Historical Society, San Francisco; Kitturah Penton Belknap, "Reminiscences," ISHD-HS, Iowa City.

6. "When Men Were Hard to Get," PAL, vol. 50, no. 11 (November 1969): 629.

7. *Iowa News* (Dubuque), June 24, 1837; Nathan H. Parker, *Iowa As It Is In 1856* (Chicago: Keen and Lee, 1856), 52.

8. Kathryn Kish Sklar, *Catharine Beecher: A Study in American Domesticity* (New York: Norton, 1976), 97–98, 102; John B. Newhall, *A Glimpse of Iowa in 1846* (Iowa City: State Historical Society, 1957), 61.

9. Johnny Faragher and Christine Stansell, "Women and Their Families on the Overland Trail to California and Oregon, 1842–1867," *Feminist Studies,* vol. 2, no. 2/3 (1975): 153.

10. "From New York to Iowa," PAL 2 (October 1921): 313.

11. Clarence R. Aurner, "Story of An Iowa Woman, PAL 28 (June 1947): 164; Catherine Margaret Haun, "A Woman's Trip Across the Plains," 1849, Catherine Margaret Haun Papers, Huntington Library, San Marino, California.

12. "Seventy Years in Iowa," AI, 3rd ser. 27 (October 1945): 98–100.

13. For a more detailed discussion of these factors, see Martin Ridge, "Why They Went West," *The American West,* vol. 1, no. 3 (Summer 1964): 40–57.

14. "Seventy Years in Iowa," 97.

15. George R. Carroll, *Pioneer Life In and Around Cedar Rapids, Iowa, from 1839 to 1849* (Cedar Rapids, 1895), 4.

16. "Seventy Years in Iowa," 98; Florence Call Cowles, *Early Algona. The Story of Our Pioneers, 1854–1874* (Des Moines: Register and Tribune, 1929), 86.

17. *Iowa News,* August 5, 1837.

18. Henry Nash Smith, *Virgin Land: The American West as Symbol and Myth* (New York: Vintage Books, 1950), 138; Roderick Nash, *Wilderness and the American Mind* (New Haven: Yale University Press, 1973), xv; *Eddyville Free Press,* April 16, 1855.

19. Annette Kolodny, *The Lay of the Land* (Chapel Hill: University of North Carolina Press, 1975), 136.

20. Amelia Murdock Wing, "Early Days in Clayton County," AI, 3rd ser. 27 (April 1946): 257.

21. Bessie L. Lyon, "Grandmother's Story," PAL 5 (January 1924): 3; Edith H. Hurlbutt, "Pioneer Experiences in Keokuk County, 1858–1874," IJH 52 (October 1954): 327; Crowder, "Pioneer Life in Palo Alto County," 156; Katharine Horack, "In Quest of a Prairie Home," PAL 5 (July 1924): 251.

22. Lyon, "Grandmother's Story," 6.

23. Emery S. Bartlett to his children and grandchildren, December 1911, ISHD-HS; Diary of Mary Alice Shutes, 1862, ISHD-MA; *Census of the Territory of Iowa,* 1838, 190–91.

24. *Census of the Territory of Iowa,* 1840, 3.

25. *Census of Iowa,* 1880, 57.

26. Leo E. Oliva, "Our Frontier Heritage and the Environment," *The American West,* vol. 9, no. 1 (January 1972): 46.

27. William J. Petersen, "Women in History," PAL 38 (April 1957): 131.

28. Bogue, *From Prairie to Corn Belt,* 23–24.

29. Diary of Mary Alice Shutes, 1862, ISHD-MA.

30. "Seventy Years in Iowa," 98.

31. Benedict, "My Early Days in Iowa," 331; Hurlbutt, "Pioneer Experiences in Keokuk County, 1858-1874," 327-28.

32. B. J. Zenor, "By Covered Wagon to the Promised Land," *The American West,* vol. 6, no. 4 (July 1974): 32-33.

33. Belknap, "Reminiscences," ISHD-HS.

34. Ibid.

35. Ibid.

36. Zenor, "By Covered Wagon to the Promised Land," 37.

37. Belknap, "Reminiscences," ISHD-HS; Diary of Mary Alice Shutes, 1862; ISHD-MA; Haun, "A Woman's Trip Across the Plains," Haun Papers, Huntington Library.

38. Horack, "In Quest of a Prairie Home," 252-53.

39. Ibid.

40. Diary of Mary St. John, 1858, ISHD-HS.

41. Diary of Mary Alice Shutes, 1862, ISHD-HS.

42. Haun, "A Woman's Trip Across the Plains," Haun Papers, Huntington Library.

43. Ibid.

44. Diary of Mary Alice Shutes, 1862, ISHD-MA.

45. Quoted in Bruce E. Mahan, "By Boat and Covered Wagon," PAL, vol. 49, no. 7 (July 1968): 247-48.

46. Isaac Galland, *Galland's Iowa Emigrant: Containing a Map, and General Descriptions of Iowa Territory* (Chillicothe, Ohio, 1840), 3.

47. Horack, "In Quest of a Prairie Home," 254.

48. Ibid.

49. Lyon, "Grandmother's Story," 4.

50. "Seventy Years in Iowa," 104.

51. For a discussion of women and children on the Overland Trail see Georgia Willis Read, "Women and Children on the Oregon-California Trail in the Gold-Rush Years," *Missouri Historical Review,* vol. 34, no. 1 (October 1944): 1-23.

52. "From New York to Iowa," 318-19; Murray, "Memoir of the William Archer Family," 369; "From New York to Iowa," 319.

53. Cowles, *Early Algona,* 122; Crowder, "Pioneer Life in Palo Alto County," 161.

54. Lyon, "Grandmother's Story," 4.

55. Diary of Mary Alice Shutes, 1862, ISHD-MA.

56. Ibid.

57. Ruth Barnes Moynihan, "Children and Young People on the Overland Trail," *The Western Historical Quarterly,* vol. 6, no. 3 (July 1975): 292.

58. Crowder, "Pioneer Life in Palo Alto County," 156; Harriet Connor Brown, *Grandmother Brown's Hundred Years, 1827-1927* (Boston: Little, Brown, 1929), 103.

59. Crowder, "Pioneer Life in Palo Alto County," 156.

60. "From New York to Iowa," 319; "Seventy Years in Iowa," 104; Diary of Mary Alice Shutes, 1862, ISHD-MA; Horack, "In Quest of a Prairie Home," 254.

61. Belknap, "Reminiscences," ISHD-HS.

62. Diary of Mary Alice Shutes, 1862, ISHD-MA.

63. "From New York to Iowa," 319.

64. Crowder, "Pioneer Life in Palo Alto County," 162.

65. Horack, "In Quest of a Prairie Home," 254.

66. Diary of Jane Augusta Gould, ISHD-HS.

67. Belknap, "Reminiscences," ISHD-HS.

68. Ibid.

69. Ibid.; Diary of Jane Augusta Gould, 1862, ISHD-HS; Diary of Mary Alice Shutes, 1862, ISHD-MA.

70. Diary of Jane Augusta Gould, 1862, ISHD-HS; Robert L. Munkres, "Wives, Mothers, Daughters: Women's Life on the Road West," *Annals of Wyoming* 42 (October 1970): 198.

71. Diary of Jane Augusta Gould, 1862, ISHD-HS.

72. Diary of Esther Pillsbury, 1863, ISHD-HS; Crowder, "Pioneer Life in Palo Alto County," 162.

73. Haun, "A Woman's Trip Across the Plains," Haun Papers, Huntington Library; Belknap, "Reminiscences," ISHD-HS; Lyon, "Grandmother's Story," 4-5.

74. "From New York to Iowa," 315.

75. Faragher and Stansell, "Women and Their Families on the Overland Trail," 160.
76. Diary of Jane Augusta Gould, 1862, ISHD-HS; Diary of Mary Alice Shutes, 1862, ISHD-MA; Diary of Esther Pillsbury, 1863, ISHD-HS.
77. Cowles, *Early Algona,* 123; Horack, "In Quest of a Prairie Home," 253; "Seventy Years in Iowa," 104; Journal of Mrs. E. A. Hadley, 1851, Caroline Phelps Papers, ISHD-HS.
78. Diary of Caroline Phelps, 1830, ISHD-HS.
79. Diary of Mary Alice Shutes, 1862, ISHD-MA.
80. Francis E. Whitly, "Across the Mississippi," PAL 15 (January 1934): 13-14.
81. Ibid., 15.
82. Allan G. Bogue, "Social Theory and the Pioneer," *Agricultural History,* vol. 34, no. 1 (January 1960): 24.
83. Katherine Clinton, "Pioneer Women in Chicago, 1833-1837," *Journal of the West,* vol. 12, no. 2 (April 1973): 324.

CHAPTER TWO

1. Julie Roy Jeffrey, *Frontier Women: The Trans-Mississippi West, 1840-1880* (New York: Hill and Wang, 1979), 3-13.
2. Hamlin Garland, *A Pioneer Mother* (Chicago: The Bookfellows, 1922); Hamlin Garland, *A Son of the Middle Border* (Chicago: Macmillan, 1927); Everett Dick, *The Sod-House Frontier, 1854-1890* (New York: D. Appleton-Century, 1937); Everett Dick, "Sunbonnet and Calico, the Homesteader's Consort," *Nebraska History* 47 (March 1966): 3-13; William W. Fowler, *Woman on the American Frontier* (1879; reprint, New York: Source Books Press, 1970); Emerson Hough, *The Passing of the Frontier* (New Haven: Yale University Press, 1921); Christine Stansell, "Women on the Great Plains, 1865-1890," *Women's Studies,* vol. 4, no. 1 (1976): 87-98.
3. Sarah Welch Nossaman, "Pioneering at Bonaparte and Near Pella," AI, 3rd ser. 13 (October 1922): 441.
4. Emery S. Bartlett to his children and grandchildren, December 1911, ISHD-MA, Des Moines.
5. Diary of Mary Alice Shutes, 1862, ISHD-MA; Abbie Mott Benedict, "My Early Days in Iowa," AI, 3rd ser. 17 (July 1930): 341.
6. Edith H. Hurlbutt, "Pioneer Experiences in Keokuk County, 1858-1874," IJH 52 (October 1954): 328, 330; Emery S. Bartlett to his children and grandchildren, December 1911, ISHD-HS; May Lacey Crowder, "Pioneer Life in Palo Alto County," IJHP 46 (April 1948): 162.
7. "From New York to Iowa," PAL 2 (October 1921): 319-20.
8. Kitturah Penton Belknap, "Reminiscences," ISHD-HS, Iowa City.
9. Diary of Mary Alice Shutes, 1862, ISHD-MA; Matilda Peitzke Paul, "Recollections," ISHD-HS; Margaret E. Archer Murray, "Memoir of the William Archer Family," AI, 3rd ser. 39 (Fall 1968): 472.
10. Crowder, "Pioneer Life in Palo Alto County," 156; Bessie L. Lyon, "Grandmother's Story," PAL 5 (January 1924): 6.
11. Crowder, "Pioneer Life in Palo Alto County," 164.
12. Nossaman, "Pioneering at Bonaparte and Near Pella," 447; Mary Ann Ferrin Davidson, "An Autobiography and a Reminiscence," AI, 3rd ser. 37 (Spring 1964): 248.
13. Davidson, 247; Belknap, "Reminiscences," ISHD-HS; Benedict, "My Early Days in Iowa," 332; "From New York to Iowa," 320.
14. Susan I. Dubell, "A Pioneer Home," PAL 12 (December 1931): 445-46.
15. Ibid.
16. Katharine Horack, "In Quest of a Prairie Home," PAL 5 (July 1924): 255; Florence Call Cowles, *Early Algona. The Story of Our Pioneers, 1854-1874* (Des Moines: Register and Tribune, 1929), 97; Sarah Kenyon to relatives, February 23, 1861, John Kenyon Papers, ISHD-HS.
17. Crowder, "Pioneer Life in Palo Alto County," 167.
18. Nossaman, "Pioneering at Bonaparte and Near Pella," 450.
19. Diary of Mary Alice Shutes, 1862, ISHD-MA; David T. Nelson, ed., *The Diary of Elisabeth Koren, 1853-1855* (Minneapolis: Norwegian-American Historical Association, 1955), 110.

20. Harriet Bonebright-Closz, *Reminiscences of Newcastle, Iowa, 1848* (Des Moines: Historical Department of Iowa, 1921), 33.

21. Dubell, "A Pioneer Home," 447; Paul, "Recollections," ISHD-HS; Crowder, "Pioneer Life in Palo Alto County," 165–67.

22. William J. Petersen, "The Pioneer Cabin," IJHP 36 (October 1938): 407–08.

23. David E. Schob, *Hired Hands and Plowboys: Farm Labor in the Midwest, 1815–1860* (Urbana: University of Illinois Press, 1975); Margaret E. Archer Murray, "Memoir of the William Archer Family," AI, 3rd ser. 39 (Summer 1968): 363–65; Paul, "Recollections," ISHD-HS; Crowder, "Pioneer Life in Palo Alto County," 173.

24. *Fairfield Ledger*, March 31, 1864.

25. Crowder, "Pioneer Life in Palo Alto County," 167; Benedict, "My Early Days in Iowa," 332.

26. Diary of Mary St. John, 1858, and Sarah Kenyon to relatives, August 29, 1856, John Kenyon Papers, ISHD-HS; Crowder, "Pioneer Life in Palo Alto County," 165–67; George R. Carroll, *Pioneer Life In and Around Cedar Rapids, Iowa, from 1839 to 1849* (Cedar Rapids, 1895), 22.

27. Belknap, "Reminiscences," ISHD-HS.

28. Ibid.

29. Crowder, "Pioneer Life in Palo Alto County," 156–68.

30. Benedict, "My Early Days in Iowa," 351–52.

31. Dick, "Sunbonnet and Calico," 4; Benedict, "My Early Days in Iowa," 342–43.

32. Ibid.

33. Petersen, "The Pioneer Cabin," 403.

34. Ibid., 402–04.

35. Ibid., 404.

36. Bonebright-Closz, *Reminiscences of Newcastle*, 33.

37. Petersen, "The Pioneer Cabin," 395; Nelson, ed., *Diary of Elisabeth Koren*, 113; Benedict, "My Early Days in Iowa," 337.

38. Ibid.

39. Paul, "Recollections," ISHD-HS.

40. Mildred Sharp, "Early Cabins in Iowa," PAL 2 (January 1921): 25.

41. Diary of Mary Alice Shutes, 1862, ISHD-MA; Lida L. Greene, ed., "Diary of a Young Girl," AI, 3rd ser. 36 (Fall 1962): 442.

42. Crowder, "Pioneer Life in Palo Alto County," 167; Cowles, *Early Algona*, 117; Lyon, "Grandmother's Story," 7.

43. Dubell, "A Pioneer Home," 452–53.

44. Belknap, "Reminiscences," ISHD-HS; Emery S. Bartlett to his children and grandchildren, December 1911, ISHD-HS.

45. Murray, "Memoir of the William Archer Family," 358; Petersen, "The Pioneer Cabin," 405.

46. Benedict, "My Early Days in Iowa," 332; Paul, "Recollections," and Sarah Kenyon to relatives, December 1, 1856, August 29, 1856, John Kenyon Papers, ISHD-HS.

47. Belknap, "Reminiscences," ISHD-HS.

48. Janette Murray, "Women of North Tama," IJHP 41 (July 1943): 288.

49. Horack, "In Quest of a Prairie Home," 255.

50. Paul, "Recollections," and DDiary of Caroline Phelps, 1832, ISHD-HS.

51. Benedict, "My Early Days in Iowa," 339; Nossaman, "Pioneering at Bonaparte and Near Pella," 453.

52. Emery S. Bartlett to his children and grandchildren, December 1911, ISHD-HS.

53. Benedict, "My Early Days in Iowa," 342–43.

54. Crowder, "Pioneer Life in Palo Alto County," 166.

55. Murray, "Women of North Tama," 287–88; Murray, "Memoir of the William Archer Family," 363; Benedict, "My Early Days in Iowa," 359.

56. Paul, "Recollections," ISHD-HS; Nossaman, "Pioneering at Bonaparte and Near Pella," 449; Bonebright-Closz, *Reminiscences of Newcastle*, 45; Dick, "Sunbonnet and Calico," 5.

57. Nossaman, "Pioneering at Bonaparte and Near Pella," 448; Paul, "Recollections," ISHD-HS.

58. Nossaman, "Pioneering at Bonaparte and Near Pella, "448; Murray, "Memoir of the William Archer Family," 358–59; Mary S. Ellis to relatives, September 25, 1856, John Kenyon Papers, ISHD-HS.

59. Dubell, "A Pioneer Home," 448–49.

60. Ibid., 448.

61. Crowder, "Pioneer Life in Palo Alto County," 168–70.

62. Diary of Caroline Phelps, 1830, and Paul, "Recollections," ISHD-HS.

63. Murray, "Memoir of the William Archer Family," 471; "From New York to Iowa," 317.

64. Alice L. Longley Papers, ISHD-MA.

65. Benedict, "My Early Days in Iowa," 332; Crowder, "Pioneer Life in Palo Alto County," 168.

66. Murray, "Memoir of the William Archer Family," 473.

67. Emery S. Bartlett to his children and grandchildren, December 1911, ISHD-MA.

68. *Burlington Daily Hawk-Eye,* January 4, 1859; *The Daily Gate City* (Keokuk), July 10, 1857.

69. "Seventy Years in Iowa," AI, 3rd ser. 27 (October 1945): 101.

70. Petersen, "The Pioneer Cabin," 405; Horack, "In Quest of a Prairie Home," 257; Paul, "Recollections," ISHD-HS; Nossaman, "Pioneering at Bonaparte and Near Pella," 450.

71. See Kathryn Kish Sklar, *Catharine Beecher: A Study in American Domesticity* (New York: Norton, 1976).

72. Jeffrey, *Frontier Women,* 10–12.

73. Michael Conzen, "Local Migration Systems in Nineteenth-Century Iowa," *Geographical Review* 64 (July 1974): 339–61.

74. Diary of Caroline Phelps, 1833, ISHD-HS.

75. Paul, "Recollections," ISHD-HS.

76. Nelson, ed., *Diary of Elisabeth Koren,* 114.

77. Gerda Lerner, "Placing Women in History: Definitions and Challenges," *Feminist Studies,* vol. 3, no. 1/2 (Fall 1975): 7.

78. Ibid., 6.

79. Mary S. Ellis to relatives, December 1, 1856, Februaary 22, 1857, John Kenyon Papers, ISHD-HS.

80. "From New York to Iowa," 320–21; Carroll, *Pioneer Life In and Around Cedar Rapids,* 34; Ruth A. Gallaher, "From Connecticut to Iowa," PAL 22 (March 1941): 70.

CHAPTER THREE

1. Irene Neu, "Women in the American Economy," *Indiana History Bulletin,* vol. 54. no. 12 (December 1977): 173.

2. Edeen Martin, "Frontier Marriage and the Status Quo," *Westport Historical Quarterly* 10 (March 1975): 100.

3. George C. Duffield, "An Iowa Settler's Homestead," AI, 3rd ser. 6 (October 1903): 210.

4. Sarah Kenyon to relatives, October 1856, John Kenyon Papers, ISHD-HS, Iowa City; Bessie L. Lyon, "Grandmother's Story," PAL 5 (January 1924): 7.

5. May Lacey Crowder, "Pioneer Life in Palo Alto County," IJHP 46 (April 1948): 171–72.

6. Janette Murray, "Women of North Tama," IJHP 41 (July 1943): 296.

7. Edith H. Hurlbutt, "Pioneer Experiences in Keokuk County, 1858–1874," IJH 52 (October 1954): 335.

8. Matilda Peitzke Paul, "Recollections," ISHD-HS.

9. Lyon, "Grandmother's Story," 7.

10. Amelia Murdock Wing, "Early Days in Clayton County," AI., 3rd ser. 27 (April 1946): 280.

11. Sarah Welch Nossaman, "Pioneering at Bonaparte and Near Pella," AI, 3rd ser. 13 (October 1922): 450.

12. Kitturah Penton Belknap, "Reminiscences," ISHD-HS; Nossaman, "Pioneering at Bonaparte and Near Pella," 446.

13. Belknap, "Reminiscences."

14. Harriet Bonebright-Closz, *Reminiscences of Newcastle, Iowa,* 1848 (Des Moines: Historical Department of Iowa, 1921), 172; Belknap, "Reminiscences," ISHD-HS.

15. Mary S. Ellis to relatives, September 25, 1856, John Kenyon Papers, ISHD-HS; United States Department of Commerce and Bureau of the Census, *Historical Statistics of the United States: Colonial Times to 1970*, pt. I (Washington, D.C.: GPO, 1975), 209; Lida L. Greene, ed., "Diary of a Young Girl," AI, 3rd ser. 36 (Fall 1962): 454; Wing, "Early Days in Clayton County," 280.

16. *Iowa Sentinel* (Fairfield), January 11, 1855, February 26, 1857; *Waterloo Courier*, April 9, 1861; Hurlbutt, "Pioneer Experiences in Keokuk County," 335.

17. Mary S. Ellis to relatives, November 7, 1856, John Kenyon Papers, ISHD-HS; Wing, "Early Days in Clayton County," 341.

18. William W. Fowler, *Woman on the American Frontier* (1879; reprint, New York: Source Books Press, 1970), 189; William J. Petersen, "The Pioneer Cabin," IJHP 36 (October 1938): 395; Nossaman, "Pioneering at Bonaparte and Near Pella," 450–51.

19. E. W. Howe, "Provincial Peculiarities of Western Life," *The Forum* 14 (September 1892): 96–97.

20. Crowder, "Pioneer Life in Palo Alto County," 167.

21. Emery S. Bartlett to his children and grandchildren, December 1911, ISHD-MA, Des Moines.

22. George F. Parker, *Iowa, Pioneer Foundations*, 2 vols. (Iowa City: State Historical Society, 1940), 2: 81.

23. Belknap, "Reminiscences," ISHD-HS.

24. Murray, "Women of North Tama," 299.

25. Paul, "Recollections," ISHD-HS.

26. Murray, "Women of North Tama," 298.

27. Wing, "Early Days in Clayton County," 280; Paul, "Recollections," ISHD-HS; Sarah Kenyon to relatives, February 23, 1861, John Kenyon Papers, ISHD-HS.

28. Margaret E. Archer Murray, "Memoir of the William Archer Family," AI, 3rd ser. 39 (Summer 1968): 360; Mary S. Ellis to relatives, December 1, 1856, John Kenyon Papers, ISHD-HS; B. F. Gue, "Early Iowa Reminiscences," *Iowa Historical Records* 16 (July 1900): 110.

29. Bonebright-Closz, *Reminiscences of Newcastle*, 39; Murray, "Memoir of the William Archer Family," 361.

30. Wing, "Early Days in Clayton County," 279.

31. Paul, "Recollections," ISHD-HS.

32. Murray, "Women of North Tama," 299.

33. *Wapello Intelligencer*, May 31, 1853.

34. Murray, "Memoir of the William Archer Family," 361.

35. Belknap, "Reminiscences," ISHD-HS.

36. Ibid.

37. Ibid.

38. Bonebright-Closz, *Reminiscences of Newcastle*, 121.

39. Clara A. Dodge to Augustus C. Dodge, January 19, 1841, Clara A. Dodge Papers, ISHD-HS; Sarah Kenyon to relatives, December 1, 1856, October 9, 1862, John Kenyon Papers, ISHD-HS.

40. Ibid.

41. *DuBuque Visitor*, July 6, 1836, September 14, 1836; *Iowa News* (Dubuque), July 1, 1837, July 15, 1837; *Iowa Territorial Gazette and Advertiser*, June 1, 1844.

42. *Burlington Daily Hawk-Eye and Telegraph*, July 23, 1855; April 5, 1859.

43. *Weekly Observer* (Mt. Pleasant), April 20, 1854; *Fairfield Ledger*, September 24, 1863.

44. *Frontier Guardian*, October 17, 1849.

45. Crowder, "Pioneer Life in Palo Alto County," 180–81.

46. Alice L. Longley, handwritten notation, Alice L. Longley Papers, ISHD-MA.

47. *Davenport Gazette*, June 14, 1855; *Burlington Daily Hawk-Eye*, January 1, 1859, January 7, 1859, April 1, 1859.

48. *Fairfield Ledger*, December 5, 1861, March 14, 1861, July 2, 1863; *Waterloo Courier*, September 18, 1860, December 17, 1868.

49. Floy Lawrence Emhoff, "A Pioneer School Teacher in Central Iowa—Alice Money Lawrence," IJHP 33 (October 1935): 378–79.

50. Ibid., 383.

51. George F. Robeson, "The Early Iowans," PAL 4 (September 1923): 299.
52. Wing, "Early Days in Clayton County," 282; *Burlington Daily Hawk-Eye,* June 18, 1859; *Fairfield Ledger,* August 27, 1863; *Waterloo Courier,* August 30, 1866.
53. Ramona Evans, "Fashions in the Fifties," PAL 10 (January 1929): 21–22.
54. *Fairfield Ledger,* March 31, 1870.
55. *Burlington Daily Hawk-Eye,* April 3, 1863.
56. Bonebright-Closz, *Reminiscences of Newcastle,* 124.
57. Murray, "Women of North Tama," 289.
58. Wing, "Early Days in Clayton County," 283.
59. Ibid., 284.
60. Murray, "Women of North Tama," 306.
61. Ibid., 307.
62. Susan Dubell, "Rural Pioneering," PAL 22 (August 1941): 236.
63. Paul, "Recollections," ISHD-HS.
64. William J. Petersen, "Diseases and Doctors in Pioneer Iowa," IJH, vol. 49, no. 2 (April 1951): 97–99.
65. Crowder, "Pioneer Life in Palo Alto County," 183.
66. Bonebright-Closz, *Reminiscences of Newcastle,* 227.
67. Paul, "Recollections," ISHD-HS.
68. Bonebright-Closz, *Reminiscences of Newcastle,* 229.
69. *Waterloo Courier,* December 2, 1862, December 30, 1863, January 20, 1864, February 3, 1864, February 17, 1864, October 29, 1868.
70. Clara A. Dodge to Augustus C. Dodge, January 28, 1841, Clara A. Dodge Papers, ISHD-HS.
71. Sarah Kenyon to relatives, March 18, 1860, John Kenyon Papers, ISHD-HS.
72. Mary Ann Ferrin Davidson, "An Autobiography and a Reminiscence," AI, 3rd ser. 37 (Spring 1864): 249–51.
73. Green, ed., "Diary of a Young Girl," 448–55.
74. Leo E. Oliva, "Our Frontier Heritage and the Environment," *The American West,* vol. 9, no. 1 (January 1972): 45; John Ise, *Sod and Stubble: The Story of a Kansas Homestead* (New York: Wilson-Erickson, 1936), 40.
75. *Burlington Daily Hawk-Eye,* January 5, 1859.
76. Ellen R. Fenn, "Sweepin' Out the Fabled Ghosts," *The Iowan,* vol. 14, no. 1 (Fall 1965): 50.
77. Fred W. Lorch, "Molly Clemen's Note Book," PAL 10 (October 1929): 361.
78. Belknap, "Reminiscences," ISHD-HS.
79. Ann Douglas Wood, " 'The Fashionable Diseases': Women's Complaints and Their Treatment in Nineteenth-Century America," *Journal of Interdisciplinary History,* vol. 4, no. 1 (Summer 1973): 26–27.
80. For a fuller discussion of this issue see Carroll Smith-Rosenberg and Charles Rosenberg, "The Female Animal: Medical and Biological Views of Woman and Her Role in Nineteenth-Century America," *Journal of American History* 60 (September 1973): 332–56, and Linda Gordon, *Woman's Body, Woman's Right: A Social History of Birth Control in America* (New York: Grossman, 1976).
81. *Fairfield Ledger,* December 5, 1861.
82. *Wapello Intelligencer,* February 27, 1854; *Iowa Capital Reporter,* April 5, 1854; *Burlington Daily Hawk-Eye,* January 4, 1859, July 15, 1866.
83. *Burlington Daily Hawk-Eye,* January 6, 1859.
84. *Waterloo Courier,* June 5, 1861; *Fairfield Ledger,* June 24, 1869.
85. Paul, "Recollections," ISHD-HS.
86. Crowder, "Pioneer Life in Palo Alto County," 160.
87. Paul, "Recollections," ISHD-HS.
88. Blaine T. Williams, "The Frontier Family: Demographic Fact and Historical Myth," in Harold M. Hollingsworth, ed., *Essays on the American West* (Austin: University of Texas Press, 1969), 40–65.
89. Duffield, "An Iowa Settler's Homestead," 210.
90. Diary of Caroline Phelps, 1830, ISHD-HS; Paul, "Recollections," ISHD-HS.
91. Sarah Kenyon to relatives, October 11, 1861, John Kenyon Papers, ISHD-HS.
92. Gilbert C. Fite, *The Farmers' Frontier, 1865–1900* (New York: Holt, Rinehart and Winston, 1966), 47.

93. Murray, "Memoir of the William Archer Family," 362, 370; Belknap, "Reminiscences," ISHD-HS.

94. Crowder, "Pioneer Life in Palo Alto County," 178, 181.

95. Paul, "Recollections," ISHD-HS; Hurlbutt, "Pioneer Experiences in Keokuk County," 331; Emery S. Bartlett to his children and grandchildren, December 1911, ISHD-HS.

CHAPTER FOUR

1. See Robert G. Athern, *In Search of Canaan: Black Migration to Kansas, 1879-1880* (Lawrence: Regents Press of Kansas, 1978); and Nell I. Painter, *Exodusters: Black Migration to Kansas after Reconstruction* (New York: Knopf, 1977).

2. *Territorial Census of Iowa*, 1840, 3.

3. *Burlington Tri-Weekly Telegraph*, August 27, 1850.

4. *Census of Iowa*, 1880, 17.

5. Sarah Kenyon to relatives, August 29, 1856, John Kenyon Papers, ISHD-HS, Iowa City.

6. According to W. Sherman Savage, *Blacks in the West* (Westport, Connecticut: Greenwood Press, 1976), 201, Kansas experienced one of the largest increases, from 627 blacks in 1860 to 17,108 in 1870. Other states undergoing significant increases in black population included Colorado, from 48 blacks in 1860 to 436 in 1870; Minnesota, from 259 blacks in 1860 to 759 in 1870; Nebraska, from 82 blacks in 1860 to 789 in 1870; and New Mexico, from 85 blacks in 1860 to 172 in 1870.

7. Kenneth W. Porter, *The Negro on the American Frontier* (New York: Arno Press, 1971), 2, 524.

8. May Lacey Crowder, "Pioneer Life in Palo Alto County," IJHP 46 (April 1948): 159.

9. Minnie M. Brown, "Black Women in American Agriculture," *Agricultural History*, vol. 50, no. 1 (January 1976): 204-8; Diary of Eliza Ann Bartlett, Grinnell College Library, Grinnell, Iowa.

10. In this case inference history may also be taken to mean that white male attitudes and actions towards blacks were representative of white females because (1) men and women in most regions tended to share racial values during this era, and (2) because there is no significant evidence of women's deviation from or resistance to such attitudes.

11. Frank Herriott, "Whence Came the Pioneers of Iowa?" AI, 3rd ser. 7 (April and July 1906): 372, 464-65.

12. Joel H. Silbey, "Proslavery Sentiment in Iowa," IJHP, vol. 55, no. 4 (October 1957): 289-93, 313-14.

13. Morton M. Rosenberg, *Iowa on the Eve of the Civil War: A Decade of Frontier Politics* (Norman: University of Oklahoma Press, 1972), 15-16.

14. Louis Pelzer, "The Negro and Slavery in Early Iowa," IJHP, vol. 2, no. 4 (October 1904): 471; William M. Donnel, *Pioneers of Marion County* (Des Moines, 1872), 70-75.

15. John E. Briggs, *History of Social Legislation in Iowa* (Iowa City: State Historical Society, 1915), 34-35; Eugene H. Berwanger, *The Frontier Against Slavery: Western Anti-Negro Prejudice and the Slavery Extension Controversy* (Urbana: University of Illinois Press, 1967), 32-33.

16. Benjamin F. Shambaugh, *The Constitutions of Iowa* (Iowa City: State Historical Society, 1934), 143.

17. Benjamin Shambaugh, ed., *Fragments of the Debates of the Iowa Constitutional Conventions of 1844 and 1846* (Iowa City: State Historical Society, 1900), 221.

18. *Constitution of the State of Iowa*, Adopted in Convention, November 1, 1844 (Washington, 1844), 3-10. *Constitution of the State of Iowa*, Adopted in Convention, May 18, 1846 (Washington, 1846), 3-9. Leola M. Bergmann, *The Negro in Iowa* (Iowa City: State Historical Society of Iowa, 1969), 15.

19. Savage, *Blacks in the West*, 179.

20. State of Iowa, *The Debates of the Constitutional Convention of 1857*, 2 vols. (Davenport: Luse, Lane, and Company, 1857), 1: 129-39.

21. Berwanger, *The Frontier Against Slavery*, 41-42.

22. *Constitution of the State of Iowa*, Adopted in Convention, March 5, 1857 (Muscatine, Iowa, 1857), 6-16.

23. Savage, *Blacks in the West*, 179-80.

24. State of Iowa, House of Representatives, *Journal*, 12th Gen. Assembly, January 23, 1868,

25. William L. Katz, *The Black West* (Garden City, New York: Doubleday, 1971), 54, 50, 284.

26. "Seventy Years in Iowa," AI, 3rd ser. 27 (October 1945): 100, 114-15.

27. Jacob Van Eck, "Underground Railroad in Iowa," PAL 2 (May 1921): 130-32, 137; Nettie Sanford, *Early Sketches of Polk County* (Newton, Iowa: Chas. A. Clark, 1874), 134; Christian S. Bykrit, "A Derailment on the Railway Invisible," AI, 3rd ser. 14 (October 1923): 95-100.

28. Mrs. Laurence C. Jones, "The Desire for Freedom," PAL 7 (May 1927): 153-63.

29. Abbie Mott Benedict, "My Early Days in Iowa," AI, 3rd ser. 17 (July 1930): 331.

30. Sarah Kenyon to relatives, October 11, 1861, John Kenyon Papers, ISHD-HS.

31. Philip T. Drotning, *A Guide to Negro History in America* (New York: Doubleday, 1968), 65.

32. Jacob A. Swisher, "The Case of Ralph," PAL 7 (February 1926): 34-39.

33. "An Iowa Fugitive Slave Case," AI, 3rd ser. 2 (October 1896): 237.

34. Ibid., 239.

35. George Frazee, "An Iowa Fugitive Slave Case—1850," AI, 3rd ser. 6 (April 1903): 37.

36. Bergmann, *The Negro in Iowa*, 24.

37. George Frazee, "The Iowa Fugitive Slave Case," AI, 3rd ser. 4 (July 1899): 127-28.

38. Ibid., 132-33.

39. Bergmann, *The Negro in Iowa*, 19.

40. Nathan E. Coffin, "The Case of Archie P. Webb, A Free Negro," AI, 3rd ser. 11 (July-October 1913): 201-13.

41. Bergmann, *The Negro in Iowa*, 29.

42. Paul W. Black, "Lynchings in Iowa," IJHP 10 (April 1912): 186-90.

43. Sarah Parker to her mother, March 10, 1860, ISHD-HS.

44. Ruth A. Gallaher, "A Race Riot on the Mississippi," PAL 2 (December 1921): 369-78.

45. *Census of Iowa*, 1880, 21.

46. Leland L. Sage, *A History of Iowa* (Ames, Iowa: Iowa State University Press, 1974), 93.

47. Amelia Murdock Wing, "Early Days in Clayton County," AI, 3rd ser. 27 (April 1946): 275; Rosenberg, *Iowa on the Eve of the Civil War*, 29-30.

48. Shambaugh, ed., *Fragments of the Debates of the Iowa Constitutional Conventions of 1844 and 1846*, 329-30, 342; (Iowa) *Constitution*, 1844, 3; (Iowa) *Constitution*, 1846, 3.

49. State of Iowa, *Debates*, 1857, 1: 129-39; (Iowa) *Constitution*, 1857, 6.

50. Frederick C. Luebke, "Ethnic Group Settlement on the Great Plains," *Western Historical Quarterly*, vol. 8, no. 4 (October 1977): 407, 425.

51. Ibid., 428.

52. Theodore Saloutos, "The Immigrant Contribution to American Agriculture," *Agricultural History*, vol. 50, no. 1 (January 1976): 46, 67.

53. Lawrence M. Nelson, *From Fjord to Prairie: Norwegian-Americans in the Midwest, 1825-1975* (Chicago: Norwegian-American Immigration Anniversary Commission, 1976), A4; Theodore C. Blegen, *Norwegian Migration to the United States*, 2 vols. (Northfield, Minnesota: Norwegian-American Historical Association, 1931); Lawrence M. Larson, *The Changing West and Other Essays* (Northfield, Minnesota: Norwegian-American Historical Association, 1937), 69-70; George T. Flom, *A History of Norwegian Immigration in the United States* (Iowa City, 1909), 190, 197, 362-65; Carlton C. Qualey, *Norwegian Settlement in the United States* (New York: Arno Press and the New York Times, 1970), 78-85.

54. Geraldine Schwarz, "Family Cohesion in a Norwegian-American Settlement," in Luis Torres, ed., *Conversations With the Recent Past* (Northeast Iowa Oral History Project: 1975), 2-3; Bessie L. Lyon, "Gunda's Coffee Pot," PAL 13 (October 1932): 416-25.

55. Letters of Diderikke Brandt, Luther College Library, Decorah, Iowa.

56. David T. Nelson, ed., *The Diary of Elisabeth Koren, 1853-1855* (Northfield, Minnesota: Norwegian-American Historical Association, 1955), 101, 110, 121-22, 130, 187, 195.

57. Ibid., 159.

58. Ibid., 114.

59. Ibid., 370.

60. Pauline Farseth and Theodore C. Blegen, eds., *Frontier Mother: The Letters of Gro Svendsen* (Northfield, Minnesota: Norwegian-American Historical Association, 1950), 40, 32.

61. Ibid., 28, 104.

62. George T. Flom, "The Growth of the Scandinavian Factor in the Population of Iowa," IJHP, vol. 4, no. 2 (April 1906): 267-68. See also Thomas P. Christensen, *A History of the Danes in Iowa* (Solvang, Calfornia: Dansk Folkesamfund, 1952); and Kristian Hvidt, *Danes Go West*

(Rebild, Denmark: Rebild National Park Society, 1976); H. Arnold Barton, *Letters From the Prom-ised Land. Swedes in America 1840–1914* (Minneapolis: University of Minnesota Press for the Swedish Pioneer Historical Society, 1975), 15.

63. Ardith K. Melloch, "New Sweden, Iowa," PAL, vol. 59, no. 1 (January/February 1978): 6–7; Barton, *Letters From the Promised Land,* 86, 100, 120, 137.

64. George T. Flom, "The Danish Contingent in the Population of Early Iowa," IJHP, vol. 4, no. 2 (April 1906): 220–21, 244; Louise Bohach, "Settlement of St. Ansgar—A Miniature Melting Pot," IJH, vol. 46, no. 3 (July 1948): 296–301.

65. Hildegard B. Johnson, "German Forty-Eighters in Davenport," IJH, vol. 44, no. 1 (January 1946): 3–6.

66. Louise Sophia Gellhorn Boylan, "My Life Story," ISHD-HS.

67. Dwight G. McCarty, *Stories of Pioneer Life on the Iowa Prairie* (Emmetsburg, Iowa, 1974), 20.

68. Ibid., 21.

69. Ibid.

70. Jacob Van der Zee, *The British in Iowa* (Iowa City: State Historical Society, 1922), 18–19.

71. Grant Foreman, "English Emigrants in Iowa," IJHP, vol. 44, no. 4 (October 1946): 409–10.

72. Lucy Rutledge Cooke, *Covered Wagon Days: Crossing the Plains in 1852* (Modesto, California, 1923), 73–81.

73. Henry S. Lucas, "The Beginnings of Dutch Immigration to Iowa, 1845–1847," IJH 22 (October 1924): 483–531.

74. Jacob Van der Zee, *The Hollanders of Iowa* (Iowa City: State Historical Society, 1912), 67.

75. Jacob Van der Zee, "Diary of a Journey from the Netherlands to Pella," IJHP, vol. 10, no. 3 (July 1912): 381; Leonora Scholte, "A Stranger in a Strange Land," IJH, vol. 37, no. 2 (April 1939): 146–54.

76. Ibid., 157–60, 166.

77. Janette Murray, "Women of North Tama," IJHP 41 (July 1943): 295, 309; Janette Mur-ray and Janet Murray Fiske, *Hurrah for Bonnie Iowa* (Lake Mills, Iowa: Graphic, 1963); "The Hungarians in Iowa," AI, 3rd ser., vol. 3, no. 30 (October 1950): 466; Harriet Connor Brown, "Schoolday Memories," PAL 30 (April 1949): 109; Rabbi Simon Glazer, *The Jews of Iowa* (Des Moines: Koch Brothers, 1904), 158, 170–75, 183, 187, 238; Mary Walters Randall, "Personal Recollections of Pioneer Life," Adda A. Lawyer Papers, ISHD-HS; Martha E. Griffith, "Czechs in Cedar Rapids," IJHP, vol. 42, no. 2 (April 1944): 114–61, and vol. 42, no. 3 (July 1944): 266–315. See also Pauline S. Merrill, "Pioneer Iowa Bohemians," AI, 3rd ser., vol. 3, no. 26 (April 1945): 261–74.

78. William J. Petersen, "Immigrants From Far and Near," PAL, vol. 49, no. 7 (July 1968): 299.

79. *Prairie versus Bush. Iowa as an Emigration Field* (Davenport, Iowa Land Office, 1859), 3, back cover.

80. A. R. Fulton, "An Invitation to Immigrants," PAL 18 (July 1937): 226; Iowa Board of Im-migration, *Immigration to Iowa. Report of the Secretary of the Board of Immigration, April 4, 1871* (n.p., n.d.).

81. *Iowa: The Home For Immigrants* (Des Moines: Iowa Board of Immigration, 1870), 63–65.

82. Ruth A. Gallaher, "The English Community in Iowa," PAL 2 (March 1921): 85.

83. Jacob Van der Zee, "The Mormon Trails in Iowa," IJHP, vol. 12, no. 1 (January 1914): 16. See also Robert B. Flanders, *Nauvoo: Kingdom on the Mississippi* (Urbana: University of Il-linois Press, 1965); Sage, *A History of Iowa,* 72–79; and Wallace Stegner, *The Gathering of Zion* (New York: McGraw Hill, 1964).

CHAPTER FIVE

1. Leland L. Sage, *A History of Iowa* (Ames: Iowa State University Press, 1974), 152–53.

2. Florence C. Cowles, *Early Algona. The Story of Our Pioneers, 1854–1874 (Des Moines Register and Tribune,* 1929), 164.

3. Sarah Kenyon to relatives, October 9, 1862, John Kenyon Papers, ISHD-HS.

4. *Burlington Daily Hawk-Eye,* September 7, 1861; Harriet Connor Brown, *Grandmother Brown's Hundred Years, 1827–1927* (Boston: Little Brown, 1929), 143; Martha Turner Searle, "Personal Experience and Reminescences [sic] of the Civil War 1861 to 1865," ISHD-HS.

5. Sage, *History of Iowa,* 153–54.

6. Emery S. Bartlett to his children and grandchildren, December 1911, ISHD-MA, Des Moines.

7. Matilda Peitzke Paul, "Recollections," ISHD-HS.

8. "Seventy Years in Iowa," AI, 3rd ser. 27 (October 1945): 116–18.

9. Mary Elizabeth Massey, *Bonnet Brigades: American Women and the Civil War* (New York: Knopf, 1966), 207; Mary McCall to Thomas McCall, January 24, 1862, March, 1862, December 19, 1862, December 26, 1862, December 30, 1862, McCall Family Papers, Special Collections, ISU Library, Ames.

10. David Logan Hauser Letters, ISHD-HS.

11. J. W. Rice to his wife, January 14, 1865, J. W. Rice Letters, ISHD-HS.

12. Ibid.; Mary McCall to Thomas McCall, November 1, 1862, McCall Family Papers, ISHD-HS.

13. May Lacey Crowder, "Pioneer Life in Palo Alto County," IJHP 46 (April 1948): 157–58.

14. Ibid., 159–60.

15. Searle, "Personal Experience and Reminescences [*sic*]," ISHD-HS.

16. M. A. Rogers, "An Iowa Woman in Wartime," pt. 1, AI, 3rd ser. 35 (Winter 1961): 523–47; pt. 2, 35 (Spring 1961): 597–611; pt. 3, 36 (Summer 1961): 20–44.

17. George Mills, ed., "The Sharp Family Civil War Letters," AI, 3rd ser. 34 (January 1959): 484–507. The Sharp letters were given by their great-great-grandson to the Iowa State Historical Department, Division of Museum and Archives in the late 1950s.

18. Harriet Jane Thompson to William G. Thompson, August 1862–October 1862, Major William G. Thompson Papers, ISHD-MA.

19. "Mrs. Ann E. Harlan," AI, 3rd ser. 2 (October 1896): 496.

20. Ruth A. Gallaher, "Annie Turner Wittenmyer," IJHP, vol. 29, no. 4 (October 1931): 525.

21. Ibid., 525–26.

22. Ruth A. Gallaher, "Annie Turner Wittenmyer, PAL 38 (April 1957): 150.

23. L. O. Cheever, "Annie Wittenmyer," PAL 48 (June 1967): 249.

24. Diary of Mary E. Shelton, 1864, Shelton Family Papers, Manuscript Collection, UI Library, Iowa City.

25. Ibid.

26. Ibid.

27. Gallaher, "Annie Turner Wittenmyer," 558.

28. Annie Turner Wittenmyer, *Under the Guns: A Woman's Reminiscences of the Civil War* (Boston: E. B. Stillings, 1895), ii.

29. Elisha D. Ely, *The Ely and Weare Families, Pioneers of Michigan and Iowa* (Cedar Rapids, 1926), 47, 62.

30. *Burlington Daily Hawk-Eye,* January 28, 1863, January 6, 1864.

31. For a more detailed discussion of relief work in Iowa see Earl S. Fullbrook, "Relief Work in Iowa During the Civil War," IJHP, vol. 16, no. 2 (April 1918): 155–274.

CHAPTER SIX

1. Amelia Murdock Wing, "Early Days in Clayton County," AI, 3rd ser. 27 (April 1946): 281–82. See also Louise R. Noun, *Strong-Minded Women: The Emergence of the Woman-Suffrage Movement in Iowa* (Ames: Iowa State University Press, 1969).

2. Robert F. Berkhofer, "Space, Time, Culture and the New Frontier," *Agricultural History,* vol. 38, no. 1 (January 1964): 28.

3. May Lacey Crowder, "Pioneer Life in Palo Alto County," IJHP 46 (April 1948): 187.

4. Glenda Riley, "Origins of the Argument for Improved Female Education," *History of Education Quarterly* 9 (Winter 1969): 455–70; *Frontier Guardian* (Kanesville, later Council Bluffs), February 7, 1851.

5. Louis B. Wright, *Culture on the Moving Frontier* (New York: Harper Torchbook, 1961), 225.

6. Ruth A. Gallaher, *Legal and Political Status of Women in Iowa, 1838-1918* (Iowa City: State Historical Society, 1918), 39.

7. Matilda Peitzke Paul, "Recollections," ISHD-HS, Iowa City.

8. Ibid.

9. Margaret E. Archer Murray, "Memoir of the William Archer Family," AI, 3rd ser. 39 (Summer 1968): 366.

10. Crowder, "Pioneer Life in Palo Alto County," 184.

11. Ibid., 186.

12. Diary of Ellen Strang, 1861, ISHD-MA, Des Moines.

13. Robert E. Belding, "Academies and Iowa's Frontier Life," AI, 3rd ser., vol. 44, no. 5 (Summer 1978): 335–38.

14. *Census of the Territory of Iowa*, 1840, 3.

15. John Plumbe, Jr., "Plumbe's Sketches of Iowa in 1839," AI, 3rd ser. 14 (April 1925): 599.

16. *Iowa News* (Dubuque) January 6, 1838, April 21, 1838; *Iowa Territorial Gazette*, February 17, 1844; Nathan H. Parker, *The Iowa Handbook for 1856* (Boston: John P. Jewett, 1856), 170; Thomas Woody, *A History of Women's Education in the United States*, 2 vols. (New York: The Science Press, 1929), 1: 378; *Northern Iowa: Containing Hints and Information of Value to Emigrants* (Dubuque, 1858), 33–34.

17. *Address and Poem: Delivered at the Laying of the Corner Stone of the Iowa Female Collegiate Institute* (Iowa City, 1853), 5–19.

18. Benjamin F. Shambaugh, *Iowa City: A Contribution to the Early History of Iowa* (Iowa City: State Historical Society of Iowa, 1893), 778.

19. *The Hawk-Eye and Iowa Patriot* (Burlington), September 5, 1839; *Burlington Weekly Hawk-Eye*, September 4, 1845, April 6, 1849, December 6, 1849.

20. *Burlington Tri-Weekly Telegraph*, October 1, 1850; *Gate City*, May 28, 1857; *Burlington Daily Hawk-Eye*, April 20, 1859, August 9, 1866, August 10, 1866; *Fairfield Ledger*, August 24, 1860, July 15, 1869.

21. E. H. Annewalt, *Mount Pleasant City Directory; Containing A Catalogue of Inhabitants* (Burlington, 1870), 6, 15–18; Belding, "Academies and Iowa's Frontier Life," 350–52.

22. Woody, *A History of Women's Education*, 1: 378; *Democratic Banner* (Davenport) April 7, 1854; *Fairfield Ledger*, April 13, 1854. Handwritten notation, n.d., Alice L. Longley Papers, ISHD-MA; *Burlington Daily Hawk-Eye*, January 12, 1859.

23. Sarah Gillespie Huftalen, "School Days of the Seventies," PAL 28 (April 1947): 123.

24. *Gate City*, August 25, 1857.

25. *Waterloo Courier*, April 30, 1862; Johnson Brigham, "The Wedding of James Harlan," PAL 3 (April 1922): 103.

26. Robert E. Belding, "Iowa's Brave Model for Women's Education," AI, 3rd ser., vol. 43, no. 5 (Summer 1976): 343.

27. Albert D. Richardson, *Beyond the Mississippi* (Hartford: American Publishing Co., 1867; reprint ed., New York: Johnson Reprint Corp., 1968), 555–56.

28. *Circular of the State University of Iowa* (Iowa City: UI, 1856), 4–14; Clarence R. Aurner, *History of Education in Iowa*, 4 vols. (Iowa City: State Historical Society, 1916), 4:20–23.

29. Woody, *A History of Women's Education*, 2:296; Aurner, *History of Education in Iowa*, 4:40–45.

30. Address of President A. S. Welch, 1870, Iowa State College, Mary B. Welch Papers, Special Collections, ISU Library, Ames.

31. Ibid.; Aurner, *History of Education in Iowa* 4:337.

32. *Poweshiek County, Iowa. A Descriptive Account* (Montezuma, Iowa, 1865), 25–26, 28; Leland L. Sage, *A History of Iowa*, (Ames: Iowa State University Press, 1974), 105.

33. John S. Nollen, *Grinnell College* (Iowa City: The State Historical Society, 1953), 58; Catalogue, Grinnell College, 1975, 13; Sage, *A History of Iowa*, 105.

34. Benjamin F. Gue, *History of Iowa*, 4 vols. (New York: The Century History Co., 1903), 1:396; B. F. Gue, "Early Iowa Reminiscences," *Iowa Historical Records* 16 (July 1900): 110; Leonard F. Parker, "Teachers in Iowa before 1858," *Historical Lectures Upon Early Leaders in the Professions in the Territory of Iowa Delivered at Iowa City, 1894* (Iowa City: State History Society, 1894), 30.

35. Crowder, "Pioneer Life in Palo Alto County," 188, 197; Floy Lawrence Emhoff, "A Pioneer School Teacher in Central Iowa—Alice Money Lawrence," IJHP 33 (October 1935): 379–84.

36. Anna H. Clarkson, "A Beautiful Life—A Biographical Sketch," AI, 3rd ser., 11 (July–October 1913): 191; Eleanor E. Gordon, *A Little Bit of a Long Story for the Children* (Humboldt, Iowa, 1934), 10–12.

37. Diary of Mary E. Shelton, November 7, 1865, Shelton Family Papers, Manuscript Collection, UI Library, Iowa City.

38. Mary S. Ellis to relatives, November 15, 1857, Kenyon Family Letters, ISHD-HS.

39. Emhoff, "A Pioneer School Teacher in Central Iowa," 385.

40. Diary of Ellen Strang, May 27, 1867, ISHD-MA.

41. Agnes Briggs Olmstead, "Recollections of a Pioneer Teacher of Hamilton County," AI, 3rd ser. 18 (October 1946): 101.

42. *Pioneer and Personal Reminiscences* (Marshalltown, Iowa, 1893), 47; Diary of Ellen Strang, January 17, 1863, ISHD-MA; *Poweshiek County, Iowa,* 34; Emhoff, "A Pioneer School Teacher in Central Iowa," 385; Olmstead, "Recollections of a Pioneer Teacher," 95–96.

43. Arozina Perkins, "Letters of a Pioneer Teacher," AI, 3rd ser., vol. 35, no. 8 (Spring 1961): 616–17.

44. *Eddyville Free Press,* March 30, 1855.

45. *Census of the Territory of Iowa,* 1836, 8–20.

46. *Business Directory and Review of the Trade, Commerce and Manufactories of the City of Burlington, Iowa, For the Year Ending May 1, 1865* (Burlington, 1856), 1–40; John Kennedy, *Iowa City Directory and Advertiser, For 1857* (Iowa City, 1857).

47. James T. Hair, ed., *Iowa State Gazetteer* (Chicago, 1865), 518–610.

48. Isaac Galland, *Galland's Iowa Emigrant: Containing A Map, and General Descriptions of Iowa Territory* (Chillicothe, Ohio, 1840), 29; Nettie Sanford, *Early Sketches of Polk County* (Newton, Iowa, 1874), 83; George R. Carroll, *Pioneer Life in and Around Cedar Rapids, Iowa, from 1839 to 1849* (Cedar Rapids, 1895), 22; Lulu Mae Coe, "Many Iowa Women Won Fame," AI, 3rd ser. 36 (Fall 1962): 459; William J. Petersen, "Women in History," PAL 38 (April 1957): 133.

49. Gue, "Early Iowa Reminiscences," 121.

50. Wing, "Early Days in Clayton County," 261, 266, 277, 281, 288, 293.

51. Gue, *History of Iowa,* 4:95, 257; Clarence A. Andrews, *A Literary History of Iowa* (Iowa City: University of Iowa Press, 1972), 45–52; Marie Haefner, "An American Lady," PAL 12 (May 1931): 169–78.

52. M. Romdall Williams, "From Mount Pleasant: Nation's First Woman Lawyer," *The Iowan* 15 (Summer 1967): 23.

53. Ibid., 23–24, 54.

54. Petersen, "Women in History," 133–34.

55. Jennie McCowen, "Women in Iowa," AI, 2nd ser. 3 (October 1884): 98.

56. *Burlington Hawk-Eye,* December 26, 1850.

57. *Address and Poem; Delivered at the Laying of the Corner Stone of the Iowa Female Collegiate Institute,* 22–34.

58. "Iowa Suffrage Memorial Association," AI, 3rd ser. 14 (July 1924); 358; "Political Equality in Iowa," AI, 3rd ser., vol. 26, no. 3 (January 1945): 197; Edith H. Hurlbutt, "Pioneer Experiences in Keokuk County, 1858–1874," IJH 52 (October 1954): 342.

59. Frank E. Horack, "Equal Suffrage in Iowa," in Benjamin F. Shambaugh, ed., *Applied History,* 2 vols. (Iowa City: State Historical Society, 1914), 2:283–84.

60. George F. Robeson, "The Early Iowans," PAL 4 (September 1923): 298.

61. Gallaher, *Legal and Political Status of Women in Iowa,* 152–55.

62. John E. Briggs, *History of Social Legislation in Iowa* (Iowa City: State Historical Society, 1915), 27–67.

63. *Constitution of the State of Iowa,* Adopted in Convention, November 1, 1844, 6; *Constitution of the State of Iowa,* Adopted in Convention, May 18, 1846, 6; and *Constitution of the State of Iowa,* Adopted in Convention, at Iowa City, March 5, 1857, 10.

64. Eleanor Flexner, *Century of Struggle, The Woman's Rights Movement in the United States* (Cambridge, Massachusetts: The Belknap Press of Harvard University Press, 1976), 185.

65. Daughters of Temperance, Broadside, Seal of Bloomington Union No. 1, Daughters of Temperance, Muscatine, Iowa, February 4, 1850, Graff Collecton, Newberry Library, Chicago.

66. McCowen, "Women in Iowa," 111; Flexner, *Century of Struggle,* 185–86.

67. Charles Negus, "The Early History of Iowa," AI, 3rd ser. 9 (January 1871): 399–401.

68. Ibid., 401.

69. Ibid., 403–04.

70. Vern L. Bullough, *The Subordinate Sex: A History of Attitudes Toward Women* (Urbana: University of Illinois Press, 1973), 314; Gallaher, *Legal and Political Status of Women in Iowa,*

238; Benjamin F. Shambaugh, *The Constitutions of Iowa* (Iowa City: State Historical Society, 1934), 305.

71. (Iowa) House, *Journal*, 11th Gen. Assembly, January, 1866, 188.

72. Ibid., March 12, 1866, 442.

73. Ibid., March 13, 1866, 444: See *Burlington Hawk-Eye*, August 8, 1866.

74. (Iowa) House, *Journal*, 12th Gen. Assembly, January, 1868, 106–7.

75. Ibid., March 31, 1868, 530.

76. Ibid.

77. Ibid., April 4, 1868, 605.

78. Noun, *Strong-Minded Women*, 91–96.

79. Ibid., 112–16, 121.

80. *Waterloo Courier*, April 15, 1869; Gallaher, *Legal and Political Status of Women in Iowa*, 238; Horack, "Equal Suffrage in Iowa," 293–96.

81. *Des Moines Bulletin*, January 11, 1870, No. 1, 1-2.

82. (Iowa) House, *Journal*, 13th Gen. Assembly, January, 1870, 95.

83. *Des Moines Bulletin*, January 19, 1870, No. 5, 2–3; (Iowa) House, *Journal*, 13th Gen. Assembly, January 20, 1870, 95; *Des Moines Bulletin*, March 22, 1870, 4; (Iowa) House, *Journal*, 13th Gen. Assembly, March 22, 1870, 417.

84. *Des Moines Bulletin*, March 29, 1870, No. 61, 1; March 29, 1870, No. 60, 4, and No. 61, 1–3.

85. (Iowa) House, *Journal*, 13th Gen. Assembly, March 30, 1870, 389; *Des Moines Bulletin*, March 30, 1870, No. 44, 1.

86. Noun, *Strong-Minded Women*, 164.

87. Gue, *History of Iowa*, 4: 38–39; and Noun, *Strong-Minded Women*, 150–51.

88. Austin Adams to Mary Newbury, February 22, 1856, Austin Adams Family Papers, Special Collections, ISU Library, Ames.

89. Noun, *Strong-Minded Women*, 113–15; Mary N. Adams to her sister, September 16, 1860, May 7, 1861, Austin Adams Family Papers; Louise Moede Lex, "Mary Newbury Adams: Feminist Forerunner from Iowa," AI, 3rd ser., vol. 43, no. 5 (Summer 1976): 323–41.

90. Noun, *Strong-Minded Women*, 91–92.

91. Ibid., 91–94, 273–77.

92. Ibid., 12–13.

93. Ruth S. Beitz, "Amelia Bloomer's Own Emancipation Proclamation," *The Iowan*, vol. 14, no. 2 (Winter 1965–1966): 40.

94. Noun, *Strong-Minded Women*, 20; Philip D. Jordan, "Amelia Jenks Bloomer," PAL 37 (April 1957): 143–48; Charles R. Tuttle and Daniel S. Durrie, *An Illustrated History of the State of Iowa* (Chicago, 1876), 669–70; Noun, *Strong-Minded Women*, 264–65.

CHAPTER SEVEN

1. Hamlin Garland, *A Pioneer Mother* (Chicago: The Bookfellows, 1922), 5–10.

2. *Constitution and By-Laws of the Pioneer Settlers' Association of Louisa County, Iowa with the Proceedings of the First and Second Annual Festivals* (Wapello, Iowa, 1860), 4, 6, Newberry Library, Chicago. A recent attempt to examine men's diaries in relation to women, family, and sex roles is John M. Faragher, *Women and Men on the Overland Trail* (New Haven: Yale University Press, 1979).

3. Richard Slotkin, *Regeneration Through Violence: The Mythology of the American Frontier, 1600–1860* (Middletown, Connecticut: Wesleyan University Press, 1973), 550.

4. Everett Dick, "Sunbonnet and Calico; the Homesteader's Consort," *Nebraska History* 47 (March 1966): 10.

5. Diary of Caroline Phelps, ISHD-HS, Iowa City; Nettie Sanford, *Early Sketches of Polk County* (Newton, Iowa, 1874), 7; Sarah Morse to her aunt, August 11, 1858, Morse Family Letters, ISHD-HS.

6. B. F. Gue, "Early Iowa Reminiscences," *Iowa Historical Records* 16 (July 1900): 115; Julian E. McFarland, *A History of the Pioneer Era on the Iowa Prairies* (Lake Mills, Iowa, 1969), 145; *The Solon Economist*, May 4, 1922 (clipping), Adda A. Lawyer Papers, ISHD-HS; George R. Carroll, *Pioneer Life In and Around Cedar Rapids, Iowa, from 1839 to 1849* (Cedar Rapids, 1895), 231; Diary of Esther Pillsbury, 1863, ISHD-HS.

7. *Waterloo Courier*, April 9, 1861.

8. "From New York to Iowa," PAL 2 (October 1921): 320.

9. John Willeford, "Biography of Susannah Willeford," ISHD-HS.

10. Sanford, *Early Sketches of Polk County*, 80; Mary D. Taylor, "A Farmers' Wives' Society in Pioneer Days," AI, 3rd ser., vol. 3, no. 13 (July 1921): 22; Diary of Esther Pillsbury, 1863, ISHD-HS; "Life and Letters of Mary Josephine Remey, Wife of Rear Admiral George Collier Remey, Daughter of Chief Justice Charles Mason, 1845-1938," 12 typescript vols., Mason-Remey Papers, ISHD-MA and HS; Virginia Ivins, *Yesterdays, Reminiscences of Long Ago* (Keokuk, Iowa, n.d.), 51.

11. Ada Mae Brown Brinton, "Sunshine and Rain in Iowa: Reminiscing Through 86 Years," ISHD-HS.

12. Mary Walters Randall, "Personal Recollections of Pioneer Life," Adda A. Lawyer Papers, ISHD-HS.

13. Ibid.; Matilda Peitzke Paul, "Recollections," ISHD-HS; *The Solon Economist*, May 4, 1922, Adda A. Lawyer Papers; Amelia Murdock Wing, "Early Days in Clayton County," AI, 3rd ser. 27 (April 1946): 270; Emery S. Bartlett to his children and grandchildren, December 1911, ISHD-MA; Sanford, *Early Sketches of Polk County*, 80; Brinton, "Sunshine and Rain"; Sanford, *Early Sketches of Polk County*, 33.

14. Bruce E. Mahan, "Frontier Fun," PAL 8 (January 1927): 38-40; May Lacey Crowder, "Pioneer Life in Palo Alto County," IJHP 46 (April 1948): 176.

15. Matie L. Baily, "Christmas of a Pioneer Family," AI, 3rd ser., vol. 3, no. 31 (October 1951): 153.

16. Paul, "Recollections," ISHD-HS.

17. Ibid.

18. Roe House, Grand Fourth of July Ball, invitation, 1859, Graff Collection, Newberry Library, Chicago; Peter T. Harstad, "The Spirit of '76 in Iowa," PAL 57 (May/June 1976): 73-74; Paul "Recollections," ISHD-HS; *Waterloo Courier*, June 25, 1862.

19. Louise Sophia Gellhorn Boylan, "My Life Story," ISHD-HS.

20. *Burlington Daily Hawk-Eye and Telegraph*, September 28, 1855, October 3, 1855.

21. *Davenport Gazette*, June 21, 1855; *Burlington Daily Hawk-Eye and Telegraph*, July 21, 1855, July 20, 1855; *Waterloo Courier*, June 5, 1861; *Fairfield Ledger*, August 13, 1863, June 11, 1863, May 28, 1868.

22. Paul, "Recollections."

23. Ibid.; Boylan, "My Life Story," ISHD-HS; "From New York to Iowa," 320; Katharine Horack, "In Quest of a Prairie Home," PAL 5 (July 1924): 256.

24. Nathan H. Parker, *Iowa As It Is In 1856* (Chicago, 1856), 83.

25. Mary S. Ellis to relatives, August 29, 1856, John Kenyon Papers, ISHD-HS.

26. Roy H. Pearce, "The Significances of the Captivity Narrative," *American Literature* 19 (1947), 9; Richard Van Der Beets, "The Indian Captivity Narrative as a Ritual," *American Literature* 43 (1972): 553.

27. Ronald J. Quinn, "The Modest Seduction: The Experience of Pioneer Women on the Trans-Mississippi Frontier" (Ph.D. diss., University of California at Riverside, 1977), i-ii, 45, 78.

28. Dawn L. Gherman, "From Parlor to Tepee: The White Squaw on the American Frontier" (Ph.D. diss., University of Massachusetts, 1975), vi-viii.

29. Leland L. Sage, *A History of Iowa* (Ames: Iowa State University Press, 1974), 48-51; Cecil Eby, *That Disgraceful Affair: the Black Hawk War*, (New York: Norton, 1973); John E. Briggs, "Indian Affairs," PAL 21 (September 1940): 261-77; John E. Briggs, "Indian Affairs in 1845," PAL 26 (August 1945): 225-38; Sage, *A History of Iowa*, 107-8.

30. Ruth Beitz, "They Guarded Iowa's Last Frontier," *The Iowan*, vol. 9, no. 3 (February-March, 1961): 12; O. J. Pruitt, "Tales of the Cherokee in Iowa," AI, 3rd ser., vol. 3, no. 30 (July 1950): 359-61.

31. Beitz, "They Guarded Iowa's Last Frontier," 12; "Frontier Fear of the Indians," AI, 3rd ser., vol. 3, no. 29 (April 1948): 317.

32. Beitz, "They Guarded Iowa's Last Frontier," 13, 46.

33. Bessie L. Lyon, "Hungry Indians," PAL 9 (October 1928): 369.

34. Lyon, "Grandmother's Story," PAL 5 (January 1924): 8.

35. Lyon, "Prospecting for a New Home," PAL 6 (July 1925): 226; Boylan, "My Life Story," ISHD-HS.

36. Diary of Caroline Phelps, 1840, ISHD-HS.

37. Ibid., 1838.

38. Dwight G. McCarty, *Stories of Pioneer Life on the Iowa Prairie* (Emmetsburg, Iowa, 1974), 20; Mary Ann Ferrin Davidson, "An Autobiography and a Reminiscence," AI, 3rd ser. 37 (Spring 1964): 256–57.

39. Harger Family Papers, courtesy Professor Dolores K. Gros-Louis, Indiana University.

40. Boylan, "My Life Story," ISHD-HS.

41. Harriet Connor Brown, "Schoolday Memories," PAL 30 (April 1949): 123–24.

42. Willeford, "Biography of Susannah Willeford," ISHD-HS; Reminiscences of Harriet M. Hill Townsend, courtesy Frank Kerlis.

BIBLIOGRAPHIC ESSAY

THE richest sources of information on frontierswomen in Iowa are their diaries, letters, and memoirs. For the most part, these documents are scattered in state and local historical society libraries and archives. Some of the most useful general discussions of frontier life include the reminiscences of Kitturah Penton Belknap, the letters of Clara A. Dodge, 1841–1849, the diaries of Sarah Gillespie Huftalen, 1858–1935, the letters of the John Kenyon family, 1856–1865, the papers of Adda A. Lawyer, the letters of the Morse family, 1856–1868, the letters of Sarah Parker, 1847–1870, the recollections of Matilda Peitzke Paul, 1938, the diary of Caroline Phelps, 1830–1860, the diary of Esther Pillsbury, 1863, the diary of Sarah Welch Nossaman, the diary of Mary St. John, 1858, and the papers of Susannah Willeford, 1820–1870, which are all deposited in the ISHD-HS, Iowa City. The diary of Ellen Strang, 1859–1872, the papers of Alice L. Longley, and twelve volumes of typescript, "Life and Letters of Mary Josephine Remey, Wife of Rear Admiral George Collier Remey, Daughter of Chief Justice Charles Mason, 1845–1938," are in the ISHD-MA, Des Moines (the Remey manuscript is also at the ISHD-HS).

Iowa frontierswomen's personal accounts are occasionally published in state and local historical journals and in book form. The most useful general accounts of frontier Iowa include Matie L. Baily, "Prairie Homesteading," PAL 23 (July 1942): 229–38; Abbie Mott Benedict, "My Early Days in Iowa," AI, 3rd ser. 27 (July 1930): 323–55; Harriet Bonebright-Closz, *Reminiscences of Newcastle, Iowa, 1848* (ISHD-MA, 1921); Harriet Connor Brown, *Grandmother Brown's Hundred Years, 1827–1927* (Boston: Little, Brown, 1929); Florence C. Cowles, *Early Algona. The Story of Our Pioneers, 1854–1874 (Des Moines Register and Tribune,* 1929); May Lacey Crowder, "Pioneer Life in Palo Alto County," IJHP 46 (April 1948): 156–98; Mary Ann Ferrin Davidson, "An Autobiography and a Reminiscence," AI, 3rd ser. 37 (Spring 1964): 241–61; Susan I. Dubell, "A Pioneer Home," PAL 22 (December 1931): 445–53, and "Rural Pioneering," PAL 22 (August 1941): 225–39; "From New York to Iowa," PAL 2 (October 1921): 311–21; Lida L. Greene, ed., "Diary of a Young Girl," AI, 3rd ser. 36 (Fall 1962): 437–59; Eleanor E. Gordon, *A Little Bit of a Long Story For the Children* (Humboldt, Iowa, 1934); Katharine Horack, "In Quest of a Prairie Home," PAL 5 (July 1924): 249–57; Edith Hurlbutt, "Pioneer Experiences in Keokuk County, 1858–1874," IJH 52 (October 1954): 327–42; Virginia Ivins, *Yesterdays, Reminiscences of Long Ago* (Keokuk, Iowa, n.d.), and *Pen Pictures of Early Western Days* (Keokuk, Iowa, c. 1905); Bessie L. Lyon, "Grandmother's Story," PAL 5 (January

1924): 1–8, and "Prospecting for a New Home," PAL 6 (July 1925): 225–32; Margaret E. Archer Murray, "Memoir of the William Archer Family," pt. 1, AI, 3rd ser. 39 (Summer 1968): 357–71 and pt. 2 (Fall 1968): 470–80; Sarah Welch Nossaman, "Pioneering at Bonaparte and Near Pella," AI, 3rd ser. 13 (October 1922): 441–53; Nettie Sanford, *Early Sketches of Polk County* (Newton, Iowa: Chas. A. Clark, 1874); "Seventy Years in Iowa," AI, 3rd ser. 27 (October 1945): 97–118; "Some Letters of James Mathews and Caroline Mathews Stone," IJH, vol. 45, no. 3 (July 1947): 311–20; and Amelia Murdock Wing, "Early Days in Clayton County," AI, 3rd ser. 27 (April 1946): 257–96.

The secondary literature dealing with women in the West is often sentimental. Examples are Dee Brown, *The Gentle Tamers: Women of the Old Wild West* (New York: Bantam Books, 1974); Everett Dick, *The Sod-House Frontier, 1854–1890* (New York: D. Appleton-Century, 1937), and "Sunbonnet and Calico, the Homesteader's Consort," *Nebraska History* 47 (March 1966): 3–13; William W. Fowler, *Woman on the American Frontier* (1878, reprint New York: Source Books Press, 1970); and William F. Sprague, *Women and the West* (1940, reprint New York: Arno Press, 1972).

Other more realistic accounts are Dorothy K. Gray, *Women of the West* (Millbrae, California: Les Femmes, 1976); Mary W. M. Hargreaves, "Homesteading and Homemaking on the Plains: A Review," *Agricultural History,* vol. 47, no. 2 (April 1973): 156–63, and "Women in the Agricultural Settlement of the Northern Plains," *Agricultural History,* vol. 50, no. 1 (January 1976): 179–89; T. A. Larson, "Dolls, Vassals, and Drudges—Pioneer Women in the West," *The Western Historical Quarterly,* vol. 3, no. 1 (January 1972): 5–16, and "Women's Role in the American West," *Montana: Magazine of Western History* 24 (Summer 1974): 2–11; Glenda Riley, *Women on the American Frontier* (St. Louis: Forum Press, 1977); and Nancy W. Ross, *Westward the Women* (New York: Knopf, 1944).

Secondary works that are useful in understanding aspects of women's role in frontier Iowa are George R. Carroll, *Pioneer Life In and Around Cedar Rapids, Iowa, from 1839 to 1849* (Cedar Rapids, 1895); Michael Conzen, "Local Migration Systems in Nineteenth-Century Iowa," *Geographical Review* 64 (July 1974): 339–61; William M. Donnel, *Pioneers of Marion County* (Des Moines, 1872); Elisha D. Ely, *The Ely and Weare Families, Pioneers of Michigan and Iowa* (Cedar Rapids, 1926); Ruth A. Gallaher, "Around the Fireplace," PAL 8 (January 1927): 18–23, and "From Connecticut to Iowa," PAL 22 (March 1941): 65–78; Benjamin F. Gue, *History of Iowa,* 4 vols. (New York: The Century History Company, 1903); Dwight G. McCarty, *Stories of Pioneer Life on the Iowa Prairie* (Emmetsburg, Iowa, 1973); Julian E. McFarland, *A History of the Pioneer Era on the Iowa Prairies* (Lake Mills, Iowa, 1969); Frank Luther Mott, *Literature of Pioneer Life in Iowa* (Iowa City: The State Historical Society of Iowa, 1923); Charles Negus, "The Early History of Iowa," AI, 3rd ser., vol. 9, no. 1 (January 1871): 393–404; George F. Parker, *Iowa, Pioneer Foundations,* 2 vols. (Iowa City: ISHD-HS, 1940); William J. Peterson, "The Pioneer Cabin," IJHP 36 (October 1938): 387–409, "Doctors, Drugs, and Pioneers," PAL 30 (March 1949): 93–96, "Diseases and Doctors in Pioneer Iowa," IJH, vol. 42, no. 2 (April 1951): 97–116, and "Women in History," PAL 38 (April 1957): 129–38; *Pioneer and Personal Reminiscences* (Marshalltown, Iowa, 1893); Irving B. Richman, *Ioway to Iowa: The Genesis of a Corn and Bible Commonwealth* (Iowa City: ISHS-HS, 1931); George F. Robeson, "The Early Iowans," PAL 4 (September 1923): 285–300; Leland L. Sage, *A History of Iowa* (Ames: Iowa State University Press, 1974); and Charles R. Tuttle and Daniel S. Durrie, *An Illustrated History of the State of Iowa* (Chicago, 1876).

The Iowa trail experience is described in "A Journey Out West," PAL 7 (July, 1925): 233–49; Lucy Rutledge Cooke, *Covered Wagon Days* (Modesto, California,

1923); Eliza Ann McAuley Egbert, "Travel Diary, 1852," California Historical Society, San Francisco; Jane Augusta Gould, "Diary, 1862," ISHS-HS; Catherine Margaret Haun, "A Woman's Trip Across the Plains, from Clinton, Iowa, to Sacramento, California, by way of Salt Lake City, 1849," Huntington Library, San Marino, California; Mrs. E. A. Hadley, "Journal to Oregon, 1851," ISHD-HS; Mary Alice Shutes, "Diary, 1862," ISHD-MA; and Francis E. Whitly, "Across the Mississippi," PAL 15 (January 1934): 10–16. Women's trail circumstances are considered in Johnny Faragher and Christine Stansell, "Women and Their Families on the Overland Trail to California and Oregon, 1842–1867," *Feminist Studies*, vol. 2, no. 2/3 (1975): 150–66; John M. Faragher, "Midwestern Families in Motion: Women and Men on the Overland Trail to Oregon and California, 1843–1870" (Ph.D. diss., Yale University, 1977), and *Women and Men on the Overland Trail* (New Haven: Yale University Press, 1979); Ruth Barnes Moynihan, "Children and Young People on the Overland Trail," *The Western Historical Quarterly*, vol. 6, no. 3 (July 1975): 279–94; Robert L. Munkres, "Wives, Mothers, Daughters: Women's Life on the Road West," *Annals of Wyoming*, 42 (October 1970): 191–224; Georgia Willis Read, "Women and Children on the Oregon-California Trail in the Gold-Rush Years," *Missouri Historical Review*, vol. 34, no. 1 (October 1944): 1–23; and Martin Ridge, "Why They Went West," *The American West*, vol. 1, no. 3 (Summer 1964): 40–57.

Works that are tangential to black women on the Iowa frontier are Eugene H. Berwanger, *The Frontier Against Slavery: Western Anti-Negro Prejudice and the Slavery Extension Controversy* (Urbana: University of Illinois Press, 1967); Minnie Miller Brown, "Black Women in American Agriculture," *Agricultural History*, vol. 50, no. 1 (January 1976): 202–12; Jean I. Castles, "The West: Crucible of the Negro," *Montana: Magazine of Western History* 19 (Winter 1969): 83–85; Philip T. Drotning, *A Guide to Negro History in America* (New York: Doubleday, 1968); William L. Katz, *The Black West* (Garden City, New York: Doubleday, 1971); Kenneth W. Porter, *The Negro on the American Frontier* (New York: Arno Press, 1971); and W. Sherman Savage, *Blacks in the West* (Westport, Connecticut: Greenwood Press, 1976).

Works that more specifically relate to Iowa blacks are: "An Iowa Fugitive Slave Case," AI, 3rd ser. 2 (October 1896): 531–39; Leola M. Bergmann, "The Negro in Iowa," IJH, vol. 46, no. 1 (January 1948): 3–90, and *The Negro in Iowa* (Iowa City: ISHD-MA, 1969); Paul W. Black, "Lynchings in Iowa," IJHP 10 (April 1912): 151–254; Christian S. Bykrit, "A Derailment on the Railway Invisible," AI, 3rd ser. 14 (October 1923): 95–100; Nathan E. Coffin, "The Case of Archie P. Webb, A Free Negro," AI, 3rd ser. 11 (July-October 1913): 200–14; George Frazee, "The Iowa Fugitive Slave Case," AI, 3rd ser. 4 (July 1899): 118–37, and "An Iowa Fugitive Slave Case—1850," AI, 3rd ser. 6 (April 1903): 9–45; Ruth A. Gallaher, "A Race Riot on the Mississippi," PAL 2 (December 1921): 369–78, "Wanted—A Servant Girl," PAL 7 (April 1926): 116–19, and "Slavery in Iowa," PAL 28 (May 1947): 158–60; Mrs. Laurence C. Jones, "The Desire for Freedom," PAL 7 (May 1927): 153–63; Bruce E. Mahan, "The Passing of a Slave," PAL 3 (July 1922): 227–30; Louis Pelzer, "The Negro and Slavery in Early Iowa," IJHP, vol. 2, no. 4 (October 1904): 471–84; Joel H. Silbey, "Proslavery Sentiment in Iowa," IJHP, vol. 55, no. 4 (October 1957): 289–318; Jacob A. Swisher, "The Case of Ralph," PAL 7 (February 1926): 33–43; "The Negro and Slavery in Early Iowa," IJHP 2 (October 1904): 471–84; and Jacob Van Eck, "Underground Railroad in Iowa," PAL 2 (May 1921): 129–43.

Few foreign-born women's diaries, letters, and memoirs are readily available for Iowa. Among those that are accessible are H. Arnold Barton, ed., *Letters From the Promised Land. Swedes in America, 1840–1914* (Minneapolis: University of Minnesota Press, 1975); Louise Sophia Gellhorn Boylan, "My Life Story, 1867–1883," ISHD-HS;

Diderikke Brandt, "Letters," Luther College Library, Decorah; David T. Nelson, ed., *The Diary of Elisabeth Koren, 1853-1855* (Northfield, Minnesota: Norwegian-American Historical Association, 1955); Gro Svendsen, *Frontier Mother: The Letters of Gro Svendsen* (Northfield, Minnesota: Norwegian-American Historical Association, 1950); and Marie C. Van Kerkhove, "Letters, 1848-1859," ISHD-HS. Two useful articles that treat the immigrant experience in the West are Frederick C. Luebke, "Ethnic Group Settlement on the Great Plains," *Western Historical Quarterly*, vol. 8, no. 4 (October 1977): 405-30; and Theodore Saloutos, "The Immigrant Contribution to American Agriculture," *Agricultural History*, vol. 50, no. 1 (January 1976): 45-67.

Other works that cover immigrants in frontier Iowa are James D. Allen, "Little Switzerland," AI, 3rd ser., vol. 3, no. 30 (July 1950): 378-84; Arlow W. Andersen, *The Norwegian-Americans* (Boston: Twayne Publishers, 1975); Elaine J. Anderson, *Old World Iowans* (Mason City: Klipto, 1949); Leola M. Bergmann, *Americans From Norway* (Philadelphia: Lippincott, 1950); Louise Bohach, "Settlement of St. Ansgar—A Miniature Melting Pot," IJH, vol. 46, no. 3 (July 1948): 296-315; Theodore C. Blegen, *Norwegian Migration to the United States*, 2 vols. (Northfield, Minnesota: Norwegian-American Historical Association, 1931); Thomas P. Christensen, "A German Forty-Eighter in Iowa," AI, vol. 3, no. 26 (April 1945): 245-53, and *A History of the Danes in Iowa* (Solvang, California: Dansk Folkesam-fund, 1952); Charles J. A. Ericson, "Memories of a Swedish Immigrant of 1852," AI, 3rd ser., vol. 3, no. 8 (April 1907): 1-12; George T. Flom, *A History of Norwegian Immigration in the United States* (Iowa City, 1909); George T. Flom, "The Danish Contingent in the Population of Early Iowa," IJHP, vol. 4, no. 2 (April 1906): 220-44, and "The Growth of the Scandinavian Factor in the Population of Iowa," IJHP, vol. 4, no. 2 (April 1906): 267-85; Grant Foreman, "English Emigrants in Iowa," IJH, vol. 44, no. 4 (October 1946): 385-420; A. R. Fulton, "An Invitation to Immigrants," PAL 18 (July 1937): 226-42; Ruth A. Gallaher, "The English Community in Iowa," PAL 2 (March 1921): 80-94; Rabbi Simon Glazer, *The Jews of Iowa* (Des Moines: Koch Brothers, 1904); and Martha E. Griffith, "Czechs in Cedar Rapids," pts. 1 and 2, IJHP, vol. 42, no. 2 (April 1944): 114-61, and vol. 42, no. 3 (July 1944): 266-315.

Iowa's rich ethnic heritage is further explored in Kristian Hvidt, *Danes Go West* (Rebild, Denmark: Rebild National Park Society, 1976); Hildegard B. Johnson, "German Forty-Eighters in Davenport," IJH, vol. 44, no. 1 (January 1946): 3-53; Bessie L. Lyon, "Gunda's Coffee Pot," PAL 8 (October 1932): 416-25; Henry S. Lucas, "The Beginnings of Dutch Immigration to Iowa, 1845-1847," IJH 22 (October 1924): 483-531; Ardith K. Melloch, "New Sweden, Iowa," PAL, vol. 59, no. 1 (January-February 1978): 2-19; Pauline S. Merrill, "Pioneer Iowa Bohemians," AI, vol. 3, no. 26 (April 1945): 261-74; Janette Murray, "Women of North Tama," IJHP 41 (July 1943): 287-318; Lawrence M. Nelson, *From Fjord to Prairie: Norwegian-Americans in the Midwest, 1825-1975* (Chicago: Norwegian Immigration Anniversary Commission, 1976); William J. Petersen, "Immigrants From Far and Near," PAL, vol. 49, no. 7 (July 1968): 295-302; Carlton C. Qualey, *Norwegian Settlement in the United States* (New York: Arno Press and the New York Times, 1970); Leonora Scholte, "A Stranger in a Strange Land," IJH vol. 37, no. 2 (April 1939): 115-203; Peer Stromme, *Halvor, A Story of Pioneer Youth* (Decorah, Iowa: Luther College Press, 1960); "The Hungarians in Iowa," AI, 3rd ser., vol. 3, no. 30 (October 1950): 465-67; N. Tjernagel, "Immigrants' Trying Experiences," AI, 3rd ser., vol. 3, no. 31 (July 1951): 64-71; Jacob Vander Zee, "Diary of a Journey from the Netherlands to Pella," IJHP, vol. 10, no. 3 (July 1912): 363-82, *The Hollanders of Iowa* (Iowa City: ISHD-HS, 1912); "The Mormon Trails in Iowa," IJHP, vol. 12, no. 1 (January 1914): 3-16, and *The British in Iowa*

(Iowa City: ISHD-HS, 1922); and B. L. Wick, "Pioneers of the Norway Community," AI, 3rd ser. 3 (July 1948): 366–78.

The travails of Iowa women during the Civil War years are described in several first-person accounts. They are George Mills, ed., "The Sharp Family Civil War Letters," AI, 3rd ser. 34 (January 1959): 481–532; the papers of the McCall Family, Special Collections, ISU Library, Ames; David Logan Hauser, "Letters, 1861–1864," ISHD-HS; Lieutenant J. W. Rice, "Letters, 1863–1867," ISHD-HS; Mrs. M. A. Rogers, "An Iowa Woman in Wartime," pts. 1, 2, and 3, AI, 3rd ser. 35 (Winter 1961): 523–48, 35 (Spring 1961): 594–615, and 36 (Summer 1961): 16–44; Martha Turner Searle, "Personal Experience and Reminesences [sic] of Civil War, 1861–1864," ISHD-HS; Shelton Family Papers, Manuscript Collection, UI Library, Iowa City; Major William G. Thompson, "Civil War Correspondence," ISHD-MA.

There are several treatments of Annie Turner Wittenmyer, in addition to her own *Under the Guns: A Woman's Reminiscences of the Civil War* (Boston, E.B. Stillings, 1895). Wittenmyer's "War Correspondence, 1861–1865," is deposited in the ISHD-MA. Useful secondary accounts are L. O. Cheever, "Annie Wittenmyer," PAL 48 (June 1967): 249–52; Ron Fisher, "Annie Wittenmyer, Iowa's Civil War Heroine," *The Iowan*, vol. 10, no. 1 (Fall 1961): 40–44; Earl S. Fullbrook, "Relief Work in Iowa During the Civil War," IJHP, vol. 16, no. 11 (April 1918): 155–274; Ruth A. Gallaher, "Annie Turner Wittenmyer," IJHP, vol. 29, no. 4 (October 1931): 518–69, and "Annie Turner Wittenmyer," PAL 38 (April 1957): 149–58.

Other works on women's involvement in the war are: Mary E. Massey, *Bonnet Brigades: American Women and the Civil War* (New York: Knopf, 1966); "Mrs. Ann E. Harlan," AI, 3rd ser. 2 (October 1896): 489–508; and Morton M. Rosenberg, *Iowa on the Eve of the Civil War: A Decade of Frontier Politics* (Norman: University of Oklahoma Press, 1972).

Reflections of Iowa frontierswomen who were involved in activities outside homemaking are found in Harriet Connor Brown, "Schoolday Memories," PAL 30 (April 1949): 107–24; Floy Lawrence Emhoff, "A Pioneer School Teacher in Central Iowa—Alice Money Lawrence," IJHP 33 (October 1935): 376–95; Sarah Gillespie Huftalen, "School Days of the Seventies," PAL 28 (April 1947): 122–28; Agnes Briggs Olmstead, "Recollections of a Pioneer Teacher of Hamilton County," AI, 3rd ser. 18 (October 1946): 93–115; Arozina Perkins, "Letters of a Pioneer Teacher," AI, 3rd ser., vol. 35, no. 8 (Spring 1961): 616–20; and the papers of Mary B. Welch, Special Collections, ISU Library.

Information pertaining to women's rights can be found in the Austin Adams Family Papers, Special Collections, ISU Library; Ruth S. Beitz, "Amelia Bloomer's Own Emancipation Proclamation," *The Iowan*, vol. 14, no. 2 (Winter 1965–1966): 40–43, 54; John E. Briggs, *History of Social Legislation in Iowa* (Iowa City: ISHD-HS, 1915); Elizabeth F. Chittenden, " 'By No Means Excluding Women,' " *The American West*, vol. 12, no. 2 (March 1975): 24–27; "Chronology of Woman Suffrage Movement in Iowa," AI, 3rd ser. 14 (October 1923): 149; Eleanor Flexner, *Century of Struggle: The Woman's Rights Movement in the United States* (Cambridge: The Belknap Press of Harvard University Press, 1976); Ruth A. Gallaher, *Legal and Political Status of Women in Iowa, 1838–1918* (Iowa City: ISHD-HS, 1918); Frank E. Horack, "Equal Suffrage in Iowa," in Benjamin F. Shambaugh, ed., *Applied History*, 2 vols. (Iowa City: ISHD-HS, 1914), 2:277–314; "Iowa Suffrage Memorial Association," AI, 3rd ser. 14 (July 1924): 357–65; Philip D. Jordan, "Amelia Jenks Bloomer," PAL 38 (April 1957): 139–48; Louise M. Lex, "Mary Newbury Adams: Feminist Forerunner from Iowa," AI, 3rd ser., vol. 43, no. 5 (Summer 1976): 323–39; Louise R. Noun,

206

Strong-Minded Women: The Emergence of the Woman-Suffrage Movement in Iowa (Ames: Iowa State University Press, 1969); and "Political Equality in Iowa," AI, 3rd ser., vol. 26, no. 3 (January 1945): 197.

A few authors directly consider the issues of loneliness and leisure time on the frontier. They are: Matie L. Baily, "Christmas of a Pioneer Family," AI, 3d ser. vol. 3, no. 31 (October 1951): 152–53; Bruce E. Mahan, "Frontier Fun," PAL 8 (January 1927): 38–42; Peter T. Harstad, "The Spirit of '76 in Iowa," PAL, vol. 57, no. 3 (May/June 1976): 66–75; and Mary D. Taylor, "A Farmers' Wives' Society in Pioneer Days," AI, 3rd ser., vol. 3, no. 13 (July 1921): 22–31.

Iowa women's relations with Native Americans are mentioned in passing in many women's source materials and particularly in Abbie Gardner-Sharp, *The Spirit Lake Massacre and the Captivity of Miss Abbie Gardner* (Des Moines, 1885); the papers of the Harger Family; and the reminiscences of Harriet M. Hill Townsend, both privately held. Other perspectives can be found in Ruth Beitz, "They Guarded Iowa's Last Frontier," *The Iowan*, vol. 9, no. 3 (February-March 1961): 10–15, 46; John E. Briggs, "Indian Affairs," PAL 21 (September 1940): 261–77, and "Indian Affairs in 1845," PAL 26 (August 1945): 225–38; A. D. Fisher, "Cultural Conflicts on the Prairies: Indian and White," *Alberta Historical Review*, vol. 16, no. 3 (1968): 22–29; Rodney Fox, "Stark Reminder of an Indian Raid," *The Iowan*, vol. 9, no. 1 (October-November 1960): 20–21, 53; "Frontier Fear of the Indians," AI, 3rd ser., vol. 3, no. 29 (April 1948): 315–22; Dawn L. Gherman, "From Parlor to Tepee: The White Squaw on the American Frontier," (Ph.D. diss., University of Massachusetts, 1975); Curt Harnack, "Prelude to Massacre," *The Iowan*, vol. 4, no. 3 (February-March 1956): 36–39; Bessie L. Lyon, "Hungry Indians," PAL 9 (October 1928): 357–70; Hubert E. Moeller, "Iowa's Other Indian Massacre," *The Iowan*, vol. 2, no. 4 (April-May 1954): 40; Roy Harvey Pearce, "The Significances of the Captivity Narrative," *American Literature* 19 (1947): 1–20; O. J. Pruitt, "Tales of the Cherokee in Iowa," AI, 3rd ser., vol. 3, no. 30 (July 1950): 359–67; Ronald J. Quinn, "The Modest Seduction: The Experience of Pioneer Women on the Trans-Mississippi Frontier," (Ph.D. diss., University of California, Riverside, 1977); and Richard Van Der Beets, "The Indian Captivity Narrative as Ritual," *American Literature* 43 (1972): 548–62.

The myths surrounding frontierswomen are embodied in Emerson Hough, *The Passing of the Frontier* (New Haven: Yale University Press, 1921) as well as in Hamlin Garland, *A Pioneer Mother* (Chicago: The Bookfellows, 1922). Critiques of western myths are found in Claire R. Farrer, "Women and Folklore: Images and Genres," *Journal of American Folklore* 88 (January-March 1975): v-xv; Dorys C. Grover, "The Pioneer Women in Fact and Fiction," *Heritage of Kansas: A Journal of the Great Plains* 10 (Spring 1977): 35–44; Barbara Meldrum, "Images of Women in Western American Literature," *The Midwest Quarterly*, vol. 17, no. 3 (April 1976): 252–67; Roderick Nash, *Wilderness and the American Mind* (New Haven: Yale University Press, 1973); Glenda Riley, "Images of the Frontierswoman: Iowa as a Case Study," *The Western Historical Quarterly*, vol. 8, no. 2 (April 1977): 189–202 and "Women in the West," *Journal of American Culture*, vol. 3, no. 2 (Summer 1980): 311–29; Richard Slotkin, *Regeneration Through Violence: The Mythology of the American Frontier, 1600-1860* (Middletown, Connecticut: Wesleyan University Press, 1973); Henry Nash Smith, *Virgin Land: The American West as Symbol and Myth* (New York: Vintage Books, 1950); Kent L. Steckmesser, *The Western Hero in History and Legend* (Norman: University of Oklahoma Press, 1965); and Beverly J. Stoeltje, " 'A Helpmate for Man Indeed': The Image of the Frontier Woman," *Journal of American Folklore* 88 (January-March 1975): 25–41.

INDEX

Abolitionism, 7, 90, 94–95, 97–99, 110, 112, 135, 144, 157
Academies, 139
Adams, Austin, 166
Adams, Mary Newbury, xv, 160, 165–67, 170
Anthony, Susan B., 160, 164, 167, 170
Antifeminism, 153
Antislavery, 7, 90, 92–95, 98, 152
Antisuffragism, 162
Apothecaries, women as, 77–79, 87
Archer, Elizabeth, 43
Archer family, 4, 20, 43, 46
Army Sanitary Commission, 131
Army women, 53, 109
Asian women, 109

Bartlett, Eliza, 71
Bartlett, Emery S., 11, 43, 45, 50, 64, 71, 87, 112
Bartlett, Hannah, 43
Beavers, Mary A., 160
Beecher, Catharine, 6, 51, 140–41
Beitz, Ruth S., 178
Belknap, George, 4, 16, 31, 34
Belknap, Kitturah, 4, 15–16, 23–26, 31–32, 34, 43, 61–62, 64, 68, 82, 86
Benedict, Abbie Mott, 31, 39–42, 44, 46, 52, 95
Benedict, Albert, 31, 44, 46
Benevolent societies, 129
Berkhofer, Robert F., 136
Bird, Alice, 160
Birth control, 82, 168
Black codes, 91, 93
Black exclusion laws, 91–93, 97–98
Black Hawk, 177, 180
Black Hawk Purchase, 8, 19
    treaty, xiii
Blacks, 90, 92
    as contraband, 89, 118
    education of, 92, 93–94, 98–99

free, 89, 91, 94, 97, 99
men, 88–99, 101, 108, 118, 158–60
miscegenation, 91, 99
rights of, 91–99, 101, 158–60, 162
slavery, 7, 85, 88, 90, 92–97, 110, 158, 170
women, viii, xv, 54–55, 88–99, 101, 108, 118, 158–60, 162
Blackstone, Sir William, 153
Bloomer, Amelia, 75, 133, 153, 168–69, 170
Bloomer, Dexter, 168, 170
Bogue, Allan G., 4, 12
Bohemians, 107
Bonebright-Closz, Harriet, 46, 62, 66, 69, 75, 77–78
Boylan, Louisa Sophia H. Gellhorn, 105
Brandt, Diderikke, 102
British, 105–6, 108, 114, 153–54
Brooks, Elisha, 22
Brown, Harriet Connor, 107
Bustles, 73–75

Callanan, James, 165
Callanan, Martha Coonley, 165, 170
Canadians, 8, 99, 107
Candles, 15, 66–67, 84, 87
Captivity narratives, 177
Carson, Kit, 168
Cassel, Peter, 104
Census data, 4–6, 11–12, 20, 53, 56–57, 85, 88–90, 99–100, 139, 148, 152, 171
Cherokee Indians, 178
Chicano women, 109
Childbirth, 81–82
Childcare, 29, 82–84, 87, 122, 166
    on the trail, 22–28
Children, 44, 79, 81, 125
    education of, 92, 93–94, 98–99, 136–48
    as laborers, 21–22, 34, 38, 42, 59, 62, 65, 72–73, 83–85, 115, 121
    as migrants, 17, 20–22, 26
Civil death, 154

210

McCormick reaper, 37, 72
McCowen, Dr. Jennie, 152
McLaughlin, Mary Moore, 16, 19, 23–24
Mallett, Mrs. R., 148
Mansfield, Arabella Babb, 150, 160
Mansfield, John M., 150
Marriage, early, 84–85
Mason, Charles, 95–96, 173
Mason, Mary J., 173
Medicine, patent, 77–79, 81–83
Mesquakies, xiii
Mexican War, 8
Middle Border, 39, 171
Midwest, 4, 107, 113, 141, 160
Migrants, xiii, xiv, 3–28, 53–54, 70, 88–91, 110
  black, 54, 88–99, 108, 118
  child care, 22, 28
  children's work, 21–22
  cooking, 24–25
  early housing, 31–32, 34–46, 48–50, 52–55, 63
Ministers, women as, 149
Miscegenation, 91, 99
Missouri Compromise of 1820, 88, 95
Money (Lawrence), Alice, 73, 145, 147
Moore, Lydia, 10, 17, 35
Moore, Milton, 10, 17, 35
Mormons, 108–9
Mormon Trail, 109
Morticians, women as, 79, 87
Mott, Alma, 4, 13, 49
Mott, Joseph, 4, 13, 34, 49
Mott, Lucretia, 152, 170
Murdock, Marian, 149
Murray, Benjamin F., 159
Murray, Janette, 65, 67, 76, 107
Murray, Margaret Archer, 32, 46, 49, 66, 68, 86, 138

Native Americans, viii, xiii, xv, 13, 18, 55, 91, 103–4, 108–11, 115–16, 118, 122, 149, 172, 175, 177–81
Newbury (Adams), Mary Ann, xv, 160, 165–67, 170
Newcomb, Jessie, 173
Newhall, John B., 6, 19, 105
Newton, Hanna, 63
Newton, Hosea, 10, 14, 31
Newton, Mary Ann, 14, 31
Nineteenth Amendment, 165
Norwegian-American Historical Society, 102
Norwegians, 102–4
Nossaman, Sarah Welch, 35, 46, 61, 63
Nurses
  men, 113
  women, 115, 131–32, 146, 160

Olmstead, Agnes Briggs, 147
Oppression history, 54

Ordinance of 1787, 88, 95

Parker, George F., xi
Parker, Sarah, 98–99, 145
Patent medicines, 78–79, 81–83
Paul, Matilda Peitzke, 42, 44, 46, 53, 60, 65, 67, 77–78, 84–85, 87, 112, 137–38, 174–76
Pearce, Roy H., 177
Peck (Harlan), Ann Eliza, 129, 133, 143
Peitzke, Matilda Paul, 32
Peitzke family, 36
Phelps, Caroline, 27, 44, 49, 53, 85, 179–80
Phelps, William, 27
Pillsbury, Esther, 27
Plumbe, John, Jr., 139
Pollard Spellers, 150
Polygamy, 109
Prairie fires, 45, 103
Prohibition party, 157
Propaganda, 9, 107–8
Proslavery, 90, 94, 98
Pyles, Charlotta, 94

Quakers, 94, 96, 109, 113

Railroads, 13–14, 27, 63, 108, 110, 173
Ralph case, the, 95–96
Ramsay, May, 59
Rebels (Confederates), 112, 116, 125
Red Cross, 129
Relief work in the Civil War, 117–19, 125–26, 128–29, 131–34, 168–69
Relocations, 38–39
Republicans, 93, 123, 158, 162, 165
Rice, J. W., 113–14
Robinson, Laura G., 160
Roe House, 175
Rogers, Dr. Samuel C., 115, 119
Rogers, Marjorie, 115–19, 128
Rorer, David, 95–97
Rush, Dr. Benjamin, 157
Rutledge (Cooke), Lucy, 106
Rutledge, Marianne, 106

Sage, Leland L., 111
St. John, Mary, 17
Saloutos, Theodore, 101
Sanford, Nettie, 160
Santee Sioux Indians, 111
Sauk Indians, xiii, 149, 178
Savery, Annie N., 160, 167–68
Savery, James C., 167–68
Scandinavians, 104
Scholte, Leonora, 107
Scholte, Peter Henry, 106–7
Scholte, Sara, 107
Schools, 139–45
Scots, 107, 155